BOOKS BY

Earl Parker Hanson

PUERTO RICO: *Land of Wonders*   (1960)

TRANSFORMATION: *The Story of Modern Puerto Rico*
   (1955)

NEW WORLDS EMERGING   (1950)

NEW WORLD GUIDES TO THE LATIN AMERICAN REPUBLICS
   (1944, 1946, 1950)

CHILE: LAND OF PROGRESS   (1941)

STEFANSSON: PROPHET OF THE NORTH   (1941)

JOURNEY TO MANAOS   (1938)

PUERTO RICO

Land of Wonders

PUERTO RICO

Land
of Wonders

BY

EARL PARKER HANSON

ALFRED·A·KNOPF : NEW YORK

1960

L. C. catalog card number: 60–7299

© EARL PARKER HANSON, 1955, 1960

THIS IS A BORZOI BOOK,
PUBLISHED BY ALFRED A. KNOPF, INC.

FIRST EDITION

Certain historical chapters in this book have been drawn from *Transformation*, Earl Parker Hanson's previous book about Puerto Rico, now out of print.

for

Don & Muriel

FRIENDS—

STAUNCH AND DEPENDABLE

Foreword

MY EARLIER BOOK on Puerto Rico, *Transformation: the Story of Modern Puerto Rico,* published in 1955 by Simon and Schuster, told the story of a new society reshaping itself and rising from the anguish of its former colonialism. Many such societies are found in the world today, and my intention was to present Puerto Rico as an example of principles and techniques that are important to the entire modern world. The book's reception was varied. In the United States it was widely regarded as a kind of "Believe it or Not" story, giving odd facts about an odd but lively society. Abroad, among the people who are trying to achieve for themselves something of what the Puerto Ricans have achieved and are achieving, its universal implications were understood much better. Kwame Nkrumah, for instance, wrote me from Accra, even before the Gold Coast achieved its independence as Ghana, that my book had persuaded him that Puerto Rico had much to offer his country by way of example and that he intended to send a number of his people to this Caribbean island to pick up ideas. In 1958, after *Transformation* was out of print, Lord John Boyd-Orr wrote me, urging that a new edition be published soon, as a rebuke and a prod to those many Europeans who seemed unable to shed their long-standing but outmoded imperialistic habits of thought. The United States Information Agency also read similar implications into the book and distributed copies all over the world—a worthy activity that did not displease either author or publisher.

A number of foreign editions helped to stimulate interest in Puerto Rico. A full-length Spanish edition was published in Mexico. Condensed versions of the book have to date appeared in Arabic, Burmese, and Hindi.

Late in 1957 the book's American edition was out of print, and the problem of getting out a new edition became acute. In this case it also involved finding a new title and a new publisher. My profound thanks and wholesome respect go to the firm of Alfred A. Knopf, Inc., and to its editor-in-chief, Mr. Harold Strauss, for being willing to go along with the venture.

Now that I have completed the job of preparing the present version, and have finally decided on the difficult question of a new title, I can assure readers, librarians, and reviewers that it is not at all a mere revised edition of *Transformation* updated and somewhat shortened. Well over half of the text had to be completely rewritten, and the present version is a "new" book in at least one important basic aspect.

The formulation of the policies described in *Transformation* was, for the Puerto Ricans, a heroic but relatively simple matter. The glaring evils of colonialism—unemployment, bad distribution of the land, hunger, illiteracy, disease—suggested and even dictated their own curative programs and policies. But now Puerto Rico has reached a new and even more difficult stage in its development and is confronted by a brand-new set of dilemmas. The Puerto Rican effort has matured and become sophisticated; Puerto Rico has emerged from its former status as a museum piece of colonial evils and is to an ever increasing extent a functioning member of the modern industrial world; by the same

token, it has taken on many of the most difficult problems
of today's capitalist nations.

The need for redistributing the land, which was so apparent twenty ears ago, now begins to give way in importance to the need for making the land produce its
maximum in economic benefits; the two needs are often in
conflict. The need for creating more jobs is at times in
conflict with the pressing need for improving industrial
efficiency, with its attendant technological unemployment.
The labor force is itself becoming more sophisticated in its
demands and activities, but in any one situation the demands
for higher wages and better conditions is often in conflict
with the society's desperate need to create more jobs,
thereby reducing unemployment.

Such are the conditions that make 1960 a turning point
in Puerto Rico's affairs which may eventually prove to be
every bit as important as the year 1940. A brilliant job was
done in twenty short years, but the changes of two decades
now demand a re-examination of all the policies under
which that job was done, a reformulation of policies, a reshaping of programs. When I wrote *Transformation,* I
didn't dream of such imminent needs; when I wrote *Puerto
Rico: Land of Wonders,* they became clearer to me daily.

My thanks also go to the government of Puerto Rico and
my many friends in it for having permitted me, since 1955,
again to play a personal role in the ferment that goes on
here unceasingly. A manumitted professor of geography, I
continue to be stimulated in my present role of consultant
and technician, of planner and writer. A former friend of
Puerto Rico, I am now a Puerto Rican, a citizen and affiliate
of the Commonwealth, as well as a citizen of the United
States.

In this foreword I could go on endlessly, giving thanks to
the many people to whom I owe them. But the list of such
people has grown immeasurably since I acknowledged my
indebtedness in the foreword to *Transformation.* Let that
foreword stand; the friends I mentioned in it will forgive

me for not repeating their names in the present book. I do, however, want to beg special indulgence of Dr. Rafael Picó and Mr. Chester Bowles for not repeating here their valiant personal contributions to *Transformation*. I appreciated and still appreciate those contributions immeasurably. But with the present volume I feel the need to go it alone, without introductory pats on the back from others.

EARL PARKER HANSON

San Juan, Puerto Rico
December 1959

CONTENTS

1   Transformation   3
2   The World and Puerto Rico   6
3   New York and Puerto Rico   24
4   The Anguish of Colonialism   44
5   Colonialism Bankrupt   63
6   The Breaker of the Cake   82
7   Climax and Disintegration   101
8   Faith in Ourselves   118
9   Tugwell   133
10 Neither Radical nor Conservative   150
11 Agriculture   167
12 The Battle for Production   189
13 Labor   215
14 Public Health   231
15 Education   248
16 Civic Employment   265
17 Culture Changes   281
18 Where Now?   301
    Index   follows page 320

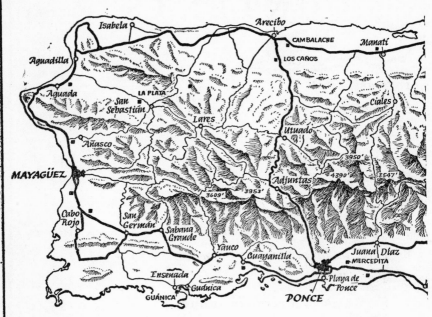

ATLANTIC

Isabela
Aguadilla
Aguada
San Sebastián
LA PLATA
Lares
Añasco
MAYAGÜEZ
Cabo Rojo
San Germán
Sabana Grande
Yauco
Ensenada
Guánica
GUÁNICA

Arecibo
CAMBALACHE
Manati
LOS CAÑOS
Ciales
Utuado
Adjuntas
3950
4390
3547'
3609'
3953
Guayanilla
Juana Díaz
MERCEDITA
Playa de Ponce
PONCE

CARIBBEAN

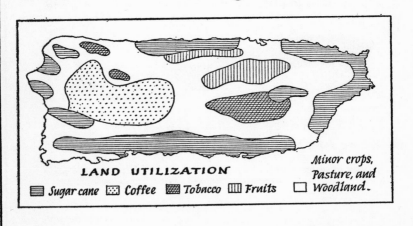

LAND UTILIZATION

▨ Sugar cane ▨ Coffee ▨ Tobacco ▥ Fruits ☐ Minor crops, Pasture, and Woodland.

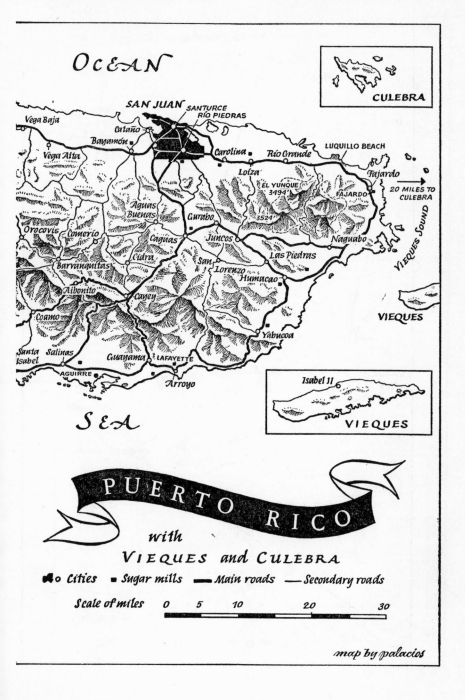

OCEAN

SAN JUAN SANTURCE
RÍO PIEDRAS

Vega Baja
Cataño
Bayamón
Vega Alta
Carolina
Río Grande
LUQUILLO BEACH
Loíza
Fajardo
EL YUNQUE
3494'
FAJARDO
20 MILES TO
CULEBRA
Orocovis
Aguas
Buenas
Gurabo
3524'
Comerío
Cagúas
Juncos
Naguabo
Cidra
Las Piedras
Barranquitas
San
Lorenzo
Humacao
Aibonito
Cayey
Coamo
Santa
Isabel
Salinas
Guayama
LAFAYETTE
Yabucoa
AGUIRRE
Arroyo
SEA

VIEQUES SOUND

VIEQUES

CULEBRA

Isabel II

VIEQUES

PUERTO RICO

with
VIEQUES and CULEBRA

Cities · Sugar mills —— Main roads —— Secondary roads

Scale of miles   0   5   10   20   30

map by palacios

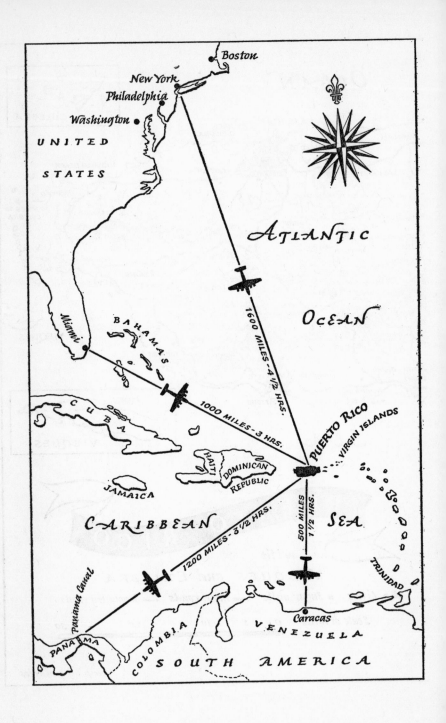

PUERTO RICO

Land of Wonders

1

Transformation

THE turning point was 1940. Before that year Puerto Rico was a run-down colony, starving and lethargic. One didn't read or hear much about the island, except when some vocal observer discovered its woes or when somebody shot somebody. A few liberal-minded people were interested in the Puerto Rican "problem" more or less as a case study, but nobody knew how to solve that problem, and few people—except, of course, the Puerto Ricans—cared very deeply about it.

Then in 1940 the Puerto Ricans staged their own brand of revolution. That year's election was a social explosion that freed the human spirit, substituted hope for despair, and released tremendous human energies for creative effort.

The world began to notice the results of that effort about 1948. The vocal observers who once, occasionally, discovered Puerto Rico's misery now discover and rediscover its phenomenal progress. Every year one reads and hears more about the progressive, democratic society the Puerto Ricans are creating for themselves.

In its own way Puerto Rico has become important in the

modern world and has made the influence of its example felt
throughout the non-Communist societies. How can that be,
as the land is small, as islands go, and incredibly poor in natural resources?

About 1,600 miles south of New York, Puerto Rico is approximately one hundred miles long and thirty-five miles
wide—about as large as Long Island. Its climate is tropical,
which, according to some observers, is supposed to rob its
bustling people of energy. Topographically Puerto Rico
consists of a complex of mountains surrounded by a coastal
plain; the amount of land suited for the orthodox kinds of
agriculture is limited. The original stands of virgin timber
have long since been cut down; not enough trees remain to
support a lumber industry of any consequence, or even to
prevent soil erosion. There are no commercial deposits of
iron, copper, manganese, gold, silver, or any other metals—
at least none that anybody knows about. There are no known
fuel deposits—coal or petroleum. Clay for making bricks,
tiles, and tableware; marble; limestone for making cement;
phosphates for making fertilizer—these constitute the total
exploitable mineral wealth discovered to date.

The rivers that tumble down from the mountains provide
water that can be and has been harnessed to produce electricity.

The excellent climate and unsurpassed scenic beauty are,
of course, also natural resources. They are being sold to
thousands of tourists and other visitors. But that more or less
finishes the list of material wealth.

The Puerto Ricans themselves are the island's greatest as-
set, but some say that there are too many of them. Two million, three hundred thousand of them divide into 650 per
square mile and make Puerto Rico one of the most crowded
countries on earth. And it has one of the highest birth rates.
If all the world's people—all the whites, blacks, yellows,
browns, all the Caucasians, Mongolians, Indians, all the
Christians, Mohammedans, Hindus, Communists, and Capi-

talists, all the people of China, the Soviet Union, India, Europe, Africa, Latin America were to move into the United States tomorrow, our density of population would also be about 650 per square mile—or about the same as Puerto Rico's, not counting the million or so Puerto Ricans who have moved to the United States.

And now people flock to the island from all over the world to see for themselves what so many people have achieved with so few natural resources.

Of course, they discover one more resource—in many ways the most important of them all. That resource is Puerto Rico's relationship with the United States, its proximity to the United States, the political system it has worked out jointly with the United States, its position within the U.S. tariff wall, its access to U.S. capital and markets, and its financial position under which it enjoys federal bounty on a basis of equality with the fifty states without contributing to the federal treasury.

That relationship compensates for the dearth of material resources; it is of inestimable value to Puerto Rico's 2⅓ million people—and incidentally also to the United States. It has made possible, though not caused, the tremendous improvements that are now attracting world attention. It has provided channels for the human energies that were released in the explosion of 1940.

After more than four centuries of lethargy, the people of Puerto Rico finally took hold of their own destiny and began to make the most of their resources, including the tremendous wealth of good relations with a powerful and friendly United States.

That is the story of modern Puerto Rico.

The present book is an attempt to deal with the questions of why that story is important, what Puerto Rico was before 1940, why and how the explosion of 1940 took place, what Puerto Rico has achieved since then, and where the island seems to be headed today.

2

The World and
Puerto Rico

THE present will go down in history as man's great age of anguish and creation, as by far the most sweeping of his fearful, recurring periods of "renaissance." That age was ushered in by the world depression.

The creative social force called *capitalism* seemed to collapse during the depression, but was not destroyed. It saved itself through an internal "revolution." In the broadest sense, it saved itself through the incipient abolition of the complex and many-faceted institution known as *colonialism*—internal, and external, political and economic. The many new nations that arose and are arising in Asia, Africa, and Oceania since World War II, the revolutionary changes being witnessed today in Latin America, did not owe their origins to the war; they were foreordained by the world depression.

The depression caught our world with the embarrassing condition known as *overproduction*, by which the industrial nations generated goods more rapidly than they created customers with the wherewithal to purchase them, and capitalism was threatened with destruction as a result. The creation of millions of new customers, through the abolition of

colonialism hand in hand with economic development to
multiply purchasing power, seemed obviously desirable.

The depression intensified what looked like a life and
death struggle between capitalism and communism. Regardless of the armaments race, it seems obvious today that
in that struggle the decisive factor will not be some secret
weapon of unprecedented destructive power; it will be nothing more complex than the loyalty, as given to this side or
that, of hundreds of millions of God's creatures who are
tired of the agonies, the lack of hope, and the hungers of
various kinds which they have hitherto suffered under colonialism.

Dramatically, the depression exposed the dangers and
fallacies of capitalism's racist thinking, by which dark-
skinned peoples are postulated as having been created for
roles in life no better than those of colonial subjects. That
those people did not believe the pseudoscientific arguments
that "proved" their inferiority to the ruling whites, and that
they were needed as customers for capitalism's goods and as
allies against communism, pointed to the need for abolishing
colonialism—in our own South and in Latin America, as well
as in Asia and in Africa.

The depression, during which the United States was itself
overpopulated by about 15,000,000 unemployed and their
families, led to the temporary popularity of the vicious system of thought known as *neo-Malthusianism*. Its adherents
maintained that the main trouble with today's world is that it
is too full of foreigners who refuse to practice birth control
for the purpose of safeguarding our high American standards of living, which they have never had a chance to enjoy.
But today it is apparent that "it is never a land that is overpopulated in terms of inhabitants per square mile, it is always an economy, in terms of inhabitants per square meal."
If the economy is expanded, and people are enabled to direct
their energies toward creative ends other than mere procrea-
tion, then—through education and the sense of responsibil-

ity that grows with improved standards of living—birth rates decrease.

The general abolition of colonialism, with all its repressive institutions, cannot go forward without friction and turmoil, as indicated in Indochina, Algeria, and Kenya. Even World War II, which was instigated by Hitler in part as a naïve effort to regain Germany's former colonial possessions in Africa, was in essence a violent delaying action. But colonialism is *being* abolished, must be abolished, in the modern world.

As a result, hundreds of millions of colonialism's former victims now find themselves with new and cherished freedoms, with new opportunities, but also with new responsibilities and terrible new problems. They have set out to develop and reshape their lands, but they have little capital and less experience for the task. They are driven by urgency, but retarded by lack of skills. The people who benefit directly from today's ubiquitous social revolution now roam the earth in search of help, knowledge, ideas, fellow workers, and sympathizers in their long uphill struggle to create a new world.

Among them, in January 1957, was Ghana's Minister of Finance, the Honorable Kohla Agbeli Gbedemah, who came to Puerto Rico while his country was still a British West African colony called "Gold Coast."

During a dinner conversation, I said: "So you get your independence on March 6 of this year."

"Yes," he answered. "That is when our troubles will begin."

"It seems to me that you've had troubles before."

"That is quite true. But until March 6 we can still blame them on the British. Now we will have to face them ourselves."

He spoke for millions. The winning of hard-bought freedoms is one matter; the prospect of having to translate them into a national way of life, with scant means for the job, can be terrifying.

The fact that Gbedemah told me this in Puerto Rico was no mere accident. A large and growing number of the pilgrims who are today in search of techniques and tools for their new tasks have discovered that relatively small Caribbean island—formerly a colony of the United States, but now its enthusiastic voluntary partner. They have discovered that Puerto Rico in recent decades has done an astonishing job of transforming itself. Between May 1950 and June 30, 1959, 10,136 official visitors, observers, students, and technicians visited the island. They came from 118 countries—in Latin America, the Caribbean area, Africa, the Near East, the Middle East, the Far East, Oceania, Europe, and the United States. The first year, when the program was inaugurated, there were 146 of them. Year by year the number grew as Puerto Rico's fame spread. In 1958-9 there were 1,362. In the beginning those visitors were sent to the island by the United States government partly because Puerto Rico was beginning to give Uncle Sam a fine reputation, partly because those from the so-called underdeveloped countries, as well as U. S. technicians, could learn much there. Eventually, as the island became known, the United Nations also began to send people there, as did private companies and organizations. Governments in Latin America, Africa, and Asia began to send observers to Puerto Rico. Such governments have no interest in propaganda to improve the United States's reputation; they send their representatives because Puerto Rico is doing a job, because the Puerto Ricans have rolled up their sleeves and are making their island over, because much can be learned from such a job, and because the island's psychological climate is today as creative as that of Israel and certain parts of India.

Even New York City is now sending observers to Puerto Rico.

In less than a decade Puerto Rico has become a showcase for U.S. decency in handling one of the world's former outstanding colonial problems, as well as a laboratory, a training ground where the world's people can acquire attitudes and techniques for improving their lives.

What is it that those thousands of visitors want in Puerto Rico?

Some seek specific skills by which they can later help to improve the economies of their own countries. Many, however, seek more than these skills. If they want to learn agricultural techniques or the technical and psychological intricacies of co-operation, they can do better in Denmark. If they are interested in soil conservation, Denmark and Germany provide excellent examples. Norway and the United States are good study areas for hydroelectric development. Puerto Rico is forging ahead in industrial techniques, sanitary engineering, city planning, budgetary practices, and many other things, but the student from Africa could obviously learn such specialties better in the United States or one of the other highly developed countries. But still they come in increasing numbers—from Africa, Asia, and other regions. Why?

What they want—and many have told me—is not some specialty, but the integrated picture. They want to learn how it is that one small society, a land dramatically poor in natural resources, a land that a few short decades previously had been all but hopeless in its lethargy—its illness, its lack of financial resources, its lack of technical knowledge— could suddenly take hold of its own affairs, embark on an "Operation Bootstrap," and become world-famous in no time at all, as human affairs go.

They want to know how the life expectancy of the average Puerto Rican, which was 46 years in 1940, could shoot up to 68 years by 1958, and how the death rate, which in 1940 was 18.2 per 1,000, could drop in the same period to a point lower than that of the United States proper.

Most of the visitors come from countries that know the agony of an average life span made short by a high death rate. They know the desperation of illness, of high birth rates in social structures of low economic opportunity, of ceaseless, hopeless, grinding toil for wages of pennies per day, of wresting crops from worn-out soils. They come from countries that may not have gathered and memorized their statistics, but that have experienced the full, living impact of those statistics. To us, who live on Park Avenue, or teach or study in universities, an increase of twenty-two years in average life expectancy may be only a somewhat interesting fact—if that. To the man from Thailand or West Africa it is the living symbol of the revolution he is trying to further when he includes Puerto Rico in the itinerary of his world peregrinations.

He is interested in revolutions because that forty-six-year life expectancy found in Puerto Rico in 1940 denoted the same conditions—grinding toil, high birth rates and death rates, high morbidity in various devitalizing illnesses, gnawing hunger, wretched clothing and housing, low standards in education, denuded soils, lack of economic opportunity, lack of political freedom for improving economic opportunity, and the loss of human dignity—the visitor knows in his own country. He feels at home in Puerto Rico. He is interested in the island because there he finds a small society that has obviously succeeded in shaking off the anguish of its former colonialism and is busily and successfully reshaping itself.

Before 1940 Puerto Rico was a colony, an "agrarian" society, as badly off as any on earth, and worse off than most. It was bankrupt financially and, to all appearances, psychologically and spiritually as well. Everybody could see and feel the suffering; nobody seemed to know how to reverse the downward spiral toward imminent destruction. Then "the man" appeared. He stirred his people out of their lethargy, taught them political awareness and morality, and promised to set them on the tortuous upward road to their own salvation. He said, in effect: "If we are to be saved, we must stop asking the ruling country to save us. The job is up to us, to do through our own indigenous power, pride, and responsibility."

That was revolutionary talk, and the resulting election, which brought Luis Muñoz Marín to political power in Puerto Rico, was a revolution, pure and simple. For when a colonial leader says "We will do this and that, regardless of what the ruling country says," he is preaching revolution because he promises to usurp power from the ruling country. When his people elect him to office on the strength of that promise, they are carrying out a revolution. *But*, when the ruling country then says "It is a fine idea and we will help you all we can," then, miraculously, that is the end of colonialism. From that point on, the course of events is foreordained.

That is precisely what happened in Puerto Rico, and that is why the United States is today pleased to send thousands of foreign visitors to San Juan. Incidentally, it is also the reason why France is not always happy to have its Algerians go to the Caribbean island, or the Union of South Africa its Liberals, or the governor of Arkansas his Negro colonial subjects.

Since the revolutionary election of 1940, Puerto Rico has, among other things:

Greatly expanded its power network and launched a remarkable program of industrialization to give employment and to strengthen and diversify the economy;

Made strong headway in the diversification, modernization, and augmented production of its agricultural plant;

More than doubled its per capita annual income in terms of purchasing power and made strides in the improved distribution of that income;

Created one of the Hemisphere's best public-health services and reduced its death rate to a figure lower than that of the continental United States;

Greatly expanded its educational system and taken drastic steps toward reshaping it to fit modern needs;

Extended that great impetus to all classes of Puerto Ricans to the point where thousands are today "civically employed" and are giving their thoughts and labors to the task of effectively improving their lives, instead of expecting their government to do everything for them;

Created social and economic conditions under which its former "explosive" birth rate has turned the corner and is declining rapidly, thus bringing the society ever nearer the point where population will finally be in balance with the productive effort;

Abolished its former colonial status and created new forms of political relationships by which it is today a self-governing country within the framework of the United States, sharing the broader independence of the latter.

The list can be expanded and detailed indefinitely. Nobody, however, claims that Puerto Rico has solved a single one of its problems for all time, or that such an effective and vitally important program can be carried forward without friction and opposition. There is friction in Puerto Rico; there is opposition. But there is also an improvement so marked that it attracts observers from all the world's areas, and a spirit of creation so dynamic and vital that it is felt immediately by virtually all visitors.

Puerto Rico's progress is precisely what Nehru and his fellow workers are striving for in India, Kwame Nkrumah in Ghana. It is what Israel is working for, as well as Thailand, Iraq, Jordan, and Indonesia. Now that democracy is invading Latin America, dictators are falling, and the medieval feudalism imported by the conquistadors is collapsing, it is what the great masses of Latin Americans have begun to expect and attempt. Hence, people come to Puerto Rico from everywhere west of the Iron Curtain, though some also come from Yugoslavia.

Nevertheless, those visitors don't go home believing that they can achieve the same results with the same techniques. No two countries on earth are the same; each demands its own techniques for salvation. If foreign visitors lament

Puerto Rico's lack of natural resources, they also envy its privileged position in the world's greatest market—the United States. Puerto Rico sells goods freely in the United States and draws so freely on U.S. capital that it has become known as "a new American industrial frontier." It enjoys nearly all the advantages of American citizenship and receives financial help from Washington comparable to that given to the various states. Unlike the states, however, it does not contribute to the federal government's expenses.

Such conditions, within the framework of which Puerto Rico is today achieving its remarkable progress, are unique and not exportable. But the idea of a society taking the initiative and making the major effort for its own progress *is* exportable. To Latin Americans the basic concept of improved relations with the United States—even though it is a two-way concept that demands something of Washington—is also exportable. Many of the techniques used to improve public health are exportable, as are the social techniques by which Puerto Rico builds thousands of sturdy, sanitary, concrete rural homes for $300 each. Innovations in education, in agriculture, in land distribution, in labor relations, and in government organization are not only exportable, but are being transported to many parts of the world.

In a basic sense the most important exportable idea is that only in a functioning, *true* democracy can progress such as Puerto Rico's occur. That leads to varied reactions.

Governor Muñoz Marín is a Latin American, and the Hemisphere's few remaining dictators, who fear democracy above all else, hate him venomously; they spend thousands of dollars to disseminate the misinformation that he and his colleagues are Communists, or are under communism's influence.

Fatayi Williams, from western Nigeria, reacted differently to the same democracy. He had spent some months in the United States, studying race relations, and told me that it was inconceivable to him that Puerto Rico could be under the same flag as Little Rock and Harlem. "This is the only place under the American flag," he said, "where I can forget that I am a Negro. Look out on the street. When twenty Puerto Ricans go past, the first may be white and the last black, but the rest are all colors in between. That is why you can make such progress. You don't waste energy on senseless racial strife."

If Puerto Rico's modern phase began with the election of 1940, its functions as a laboratory began with what many still regard as the most important statement made by a world leader since World War ii. Truman was elected President in 1948, and his inaugural address included the sensational "Point IV" statement. "We must embark," he said, "on a bold new program for making the benefits of our scientific advances and industrial progress available for the improvement and growth of underdeveloped areas. More than half the people of the world are living in conditions approaching misery. Their food is inadequate. They are victims of disease. Their economic life is primitive and stagnant. Their poverty is a handicap and a threat both to them and to more prosperous areas."

Shortly after saying those things, Truman was visited by Puerto Rico's governor—the first ever to be elected by the island's people. There is no written record of the conversation between the two. In general, however, it went as follows:

The President said: "What can I do for you?"

"Nothing," Muñoz Marín answered. "During the past ten years we have changed from 'Operation Lament' to 'Operation Bootstrap.' We have begun to do the things that you call for in your Point IV. We have worked out techniques for doing them and are well on the way to solving our basic problems. Within the framework of the American scheme of things we have also strengthened and widened our democracy immeasurably. Now we want to do what we can to help you implement Point IV.

"We believe that we have something to show and teach

the so-called underdeveloped regions and their people. If you will send us their representatives and your technicians, we will gladly show and teach them whatever we can—as a result of our past ten years of experience. We believe that we will thereby also help to strengthen the good reputation of the United States throughout the world, because what we have done, and are doing, is to a large extent a result of American fairness, co-operation, and democracy."

Truman sent a commission, which reported favorably on possibilities for carrying out the governor's proposal. Muñoz talked to his legislature, asking that Puerto Rico—still a colony in the technical sense—appropriate funds for the program. These funds were voted even before the U. S. Congress had passed the legislation that made a small reality out of Point IV. They have been voted every year since then and have in recent years been increased considerably. Little Puerto Rico, struggling to solve its own problems with inadequate means, poorer by far then our poorest state, is the only part of the American Union that contributes to the world-wide federal Point IV effort.

Appropriate government machinery was set up in San Juan and in Washington, and foreign visitors—at first largely from Latin America—began to arrive in 1950. Since then the procedure has been changed considerably, with Puerto Rico itself taking on more responsibility and paying more of the cost than formerly. Today Puerto Rico's Department of State is perhaps the most cosmopolitan spot in the Caribbean area. A constant stream of visitors from all parts of the world fan out from the department to visit other government agencies, inspect the work done in the field, talk to Puerto Ricans of all classes, and absorb the atmosphere in what has been called "America's answer to communism."

One visitor in 1957 was a newspaper publisher from Indonesia. He told me that he had come to the island because in his own country the politically strong Communists were constantly pointing to Puerto Rico as a suffering, starving, demoralized victim of the United States's imperialistic greed. He wanted to see for himself, and he did see. He saw many poor people, but he also saw them striving with hope and in freedom to improve their lives. When he returned to Indonesia, he published articles in his paper refuting the Communists' claims. Such articles, pointing to Puerto Rico as the *refutation* of imperialistic charges against the United States, are beginning to appear by the dozens in Latin America, in Africa, in Asia, and in Europe. Many Puerto Ricans regard these articles as a partial repayment of their great indebtedness to the United States. In today's strife-torn world, where reputation is at least as important as technical advance in armaments, they and the spirit behind them may well be worth every penny of financial help and advantage the United States gives Puerto Rico.

Dr. Arturo Morales Carrión, erstwhile professor of history at the University of Puerto Rico, and now Undersecretary of State in charge of the Commonwealth's several foreign-visitors programs, is a busy man. His department's "Program of Technical Co-operation," directed by Señor José Luis Colom, formerly of the Pan American Union, is carried out in full co-operation with the United States International Co-operation Administration, although it also receives and handles many visitors sent by other bodies, public and private, or by their own governments. The program includes the granting of hundreds of scholarships to students from the Caribbean area, and specializes in training in specific fields. It accounted for 6,484 of the total number of official visitors through June 1959, and these came from 118 countries. Today it is attracting visitors at a rate of well over 1,000 per year.

The Program of Educational Exchange, carried out with the co-operation of the International Exchange Service of the U. S. Department of State, is headed in San Juan by Señor José Ramón Piñeiro, Master in Political Science from the University of Chicago. It was started in 1955 and has since then, through June 1959, attracted 1,444 official visitors from seventy-five countries. Unlike the Technical Cooperation Program, it offers no training in specific fields; it does, however, attract a large number of eminent men and women. Sir Arkuh Korsa, Chief Justice of Ghana's Supreme Court, Dr. Hussein Bushnaq, Jordan's Director of Public Welfare, and the charming Madame Ella Koblo Gulama— Sierra Leone's only woman Paramount Chief, member of Sierra Leone's legislature, a leader for her country's eventual independence, and a hereditary African queen in her own right—are examples of the type of people attracted. Important, also, are the many foreign journalists who come under "educational exchange." These include individuals like my Indonesian friend, as well as groups of journalists who periodically visit Puerto Rico from Latin America. When Asian Communists use Puerto Rico for attacking American imperialism, when die-hard Latin Americans refurbish the old, dogmatic line of "dollar diplomacy," despite its rapidly waning validity, when mobs attack the Vice-President of the United States as a symbol of America's ill will toward lesser peoples, these journalists are in a position—as a result of their Puerto Rican experiences—to refute much outmoded thinking still current in the Hemisphere.

In the Latin-American field, especially, such leadership is vitally important. Outstanding Latin-American leaders for democracy, such as President Betancourt of Venezuela, and ex-President Figueres of Costa Rica, acknowledge their indebtedness to Puerto Rico for their present ideas on the possibilities of strengthened relations with the United States—sustained mutually and in good faith, to the advantage of both. In Washington 1958 was a turning point: a number of important voices were raised in favor of a "hard new look" at our relations with Latin America. Vice-President Nixon, for instance, raised such a cry after his disastrous South American visit—but also after he had spent the

better part of a night talking to Muñoz Marín in San Juan
about the lessons to be learned from his sobering experiences in Peru and Venezuela.

The Senate Committee on Foreign Relations invited
Muñoz Marín to Washington in 1958 to give advice. He outlined a broad new policy toward Latin America, which was
reported to be taken very seriously at the time, and to be
taken even more seriously after the Nixon debacle.

Another important activity of Puerto Rico's Department
of State is that of sponsoring and arranging international
conferences and seminars. Twenty years ago, when Puerto
Rico was still a starving, stricken colony with nothing to
teach except woe, and when the needed hotel and other facilities were lacking, nobody would have dreamed of such
conferences being held on the island. Since 1953 more than
twenty have been held, under favorable coauspices, attracting 2,500 official delegates from a large number of countries. Naturally these also broaden the Puerto Ricans' hori-
zons. There have been large international conferences on
such diverse subjects as: health problems in the Americas;
the exchange of persons as a means of strengthening international good will; social service in the Hemisphere; the
plantation system; Caribbean problems. There have been
seminars, well attended by people from many nations, on:
the teaching of history; education for planning; the history
of ideas in the Americas; industrial development; and several other subjects.

The fifty-first annual conference of United States governors, held in San Juan in August 1959, was by far the
most important and the best-arranged conference ever held
in Puerto Rico. It was also the first meeting of state governors to be held outside of the continental United States,
and resulted in a large number of governors obtaining an in-
timate view of Puerto Rico's progress and problems—social,
economic, and political.

Such activities focus attention on modern Puerto Rico as a seed bed for ideas that are important to the modern world, where many new worlds are emerging.

Many Puerto Rican technicians and advisers have gone to other countries in recent years to lend help to those countries' efforts; and they continue to go in a swelling stream. Meanwhile, the United States has been using Puerto Ricans in yet another of its international activities. The Caribbean commission grew out of wartime co-operation in the Caribbean area by the United States and Great Britain. It developed into a commission of the imperial powers—the United States, Great Britain, France, and the Netherlands—though the United States included Puerto Ricans among its delegates from the first. Though glad to help, Puerto Rico would have preferred to represent its own country, rather than the United States; after 1952 they said so, openly and officially. It was in 1952 that Puerto Rico attained its present Commonwealth status, under which the United States ceased being an imperial power in its relations with the island. Imperialism, said the Puerto Rican delegates of the United States, was rapidly being liquidated in the area; the imperial commission should therefore also liquidate itself and thus make room for a new body that would represent the Caribbean's people and societies, rather than their metropolitan present and former rulers.

The United States backed the proposal immediately; the other powers followed suit in the ensuing years, with France hesitating somewhat. Developments in the Caribbean area, following the granting of Commonwealth status to Puerto Rico, gave ever increasing validity to the Puerto Ricans' proposal. The "statute" under which the former Dutch colonies now enjoy full autonomy went into force December 29, 1954. On March 25, 1958, the new, self-governing British West Indian Federation held its first election and began to tackle its own problems with its own nascent powers. Earlier, perhaps in an effort to stave off more drastic measures,

France had made the gesture of redesignating the former colonies of Guadalupe and Martinique as Departments of Greater France; there is some doubt, however, as to whether the inhabitants of those Departments feel as free in their present roles as "full citizens" as do the people of Paris.

The Puerto Rican delegates worked year after year toward the voluntary liquidation of the Caribbean commission and the substitution of a new body that would truly represent the region's people. In August 1959, at the meetings in the Virgin Islands, their efforts came to fruition. At the time of the present writing, only a certain amount of technical paper work remains to be done before the new organization becomes a working reality. The four former imperial powers have agreed to abolish their commission, and a new body, the "Caribbean Organization," is about to take its place. In that body the former American, British, Dutch, and French colonial subjects will now work for themselves, as self-governing peoples, toward collaboration in social and economic matters, and especially in tackling problems of economic development, industrialization, agriculture, fisheries, education, health, and the like. A truly regional body would, of course, also include the three Caribbean sovereign countries —Cuba, Haiti, and the Dominican "Republic." Although someday they may be invited to join, it is at present unthinkable that a place can be found—in an international, democratic organization—for the "well-ordered graveyard" Generalissimo Trujillo rules with an iron hand from the ancient city he has modestly renamed after himself.

The secretariat of the defunct Caribbean commission is now to be reorganized to serve the new body, and to be moved from Trinidad to San Juan. With it will come its library of about 35,000 items—the world's largest on the Caribbean. In the future that library will attract scholars to Puerto Rico from all parts of the world.

The American educational system is also, though too slowly, becoming aware of Puerto Rico. The so-called crisis in U.S. education, about which much is being said and written today, stems from the growing realization that our modern education fails to condition its students to play their full roles in a rapidly changing world. Old educational concepts and compartmentalizations, inherited from a former world now doomed, fail to meet the problems of the new. World realities have outgrown the "social sciences" that were designed to train people to deal with those realities. Hence there is increasing emphasis in American universities on field studies, area studies, work among people, rather than texts, and laboratory work abroad to check the classwork at home. But universities cannot send students everywhere; time, money, and travel facilities don't permit it. Then, why not send them to Puerto Rico, where American students can meet other students and observers, from all the free world's countries, in search of the same world realities the Americans will need?

In 1952 the University of Delaware's Department of Geography sent a class to San Juan for a summer-school course, the subject of which was not geography, sociology, history, education, or any other specialty, but Puerto Rico, as an emerging society that must draw on all these fields *in an integrated manner*. Haverford College and Sarah Lawrence College are among those that have in recent years, with the full support and co-operation of the Commonwealth Department of State, sent groups to Puerto Rico for similar purposes. A few years ago Colgate University developed an imaginative scheme by which a number of students would spend their entire senior year in Puerto Rico, working in various government departments, hearing lectures, discussing what they saw and heard, writing term papers. Unfortunately that important experiment in modern education was thwarted by the last-minute death of the professor who had organized it.

But the idea did not die. It is important that American education play an effective, realistic role in training students for the world leadership the forces of history have thrust on the United States. Puerto Rico is itself proof that the world in which we must exercise that leadership is changing with a speed so dizzying that the academic precepts of our various compartmentalized social sciences hardly fit it any longer. Increasingly American education is turning to Puerto Rico for help in its large tasks of reorganization and reorientation.

3

New York and
Puerto Rico

*"IF THEY got it so good down there," says the New York taxi driver, "what are they all coming up here for? The Puerto Ricans are taking over the city, and it's bad. They come here without any money, and bingo, the next day they're on relief. We ought to give them independence, that's what we ought to do. Then they can't come flocking in by the thousands. This used to be a nice, quiet, peaceful town, but it's getting so now that you can't hardly walk down the street without some Puerto Rican comes and tries to stick a shiv into you. And you know the movement to the suburbs. Know who started it? It's them Puerto Ricans, that's who. They're chasing everybody out of town. They join gangs and take dope, and they can't even speak English—most of them. It's not right, I'm telling you."

One gathers, on visiting New York, that the city's "average" taxi driver and even the "average" New Yorker regard Puerto Rico and the Puerto Ricans with somewhat less affection than do the visitors to San Juan from Brazil, Ghana, Indonesia, or Jamaica. When Puerto Rico is mentioned to the average New Yorker, he is likely to conjure up a fantastic picture of burglaries and murders, teen-age troubles, mug-gings, housing shortages, dope, and other ills. That the pic-ture is greatly exaggerated is less important than the fact that it exists and gives rise to much hostility against the New York Puerto Ricans.

While it is true that many Puerto Ricans inhabit New York and that Spanish is by now the second language of Times Square, their numbers are often exaggerated—usu-ally for budgetary purposes. When the departments of hous-ing or hospitals want money, they talk at budget time about the three quarters of a million Puerto Ricans now in New York and the 50,000 per year who are supposed to be streaming in, all of them equally indigent, bewildered, and in need of help. The same kind of talk is now being heard in Chicago, Philadelphia, Hartford, Youngstown, Bridgeport, and Cleveland, as Puerto Ricans spread to the rest of the country.

Actually the "net migration"—the difference between the Puerto Ricans leaving the island and those who return to it —varies widely. In 1956 it was almost 62,000, though not entirely into New York's slums. By 1958 it had decreased to nearly 26,000.

Such variations follow the pattern of general economic trends in the States; during a good year the stream of mi-grants increases; during a bad year it tends to decrease, while the number who return to Puerto Rico grows larger. Every improvement of economic opportunity on the island also serves to slow down the out-migration. The United States has seen similar variations before, as, for instance, in relation to Iceland. During the 1870's when that sub-arctic island had fewer than 100,000 people, but no economic de-velopment to speak of, there was a flood of Icelanders to America, escaping from poverty at home. Meanwhile, how-ever, the Icelanders have accomplished wonders in develop-ing their homeland and in improving their standards of liv-ing. Today, despite the fact that Iceland's population has risen to over 150,000, it is almost impossible to lure an Icelander to America's fleshpots. A reversal of the migration trend is already in sight in Puerto Rico. Very few Puerto Ricans would choose to move to New York if they could find at home, in their own hills and valleys, the opportunities New York now seems to offer, while retaining the human dignity too often withheld from them by the New York taxi driver, landlord, labor racketeer, dope peddler, and the like.

The Puerto Ricans, however, have in recent years become New York's greatest single topic of conversation, as well as the theme for an ever increasing number of books, articles, learned studies, doctoral dissertations, and term papers written by earnest students. As subjects for sociological and pseudosociological studies of various kinds, the Puerto Ricans have managed to usurp the supreme position once held by Minsky's burlesque shows.

New York receives the greatest number of Puerto Rican migrants for the simple reason that the city is and has always been America's principal port of entry. New Yorkers have therefore had similar "troubles" before. The same Gothamites who today resent the Puerto Ricans, yesterday resented the Italians, the Russian Jews, the Poles, the South Carolinians or Alabamans with dark skins. New York has had that kind of problem since the earliest days when the original inhabitants of Manhattan had their own Dutch "problem" and moved to the suburbs because of the many palefaces flocking in. The city has received wave after wave of migrants, has housed them—though inadequately, to judge from the lot of today's Puerto Ricans—has given them much work for little pay, and has begun the task of teaching them English, "Americanizing" them, blending them with their predecessors in the great melting pot that is the United States.

And today the taxi driver asks: "If they got it so good down there, why do they come here?"

Well may he ask. The current mass out-migration is a

new phenomenon in Puerto Rico's life and culture. Its sudden rise marks a decided culture change. Previously, throughout four centuries, the island's people had been homebodies, clinging to their beautiful but poor land with a desperate love that may have been mixed with a certain amount of fear. True, after learning of the dramatic news of Pizarro's conquest of Peru, Puerto Rico's early settlers wanted to leave in order to get in on the loot; at that time their governor thought it best to threaten the death penalty for anybody so unpatriotic as to want to abandon an important strategic position. Succeeding governors and the Catholic Church also did what they could to discourage the kind of exodus that didn't begin until about the turn of the twentieth century—and then very slowly. The Puerto Ricans developed into a provincial lot, with no seafaring tradition; during their first two centuries most of them saw "foreigners" only in the shapes of Spanish administrators and businessmen, or in those of the even less popular pirates, soldiers, invaders from northern Europe. Many Puerto Ricans may well have been afraid to leave "lest the Dutchman catch them" once they got on the high seas. Staying at home became a definite culture trait.

Especially during the early nineteenth century the Puerto Ricans had their own immigrant problem. At the beginning of the nineteenth century, when the French began to have serious troubles with their Haitian slaves, a number of Frenchmen left Haiti to establish themselves in Spain's peaceful colony of Puerto Rico. After the Louisiana Purchase in 1803 many Creoles, Frenchmen, and Spaniards left the affected territory and moved to Puerto Rico to escape being ruled by the Protestant, Republican United States. For decades after the outbreak of the Latin-American revolutionary wars, beginning with Miranda's ill-fated expedition from New York to Venezuela in 1806 and ending with the establishment of the various Latin-American republics in the 1820's, thousands of royalists left the col-

onies and sought refuge in royalist Puerto Rico. Many
Corsicans came after Napoleon's fall.

The flow of people in those days was into Puerto Rico.
The island's population grew dramatically. Not until the
1890's was there a recorded outward movement of any
appreciable size. The Puerto Rican sugar culture had been
ruined by the imposition of a U.S. tariff. Thousands of
Puerto Ricans were left, not only poor and unemployed,
but landless as well. But Hawaii, about to be joined to the
United States, needed field hands because it had already
received large amounts of American capital to mechanize
its agriculture. Puerto Ricans were recruited to go to Hawaii, where their colony today numbers about 10,000.

During the early years of American rule a number of
Puerto Ricans were sporadically recruited for agricultural
labor in the United States. Most of them were unhappy—
especially the dark-skinned. Coming from their patriarchal
society, where a man's color was hardly noticed and where
he was respected no matter how poor, it was difficult for
them to adjust to their treatment by American employers:
to be abused and treated as second-class, colored cheap
labor speaking a foreign language. However, some did come
to find new homes in the United States, of which all Puerto
Ricans became citizens in 1917. The 1930 census reported
Puerto Ricans in all of the forty-eight states. By 1940 their
number had become appreciable. New York then had 63,000
Puerto Ricans. But it was not until after 1945 that the
stream of migrants became so large that it began to have a
considerable effect on Puerto Rico's population problem.

Why? Why that sudden exodus at precisely the time
when Puerto Rico itself was turning the corner toward a
better life? There are those who accuse the Puerto Rican
government of encouraging and even financing migration,
with the idea of easing unemployment at home. That is
not true. The Commonwealth government is scrupulous
neither to encourage nor discourage migration, though it

takes a responsible attitude toward those who want to leave, and does everything possible to help them. As will be seen later, it also helps the migrant laborers, those who bring in the sugar harvest in Puerto Rico and then go north to bring in various other crops in such states as New Jersey and Connecticut, returning home when that chore is done to bring in the next home sugar crop.

There are many explanations for the present exodus, and one of the most important is undoubtedly to be found in the significant psychological changes that resulted from the 1940 turnabout. Previously the great masses of Puerto Ricans had been all but hopeless in their miseries; now, almost for the first time in their history, they began to realize that they themselves, by their own efforts, could do something to ease their lives. Many pitched in at home to do what was possible; many others, with new faith in themselves, migrated to where the pay checks were higher than in Puerto Rico, the opportunities still greater. ⸢That their hardships also became greater was and is self-evident; even those who complain about the New York Puerto Ricans cannot claim that their life is a bed of roses. They are beset by thousands of enemies, from the cockroaches and rats that too often infest their miserable quarters to the more vicious two-legged swindlers who prey on them. But they see more immediate opportunities ahead for their children, and so they face their numberless tribulations. In many ways the Puerto Ricans who move to New York are more courageous as pioneers than those who stay at home. ⸥

There are other and related reasons for the exodus. In many subtle ways the 1940 election turned the United States—in the thinking of many Puerto Ricans—from a covert enemy into an open friend. Then, too, thousands of Puerto Ricans served in the U.S. armed forces during World War II, in Europe and in the Pacific Theater; they came back with new ideas about the formerly hostile alien world and its people. In line with such psychological changes, Puerto Rico suddenly changed itself from a haven of refuge surrounded by enemies, into a crowded place surrounded by frontiers of opportunity. The very word "opportunity" was all but coined, as far as the masses of Puerto Ricans were concerned, after the 1940 election.

Then came the airplane, with its rapid and inexpensive transportation. It did much to accelerate migrations to the mainland.

Meanwhile the economic pressure not only remained, but—paradoxically—grew greater. Though today's Puerto Rican is much better off, he is under far greater pressure to improve his life than was his father, who accepted his abject poverty, his gnawing hunger, the deaths of his children, with a hopeless fatalism. Faith in oneself also breeds impatience.

There is also the matter of geographical distribution of progress. The statistics on modern Puerto Rico reflect a tremendous achievement, but it would be wrong to believe that the social progress they indicate is evenly distributed throughout the island. Puerto Rico's progress is concentrated in certain well-defined regions; some of the others remain virtually as stricken as they were twenty years ago; some have quite possibly retrogressed. People move from these into the more prosperous areas, as they have been doing for a number of decades. Today, however, they also have the airplane and a new culture trait—restlessness— which permit them to move to New York if they wish. Eventually, when the island's progress becomes more evenly distributed, the exodus will slow down and may even be reversed.

By means of its program of economic development, Puerto Rico is today creating thousands of new jobs every year. Health conditions and indices improve dramatically, but also complicate the task. A modern birth rate that has fallen to 31.8 per 1,000 per year and a death rate that has sunk to 7.2 indicate sound social health; they also mean that for every seven Puerto Ricans who die, thirty-two are born, to demand education and health services, jobs when they come of age, decent opportunities for themselves and their families. Those thirty-two formerly had a life span of forty-six years. Now they live sixty-eight years and hence demand that much more of their society.

Puerto Rican officials are frank to admit that migration helps them in their work. Not only does it tend to keep the island's total labor force at a more or less constant level, so that every new job created means a reduction by that much in unemployment, but the money sent back from Puerto Ricans in the States to their relatives at home has become a real contribution to the island's economy.

A number of hostile New Yorkers realize some of those things and increase their hostility as a result. Many of them use the cause of "freedom" as a means of retaliation. Like the taxi driver previously quoted above—and he was a real taxi driver whose number is legion—they advocate the island's political independence as a means of keeping Puerto Ricans out of New York. Indeed, when Congressman Morgan H. Moulder, of Missouri, in January 1959 presented a bill for Puerto Rican independence, he gave as one of his reasons the fact that a great number of Puerto Ricans, being citizens of the United States, were flowing freely into New York and other centers.

The Missouri legislator and the many New Yorkers who think as he does need to consider realities. Citizenship in the United States cannot be taken away by the simple expedient of an independence law. If the island were to become a republic tomorrow, every Puerto Rican would be required to step before a magistrate and choose for himself whether he wanted to retain the status and the rights of his United States citizenship or become a citizen of the newly formed sovereign country. And which way would a large proportion in all probability choose to go, as it is self-evident that independence would rob the Puerto Ricans of their greatest resource—their present relations with the world's greatest industrial nation? Which way would they go when confronted with the prospect of factories shutting down for loss of markets, schools closing for lack of funds, health services being shut off? It is safe to say that perhaps three quarters of them would choose to retain their U.S. citizenship, and that most of *those*—virtually all who had the airplane fare—would catch the first available planes for New York.

It is a safe guess that in the event that Puerto Rico became a soverign republic, a million or more Puerto Ricans would almost immediately descend on New York.

And what would happen to New York if all its Puerto Ricans were suddenly to leave the city? It is not true that most of them go on relief. The number of those who do varies from five to about ten per cent, according to the methods used in computing and the attitudes of the computers. The testimony of a large number of employers praises them as steady, earnest, hard workers. What would happen to the needlework industry, to building maintenance, to the hotels and restaurants, to the toy, novelty, and plastic plants, and to many other branches of the city's economy if the Puerto Ricans who now virtually support those branches with their labor decided to go somewhere else? Some other ethnic group would have to be brought in to take their places. As somebody has to do the work, New York would simply exchange its Puerto Rican "problem" for a Haitian, Jamaican, British West Indian, Polish, Hungarian, or Mexican "problem."

Virtually all lower-class Puerto Ricans who migrate to the States do so for the purpose of improving their economic conditions more rapidly than they can at home, where there is still a pressing unemployment problem. The aim is laudable, but the wrench is often terrible.

A man wakes up and has breakfast in the beautiful hills of his beloved "Borinquen" (the old Indian name for Puerto

Rico, still often used as a term of affection). He is poor and lives in a small, dilapidated, but immaculately clean, shack. However, he is a man, respected as such regardless of his color or economic condition. In his easygoing, paternalistic society he is among equals. If he has troubles or problems, he seeks help from his *patron* or from his relatives—in a society that is characterized by strong family ties. The climate is mild, and it makes little difference if his children wear few clothes or no clothes at all. He is the undisputed head of the family; his word is law. His language is Spanish, and despite his lack of formal schooling, he may be extremely eloquent in that language. It is not a bad life, except for hungers of various kinds. Don Luis in San Juan is doing everything that any man possibly can; he is creating factories where none had existed before, schools by the dozens, new hospitals and health units, and electric light in the homes. Nevertheless, this man's needs and his children's needs are growing even more rapidly than are the facilities Don Luis is providing for meeting them. The man has had letters, some of them with money orders, from relatives in New York. He has decided to migrate.

That afternoon, after a brief six-hour hop, he is dropped into the seething human mess of Idlewild Airport. The weather is cold to an extent that he had never before thought possible. He and his wife and children must suddenly be bundled up; God knows if they have the clothes for it. His native language marks him as an alien. A hop of only six hours, just between meals, has brought him from his own easygoing society into the world's most bustling and sophisticated metropolitan center.

Immediately he becomes the victim, not the creator, of a desperate housing shortage. Often he is also the victim of a chiseling landlord who has discovered that low-rental housing is the world's most profitable, and has therefore remodeled a one-family apartment to accommodate three, four, or five families. The Puerto Rican, who may even have his mother or aunt with him, as well as his wife and children, must make do in one room, often with a leaky ceiling, plaster falling off in chunks, no heat, infested with rats, cockroaches, and other vermin. After a while he may start complaining to the landlord, who may—and usually does—tell him to leave if he doesn't like it.

The man starts looking for a job, but the fact that he knows little or no English imposes difficulties. But his oldest daughter has learned some English in the Puerto Rican school, and goes along to help him. It is a humiliating thing, and from that point on he loses some of the respect he enjoyed as a man and as the head of his home. His wife, who is a skilled needleworker, gets a job before he does, and he loses more of his former position. His children are sent to school, where they may or may not learn English, reading, and writing. The children, learning new "American" ways, depart from the Puerto Rican rules of strict conduct by which they had been raised. They may want to go to school parties unchaperoned, or do other "awful" things. There is conflict in the home, but the children take their Americanization into their own hands and use various dodges to get around the parental authority. However, the children, too, are subjected to the erosive processes of abject poverty and lack of human dignity. Their world is often hostile to them because they are Puerto Ricans. Some of the boys may join gangs and even take to dope—as addicts or as peddlers. Some of the girls may become prostitutes, not because they are Puerto Ricans, but for the same reasons for which millions of other girls, from time immemorial, have become prostitutes.

Meanwhile the parents are preyed upon by labor racketeers and political ward heelers, while also being subjected to a special and bewildering kind of racial discrimination. In most communities in the United States anyone who is known to have a drop of Negro blood in his veins is considered a Negro and receives special treatment as such.

In Puerto Rico, at the social level of the hypothetical man I am talking about, there is no discrimination, no special treatment reserved for Negroes. However, there is a special kind of classification, just as valid as ours: anybody with a drop of white blood is a white man. The effects of such differences in attitudes are apt to be traumatic, and our hypothetical Puerto Rican may make one of three well-known adjustments. If he is very dark, he may merge with the Harlem Negroes, though claiming to be from some part of the West Indies other than Puerto Rico. If he is very light, he may in self-protection disown his Puerto Rican heritage, claiming to be Spanish. If he is *trigueño,* as the people somewhere in-between are called in Puerto Rico, he may well cling to his Puerto Rican nature and origin with a fierce passion that is generated in part for expediency; he may associate almost exclusively with other Puerto Ricans and may even refuse to learn or speak English, in order to set himself apart from the American Negroes of all colors who live in Harlem.

There are bewilderments; there are troubles; there is much unhappiness; but there is always also that airplane that takes only six hours—less than the time between supper and breakfast—to span the distance between this terrible new world and the more peaceful and understandable old one. Having all my adult life been interested in the world's frontier regions, I was once convinced that only one thing is needed to make a man a good pioneer: he must *not* be able to return to where he came from. Now I am not sure. I believe that the presence of that airplane, its speed, and its low fares sustain many Puerto Ricans through their first terrible years in New York.

I have chosen and possibly exaggerated a hypothetical case, but it is precisely that case that creates the Puerto Rican "problem." Thousands of Puerto Ricans slip quietly into New York or some other United States city and manage almost immediately to establish themselves as good citizens. But it is not fashionable to talk about *them*. What *is* fashionable is to talk in round numbers of perhaps 700,-000 Puerto Ricans in New York and to lump them all as "they," with no idea of how many of them actually create civic problems.

In 1959 a number of teen-age murders in which Puerto Rican children were involved led to a new wave of anti-Puerto Rican feeling, caused the city to reexamine its juvenile delinquency problem drastically, and gave rise to several statements to the effect that Puerto Ricans should thenceforth be barred from the city. The situation resulted in accelerated activity among the many civic groups working with and for the resident Puerto Ricans. One hundred and sixty-two of them published a full-page advertisement in the papers, informing the New Yorkers—many of them skeptical—that Puerto Ricans are essentially decent and law-abiding citizens, that they have produced many notable men and women, and that they are doing all in their power to combat lawlessness. The question of whether the situation was created by "the Puerto Ricans" or by conditions in New York was debated far and wide.

In that debate the city's own ceaseless activities—providing decent municipal housing for thousands of indigent families, hiring a large number of Spanish-speaking teachers, reforming the school system in a mad scramble to meet overwhelming needs—were apparently given scant consideration. Obviously, the wave of crime—regardless of whether committed primarily by Puerto Ricans or by others—showed the city's efforts to have been "too little and too late," though how a harassed city official is to anticipate such a condition is not known.

New York has had such crime waves before, and always there have been resentments against the latest immigrants who participated in them. Many a sociological study has established, almost as dogma, that the true assimilation of migrants from other shores and other cultures requires three generations; the average New Yorker seems to demand that the Puerto Rican migrants achieve that readjustment in six hours' flying time.

The airplane sets the Puerto Rican migrants apart from all other ethnic groups that have left their homes—in Sicily, Poland, Russia, Germany, Ireland—to seek new lives in the great United States, usually via New York. Another important matter that sets them apart is the continued realistic interest of their home government in their welfare even after they have left Puerto Rico. Let us grant that in the old days Sicily, Germany, Poland, or Russia could not have been expected to send agents to New York or other American cities to help their migrant nationals there. Let us grant that Puerto Rico is under the American flag, that the Puerto Ricans are United States citizens, and that the movement of Puerto Ricans northward is merely a part of the well-established general larger northward movement within the United States proper. Let us realize in that connection that the northward movement of Puerto Ricans, no matter what is said about it, is proportionally *smaller* than that from the southern states, which have for decades been sending so great a stream of migrants to the north that they are known as the nation's seed beds of people. Nevertheless, it is still remarkable that little Puerto Rico, far poorer than Mississippi, should spend thousands of dollars annually out of its inadequate budget to help the Puerto Ricans who have left home in search of greener pastures. Imagine Governor Faubus or Governor Jimmy Byrnes spending money for the welfare of the thousands of citizens of Arkansas or South Carolina who have chosen to move to Harlem!

But the Puerto Rican Department of Labor, headed by Secretary Fernando Sierra Berdeciá, has long maintained a busy office in New York to help the Puerto Ricans there, and now has similar offices in Chicago, Cleveland, Detroit, Harrisburg, Camden, Hartford, and Boston. Indeed, the "Migration Division" of the Commonwealth's Department of Labor, headed by the former social worker Petroamérica Pagán de Colón, is one of the liveliest and most vital of all of Puerto Rico's governmental organizations. "Petro" is an embattled fighter for her people, whose tenacity, ready wit, and biting sarcasm are well known to many a mainland employer or landlord. Her superior, cabinet member Sierra, has on a number of occasions roamed incognito through such Puerto Rican slums as Spanish Harlem, talking to his people and learning about their problems.

The New York office of the Migration Division is run by Mr. Joseph Monserrat, who fights for his people with the same enthusiasm he gives to fighting for Latin-American democracy and against dictators.

In Puerto Rico the Migration Division helps all those who need and ask help, primarily through orientation. It tells them about United States realities in terms of weather, housing, jobs, and racial discrimination. It attempts to convince them—now with increasing success— that New York is not the mainland's only city, so that the migrants may settle in other areas. Workers in the Division talk to would-be migrants about the need for job skills and about the differences that often exist between such skills in Puerto Rico and in the States. A man may, for instance, believe that he is a skilled construction worker and should therefore be able to get a job without too much trouble. But he knows nothing about plastering walls because that is not done on his island; when he goes north he may find that construction jobs are open only to plasterers. A man may be an expert radio mechanic in Puerto Rico, but not in New York, because the city uses only the newest gadgets, which have not yet made their appearance on the island. Through vocational-school training, either in San Juan or in New York, the Division helps such a man to round out his skills to fit the city's needs. In New York he may have to work for a while as a dishwasher in the Waldorf Hotel, but he is encouraged to go to night school to improve himself and his employment possibilities.

Before leaving Puerto Rico, prospective migrants are urged and helped to attend adult classes in English, which have now been organized even in the island's rural areas. In New York, too, they are helped to attend such classes.

The New York office does not run an employment bureau, but it is militant in demanding protection for the Puerto Ricans against labor racketeers. By means of its program of community organization the office helps Puerto Ricans to organize themselves and their neighbors for protection against, let us say, chiseling landlords. The tenants in a block of filthy, crumbling tenements may be Italians, Poles, Negroes, etc., all mixed together; when they do manage to get together for the purpose of presenting their complaints to the city, it is nearly always the Puerto Ricans among them who take the lead, partly because their own government backs them.

Through its offices in various cities the Migration Division keeps after the Puerto Rican migrants, encouraging them to vote, to join the parties of their choice, to join good labor unions, to identify with the union movement and with the life around them. Many are timid about such things, clinging to each other because of fear. The New York office also encourages and helps various civic groups composed of Puerto Ricans and non-Puerto Ricans and devoted to improving the city's life.

Constantly, too, the Division scouts the United States for new opportunities for Puerto Rican workers, trying to get them out of their clannish lives in New York and to scatter them throughout the country. An experiment of some years ago, under which 500 Puerto Ricans were placed as workers in the steel mills of Gary, Indiana, worked so well—from the point of view of both the workers and the employers—that Puerto Ricans are now moving to that part of the Middle West in increasing numbers. Many a prospective employer—in Connecticut, in the Delaware River Valley, in Massachusetts, and elsewhere—has been afraid of Puerto Ricans because of what he had heard about them, but, after being persuaded to hire them, has been delighted with them as adaptable and reliable workers. True, even in their new locations the new workers often have housing problems because these problems existed before they came. They also have adjustment problems, but they do adjust, thereby easing the problem in New York considerably.

With the help of Dr. Clarence Senior, the New York office sponsors scholarly studies of the Puerto Rican "problem" and issues circulars aimed at solving it through knowledge.

In San Juan the Migration Division strives to orient not only the Puerto Ricans who intend to migrate, but also the people who have contact with them in the States. Orientation, according to the Division's norms, is only partly a matter of attempting to improve the readiness of a person to adjust to conditions new to him; it is also an effort to improve the readiness of the northern community to receive him.

Every summer Puerto Rico is invaded by "workshops" of teachers, principals, and social workers from the States, who go through an intensive course of training in the home culture of the Puerto Ricans with whom they deal in their own communities. The Commonwealth pays for their room and board. They return after six weeks or so with far more informed and sympathetic attitudes than they had had before. The Department of Labor has also organized intensive seminars in San Juan for a number of New York's highest city officials in order to discuss the Puerto Rican problems and the various means by which New York and Puerto Rico can help solve them. Puerto Rican government officials are included in those seminars. Recently groups of policemen from various mainland cities have begun to be brought to Puerto Rico so that their understanding of the Puerto Ricans in their home towns, might be increased.

Another important activity of the Migration Division is the protection and preparation of the Puerto Ricans who go north on contract for seasonal work. Shortly after World War II a number of unscrupulous agents, working hand in glove with new, small airlines, opened offices in San Juan. They painted glowing pictures of life in the United States, talked about jobs on the mainland, arranged for the shipment of whole planeloads, and charged fees for their services. On several occasions the second-hand planes fell into the ocean, and dozens of Puerto Ricans were killed. At times the agents shipped their clients to places on the continent where no work existed for them; then arose the problem of how to care for the penniless newcomers.

A Puerto Rican law of 1947, however, changed all that. It prohibited all fee-charging agencies in Puerto Rico and stipulated that all contracts for workers on the island must be approved by the Secretary of Labor. Moreover, today no Puerto Rican worker can be recruited for the continent unless a labor shortage is certified at his place of destination by the responsible local, state, and federal officials. After a number of labor scouts had been arrested, tried, and jailed, the 1947 law began to work fairly well. Fee-charging, racketeering agents are still caught occasionally. White slavers at times go to the island to recruit "servant girls"; Spanish-speaking agents, possibly Puerto Ricans themselves, have been known to meet bewildered, newly arrived migrants at Idlewild Airport, hustle them into station wagons, and drive them to agricultural jobs that require them to labor under conditions of peonage. But the Commonwealth government is alert to such practices and does everything in its power to combat them.

The Labor Department's employment service in San

Juan now supervises contracts for work in the States. Occasionally it sends needleworkers, but usually it sends seasonal agricultural workers, more than 17,000 of them per year. These are sent on contract with the employers; the latter pay the transportation costs, which are subsequently taken out of wages.

As a result of Secretary Sierra's labors, the Puerto Rican employment service is affiliated with that of the United States government, and Puerto Rican workers are now officially a part of the U.S. labor force. Thus, employers who contract for their services cannot get them at a lower rate, as "West Indians." They must pay the full wage prevailing in their neighborhoods at the time, and they don't always like it. Also, no "West Indians" or other noncitizens may be brought in to do the work as long as Puerto Rican workers are available. Under U.S. law the supply of available citizens must be exhausted before aliens can be imported.

Finally, the Commonwealth's Department of Labor does *not* negotiate contracts for Puerto Rican agricultural workers in the South, where they might get the full, degrading racial treatment. The Commonwealth's constitution bars discrimination or selection on the basis of race or color.

After the farm workers have been oriented and shipped north, their government continues to take an interest in them. It is always ready to step into disputes about wages, living quarters, food, and general working conditions. The employers don't always like it, but they can do little; the Puerto Rican government representatives know the law very well. Eventually the employers often develop a respect bordering on a cross between love and awe for Petroamérica and her several co-workers.

However, not all Puerto Rican seasonal workers go north under the aegis of their government. A large number have made their own contacts, have developed good working relations with specific farmers, and have gone back to the same farms year after year to bring in the harvests in

Delaware, New Jersey, Connecticut, etc., after completing the sugar harvest on their island. Others, perhaps 3,000 of them, go on their own to join the annual migratory stream of workers who move southward from New Jersey to Florida, harvesting as they go.

In one way or another, the ferment is on. Through many direct means, some of them painful, but all of them instructive, many thousands of Puerto Ricans are learning to know the United States and are slowly beginning to feel at home there.

American industry has begun to flow into Puerto Rico, and Puerto Rican labor has invaded the United States. The trade is not always fair; the industry generally earns more money than does the labor. But, nevertheless, the ties between Puerto Rico and the United States become stronger daily.

4

The Anguish of Colonialism

THIS was Puerto Rico in the early seventeenth century, as described by Dr. Arturo Morales Carrión: "In the country, under the most primitive conditions, a people which seeks its elemental sustenance from the earth, and lives by clandestine commerce is slowly forging itself. A social dichotomy arises between the city and the country, between the fortress and the hinterland. These are two worlds, obeying different motivations. The walled city is a creation of imperialism, bulwark of a political structure which embraces vast territories. It is a stronghold in seas of enemies and heretics. Hence it develops a psychology of suspicion, and its citizens do not venture on the surrounding waters lest the Dutchman catch them. Within its walls the predominant elements of its society are at each other's throats: the bishops and the governors, the governors and the councils. The country, on the other hand, produces a much more homogeneous rustic society, which lives in a primitive manner and develops its own norms and customs, alien to the great metropolitan conflicts and disdainful of the rigid metropolitan commands. So Puerto Rico develops during the seventeenth century: a land largely virgin, exuberant and forested, with a small pauperized population, which does not succeed in creating a plantation economy with a wide base of slavery, like that which is beginning to appear in the neighboring British and French colonies."

The city was characterized by its fortifications, the most massive in the Caribbean except for those of Barranquilla, Colombia. To build El Castillo del Morro and Fort San Cristóbal, money was diverted from Mexico, and coolies from China. When the latter had completed their work they were loaded on ships for the long haul home, but were soon dumped overboard on the high seas to save time, travail, and cash. Again and again the English, the French, and the Dutch tried to storm the forts and wrest Puerto Rico from Spain; again and again they were repulsed. Once I showed the forts to a visiting Englishman, but the sight only saddened him because they represented one of "Sir Francis Drake's great failures." Drake attacked San Juan in 1595 in an unsuccessful attempt to capture a treasure ship that had put in on the way to Spain. The English took the city three years later, but had to abandon it after three months of occupation because of illness among their troops.

During the sixteenth, seventeenth, and eighteenth centuries the recorded history of Puerto Rico's people was far less one of internal growth and development than of tribulations suffered in the defense of somebody else's empire. The North Europeans didn't concentrate exclusively on San Juan. Other, and defenseless towns and settlements were repeatedly sacked and burned by the French during the 1500's, rebuilt, and burned again. Raids and attacks by French and English privateers occurred periodically until the advent of the nineteenth century. And during those dismal years various hurricanes ravaged the island even more than did Spain's human enemies.

The last attack on San Juan, before Admiral Sampson finally managed to take the city during the Spanish-American War, was made by the English in 1797. By that time, however, efforts had already been made to substitute horse trading for military action. England desperately wanted Puerto Rico because of its strategic location; that the attempted trades came to nothing enhances the fascination of speculating on "what might have been" had Puerto Rico become a British colony.

This was the sequence:

In 1704 the British and the Dutch stole Gibraltar from Spain, and the British immediately stole it from the Dutch. After the American Revolution, Britain offered to swap Gibraltar back to Spain in return for Puerto Rico. The Spanish held out for a better deal, wanting West Florida in addition. Later they changed their minds, decided to keep Puerto Rico after all, and offered to exchange Spanish Santo Domingo for Gibraltar and West Florida. Nothing came of that, either. Today Britain still has Gibraltar, Puerto Rico has Commonwealth status, Spanish Santo Domingo has its *benefactor*, Generalissimo Rafael Leonidas Trujillo Molina, and retired U.S. farmers and executives have West Florida as a pitching ground for horseshoes.

While such things were going on, the Puerto Ricans proper, as opposed to the Spanish elements in their society clung to their beautiful island and got along as well as they could. Because they had to manage in abject poverty, they did so in the democratic fraternity that is still one of their distinct culture traits; nothing welds people together more closely than does poverty enforced by political oppression.

The fact that their poverty prevented them from "creating a plantation economy with a wide base of slavery" saved them a good many headaches later. It meant that the imported Negroes were relatively few, treated well, and not feared as a social menace. Shortly after the U. S. Civil

War a group of Puerto Rican slave owners petitioned Spain on their own initiative to abolish slavery on the island, with or without compensation. The racial attitudes resulting today from the long-standing, easygoing relations between Negroes and whites were felt recently by a liberal-minded, though dogmatic and embattled, North American woman who had a job in one of the island's government departments. She was indignant because she saw no Negro employees in the office; she thought that a decent government would take pains to hire people of both races. But her chief, a power in modern Puerto Rican affairs, said to her: "Just look around you. Look at me and all the rest of us. I doubt if you will see a single one who might not be classed as a Negro in the United States."

Under Madrid's trade monopoly the Puerto Ricans could trade with nobody but Spain, shipping their cargoes in Spanish ships and dealing with the middlemen imported from Spain. The modern counterparts of these middlemen, known as "Spanish merchants," still powerful in the wholesale and retail trade, have their own exclusive, Fascist-minded social club and often today mutter darkly about "all this democracy that has hit the island and is ruining it." But to believe that the Puerto Ricans obeyed the trade decrees would be as naïve as to believe that there was no drinking in the United States during Prohibition, or that the thirteen North American colonies that preceded the United States obeyed Britain's commercial regulations. An exuberant trade of smuggling developed—most of it between Puerto Rico and those thirteen colonies.

Since early in their history the people of Puerto Rico have needed free trade with the United States for their economic survival. Today they need it more than ever. That inescapable fact has shaped the island's modern development, as well as its political thinking. What is bad for the Puerto Ricans economically is also bad for them politically; out of bilateral recognition of that basic fact has grown a new political status and a close, ever strengthening relationship between the island and its former imperial rulers.

During the nineteenth century, after losing most of its former colonies in the New World, Spain read the handwriting on the wall and began gradually to lighten her rule in Puerto Rico. Freedom of the press was established, military powers were separated from the civil, and the Puerto Ricans were permitted to create two cultural societies for the purpose of stimulating their intellectual life. They were also permitted, legally, to trade with the United States and with the colonial possessions in the Caribbean, with whom they had long enjoyed a thriving illicit commerce. The plantations on the coastal plain developed a good business, selling sugar to the United States. But American farmers began to plant beet sugar, and in 1870 they managed to protect their infant industry with a tariff. Puerto Rican planters went bankrupt and clamored for the free trade the United States could not grant to a Spanish colony without incurring the wrath of its own farm lobby. Much of their fertile, level sugar land reverted to the raising of tick-infested scrub cattle. Not until after the Spanish-American War did Puerto Rico achieve that free trade. But then it discovered that its industrial plant for processing sugar, to say nothing of its agricultural techniques, was so antiquated and inefficient that it could not take advantage of the situation. American capital and American technology poured in and forced many Puerto Ricans out of business. As long as the island retained a "one-crop" sugar economy, the major benefits of its inclusion within the United States's tariff structure were reaped by American, rather than Puerto Rican, interests.

That the United States should take over Puerto Rico was a foregone conclusion the day it was decided that we would build the Panama Canal and would therefore need Caribbean bases from which to protect it. Then somebody con-

veniently sank the battleship *Maine*. We went to war with
Spain in solidarity with Cuba's revolting elements and acquired Puerto Rico through the Treaty of Paris, December
10, 1898. Our General Miles, marching across the island
with his troops, was hailed as a liberator, and gave lavish
promises of cordial, democratic relations with the United
States. However, the cordiality of those relations began to
deteriorate after the "Colossus of the North" took over the
island's government.

In Puerto Rico Luis Muñoz Rivera, father of the present
governor, had earlier become one of the island's outstanding leaders and patriots. In 1897 he had been instrumental
in obtaining from Spain Puerto Rico's first real constitution, its first charter for home rule. Hailed with jubilation
at the time, that constitution was in effect less than a year.
During the years immediately following our assumption of
power in San Juan—when "alien" American governors
clashed repeatedly with the Puerto Ricans, who were frantically determined to preserve what few political and civil
liberties they had won after four centuries as Spanish subjects—the idea arose in the United States that the Puerto
Ricans were an unruly lot, ungrateful, and unfit for self-
government. Most of the rights and freedoms they had acquired from Spain in 1897 were abrogated during the first
year of American occupation. Many of the Puerto Ricans
had once hailed us as liberators began to change their
minds.

Nevertheless, despite much classical Latin-American
clamor to the contrary, and despite such inhumanities as
the Little Rock troubles, we Americans were and are a decent people with kind intentions toward colonial under-
dogs. No matter what we succeeded in doing, and no matter what the island's hotheads accused us of wanting, we
never intended to grind the Puerto Ricans into abject misery.

Our greatest trouble was our inexperience in matters of

colonial administration, coupled with our naïve belief that what's good for American business is good for everybody. We made fiscal and other arrangements that were notable as colonial matters went, and outstanding in contrast to Spain's earlier ruthless exploitation. However, while giving the Puerto Ricans a measure of "autonomy" in the management of their internal affairs, we kept the ultimate control always in our own hands under the pretext of guiding a "lesser" people toward eventual self-government, thereby draining the form of autonomy of all real substance. What we didn't know and what the free world is only now discovering is that government is much too complex and vitally important a matter to be left in the hands of experts.

With admirable energy and good will we began to clean house on the island immediately after the Spanish-American War. Roads, schools, and public-health programs attested to that energy and good will. The armed forces, which in Spanish days had been a drain on the economy, now began to contribute to it. Military and naval constructions, pay and pensions for Puerto Rican soldiers, benefits for their families—all these and many more, mounting steadily in volume through World Wars i and ii, through the Korean Police Action, and into the present era of fearful alert, have poured millions of dollars into Puerto Rico.

While Puerto Rico was given free entry into the tariff-protected American market, it was also stipulated that customs receipts on foreign cargoes landed in insular ports be turned over to the island's government instead of into the federal treasury.

The Puerto Ricans have never paid taxes to Washington. Even today their income taxes are paid exclusively to their own government, and excise taxes on such goods as rum and cigars, manufactured locally, remain in Puerto Rico. The principle involved is the old American one of no taxation without representation. Since the early years of its relations with the United States, Puerto Rico has been represented in the U. S. Congress only by a Resident Commissioner who has a voice, but no vote, who can prepare bills and argue for or against legislation related to Puerto Rico, but cannot vote on such legislation. Residents of Washington, D. C., who also have no representation in Congress and lack all vestiges of self-government, would like to see that old American principle invoked for their own benefit to relieve them of federal taxation.

The fiscal arrangements were stipulated in Puerto Rico's first "organic act," the Foraker Act of 1900, unilaterally drafted and passed by Congress. Today they form the solid foundation on which the island's present political status rests. "Patriots" may cry for either sovereign independence or statehood on emotional grounds, with the choice between the two depending on their personal orientations. The hard, practical questions are still: (1) Could an independent Republic of Puerto Rico survive the loss of free markets in the United States, as well as that of federal contributions to the island's economy? (2) Could a "State of Puerto Rico" afford to make the contributions to the expenses of the federal government which would be demanded under that status?

The principal trouble with those admirable fiscal arrangements was that they failed to benefit the great majority of the Puerto Rican people—the laborers, the men in the hills—and soon began to lean more toward United States interests.

The Spanish-American War had marked a turning point in American affairs, the point at which we became a world power in the financial as well as the military sense, turning from a debtor into a creditor nation. The nineteenth century had seen the industrial development of the United States—with the help of European, mostly British, capital. By the century's end we had generated sufficient capital of our own to want to export some of it. Hence, when Puerto

Rico came under the American flag, it also became a fertile field for millions of American investment dollars, which poured into the island and came to dominate its entire life. That capital poured primarily into the sugar industry. Great new mills were erected; industrial efficiency was introduced in the sleepy, poverty-stricken former Spanish colony. Puerto Rico's sugar production of 70,000 tons in 1897 grew to over 1,000,000 by 1934. The acreage planted to sugar cane trebled during the first thirty-five years of the century, but the tonnage produced multiplied tenfold.

All that looked fine on paper. The main trouble was that too much of the acreage involved came to be owned or controlled by the powerful absentee corporations, under rules of "good management," which had a certain amount of validity in those days. The owners of expensive mills felt that they had to protect their investments of millions, had to assure efficient agricultural production, by acquiring control of the lands surrounding those mills. Too many Puerto Ricans thus lost their lands and were thrown either into destitution or into employment at miserable wages by the sugar companies. Meanwhile, the birth rate and the population increased.

Four great U.S. sugar companies came to control 166,-100 acres of the island's best lands, though working only 75,900 acres. The remainder was left idle—held in reserve or, at the most, used for pasturing oxen, while starving, landless Puerto Ricans looked on.

The grabs for land continued until the depression's advent, despite the fact that such acquisitions were illegal under the federal Foraker Act. That first organic document included a provision that is still in effect—the Five-Hundred-Acre Law—under which no corporation is permitted to own or control more than 500 acres on the island. Senator Foraker had ostensibly added the provision to his act in order to protect Puerto Rico from the inroads of large mainland corporations. There are those, however, who claim

that he was influenced by the farm lobby, which wanted to
protect the U.S. beet-sugar industry against the growth of
a new cane-sugar rival in our newly acquired territory.
Whatever Foraker's motivations, the fact is that he put no
teeth into his law, no penalties for ignoring it. Therefore it
was ignored; one of the "big four" U. S. Corporations, the
Eastern Puerto Rico Sugar Company, came to control 54,-
700 acres, or more than a hundred times its legal limit.

Not until 1940 were the legal battles won, permitting the
enforcement of the Five-Hundred-Acre Law; then that enforcement, if only in part and for about half the total acreage involved, became the solid foundation for Puerto Rico's
present enormous progress.

Independent Puerto Rican sugar plants could not hold
out against the inroads of the corporations. A number, of
course, sold their land voluntarily and thus also their
means of livelihood. Others, among those who tried to continue to grow cane for sale to the company-controlled mills,
had to sell at corporation prices, with no power either to
bargain or to audit accounts. Often they were squeezed out
of the picture entirely. Credit for their operations was available to them only from the sugar companies; the banks
would not grant it. Interest rates were high. When the planters borrowed, they later often lost their lands through
mortgage foreclosures. It was these *colonos*, independent
sugar growers, who came to be the first supporters of
Muñoz Marín in the struggles that led to the revolutionary
election of 1940.

That is not saying that all Puerto Rican planters were
ruthlessly weeded out. Like the Firestone Rubber Company
in Liberia and the United Fruit Company in Central America, the absentee sugar companies took care to surround
themselves by a kind of reverse *cordon sanitaire* of in-
fluential native planters who were encouraged and helped
to become rich. A few fortunes were made; Puerto Rico's
first native millionaires appeared on the scene after World

War I, during the early 1920's. Today they are among the most ardent advocates of Puerto Rican statehood, as a sure hedge against the possible independence that would cost them their free American market. But the creation of paupers was much more rapid than was that of tycoons.

By 1930 the island's social, economic, and political system was geared almost exclusively to sugar. Transportation by highway or railroad was constructed to serve sugar; agricultural credit—the first essential for growth and development—was available only in sugar; with the exception of needlework—a sweatshop industry dominated by New York jobbers and based on the cheap labor of a stricken society—nearly all existing industries served sugar; business depended largely on sugar for its well-being; politics was dominated almost completely by the absentee-controlled sugar industry.

Not only were the various U.S.-appointed governors concerned with protecting U.S. interests, which meant sugar, but sugar also permeated the island's internal political life. The political parties that received financial donations from sugar and its associated interests could survive; the rest could not. The governor had veto power over local legislation and he also controlled government patronage. If a party were to pass local legislation to enforce the Five-Hundred-Acre Law, the governor would veto it, and even the threat, even the power of such veto was enough to make any party think twice. If the law was passed again, over the governor's disapproval, the veto power passed into the hands of the President of the United States; no president was ever known to fail to back up his governor in such a matter. The fact that the governor controlled patronage meant that he also had the power to punish any recalcitrant party by withholding from its members the jobs they needed so desperately. Without either financial contributions or patronage no party could survive. As political parties don't like to be destroyed, they behaved themselves, if

only because the United States, as the imperial nation, had
the power to destroy them if they *didn't* behave.

During the late twenties Luis Muñoz Marín was living in
self-imposed exile in New York. His reputation among the
San Juan elite was that of a Bohemian, a wastrel, who did
nothing but write an occasional poem and a rare article for
the liberal and avant-garde press. But the things he did
write were among the most penetrating analyses of Puerto
Rico's ills being produced anywhere. In an article in *The
Nation* in 1929 he pointed out that no local steps had ever
been taken to enforce the Five-Hundred-Acre Law because
no governor had ever announced that such steps, far from
drawing reprisals from him, would enlist his co-operation.

The sugar interests controlled the island's political life,
not only indirectly through the workings of the colonial
government, but also directly by the controlling of
elections. Thousands of laborers in the sugar industry voted
as they were told lest they lose their paltry jobs, with no
others in sight. Other thousands of workers and small
farmers in the hills sold their votes because they needed
the money for buying beans and rice for their gaunt families. For such vote buying the sugar companies donated
lavishly to the parties that could be trusted not to displease
the industry when in power. The legislature came to be
composed largely of Puerto Rican sugar lawyers.

Sugar, on the other hand, paid the major part of the island's taxes, employed the major part of its workers,
created the major part of its business, and supported seventeen of Puerto Rico's twenty seaports by giving them shipping.

In 1935 sugar employed some 100,000 workers, or about
twenty per cent of all who worked for wages. About 93,000
of these were farm laborers, most of whom worked four or
five months a year during the harvest season and were idle
the rest of the time. Most of the sugar workers lived in company houses, which were often better than were other rural

living quarters; they traded in company stores at prices that were generally lower than those in other stores; they had credit at some of the company stores, which helped to tide them over the long dead season; their wages were usually somewhat higher than those they could receive elsewhere. Nevertheless, Estéban Bird accused sugar of gross injustices in its treatment of labor while reaping impressive dividends for its absentee stockholders.

Bird's report on the sugar industry was prepared in 1936 at the request of the U. S. Puerto Rico Reconstruction Administration. However, it was kept under cover until 1941, when the Puerto Rican government published it. It read: "After making allowance for seasonality of employment, for supplemental labor of women and children, for the average number of idle days during the week, various agencies have estimated that the typical wage income of sugar laborers is around $170 per year." That was, of course, a tragic wage on which to raise and support a family, clothe it, educate it, and feed it largely on imported foods at prices higher than those paid in the continental United States. Bird goes on to cite the earlier study made in 1929 by the Brookings Institution, according to which the average weekly wage of a Puerto Rican working-class family was "$6.47 per family, $3.49 per worker, and $0.85 per person—approximately $0.12 per day to cover all their daily requirements. These families spend 94 per cent of their weekly earnings for food, the largest single item being polished rice—*a coolie's diet*."

"Twelve cents per person per day," writes Bird indignantly "is only four cents more than the food expense required for feeding a hog in the United States! No wonder these laborers have even lost combativeness to do what was witnessed in the United States during the recent depression—farmers in the West holding up trucks in transit laden with food, picket lines formed by a harassed and embattled farm group ready to combat by any means the des-

perate situation created by a social structure on the verge of
collapse. Twelve cents per person per day explains why
birth, sickness, accident, and death are suffered with a
helpless fatalism.

"Twelve cents per person per day is the root of all evil; it
ought to dispel the brutal contempt for this laborer held by
many defenders of the present state of affairs who accuse
him of laziness. Twelve cents per person per day plays a
prominent part in a death rate of 575 (per 100,000) for enteritis and diarrhea, 237 for tuberculosis, and 221 for malaria in the sugar cane areas of Puerto Rico."

To Bird's statement should be added that tens of thousands of Puerto Ricans were totally unemployed during the
depression and had no land on which to grow subsistence
crops, and that thousands of women were working at home
for the needlework industry, for pay that began in New
York at sweatshop rates and was divided and fractioned by
various contractors and subcontractors until at times,
when it finally reached the workers, it amounted to three
cents per dozen for hand embroidering and hemming hand-
kerchiefs.

Twelve cents per person per day, no cents at all for
150,000 unemployed, and three cents per dozen handker-
chiefs go far to explain the lethargy and spiritual corruption of Puerto Rican politics before 1940. The man who
earned that twelve cents voted as he was told lest he lose
it. The man who didn't earn it voted as he was told because
somebody paid him two dollars for so doing. From the
United States, progressively lightening its political control
through the decades, Puerto Rico had achieved a measure
of home rule that was on paper notable as colonial affairs
go. At twelve cents per person per day it tended to be a
sham, operating largely for the perpetuation of evils and
for the benefit of the entrenched interests that could afford
to pay two dollars every four years for the vote, instead of
two dollars daily for the work.

While such conditions were tragic, and while the absentee sugar corporations dominated the island's political, as well as economic, life, it must be recognized that those corporations were not the only devils on the scene. They were, however, the symbols of American "imperialism," just as similar absentee corporations, in copper, petroleum, bananas, and the like, were symbols of "Yanqui" imperialism throughout Latin America. Like the latter, the sugar corporations defended themselves by pointing out, quite correctly, that their wages and their treatment of labor were better than those that had prevailed during Spanish days, and also better than those in the branches of Puerto Rico's agriculture which had remained in Puerto Rican hands. That phenomenon was common throughout Latin America. To be sure, United States corporate interests have exploited Latin America by North American and world standards, but they have not exploited the people of Latin America nearly as much as have the Latin-American feudal barons themselves. The kind of exploitation with which we "Yanquis" have so often been charged could not exist except in the setting of even greater local exploitation by intrenched indigenous feudalism.

In Puerto Rico the tobacco- and citrus-fruit industries began to flourish after the Spanish-American War, though they were of minor importance when compared with sugar. There, too, however, U.S. capital poured in to improve conditions somewhat, but also to drain off a large share of the profits. The only part of the economy that remained exclusively in Puerto Rican hands was the production of coffee in the island's western hills. That crop, which had once commanded top luxury prices in Europe, had been Puerto Rico's economic mainstay until the advent of the twentieth century and had done relatively well until it was ruined by a disastrous hurricane and the disruptions caused by World War I. It survives today, but as a "sick" crop, and living conditions in the coffee hills are today the worst in

Puerto Rico. That they were even worse six decades ago, when the coffee business was relatively prosperous, is attested by Dr. Bailey Ashford, who served in Puerto Rico as a Major in the Medical Corps of the U.S. army. Bailey writes:

"Rose, Director of the Rockefeller Sanitary Commission, saw the poor mud-stained laborer degraded by his disease and literally submerged in the monotonous routine of coffee culture, living from hand to mouth; his children starving and sick; and his wife, no better off than he, working a bit in the coffee grove and a listless bit in the bare shack. He saw the exquisite beauty of these tropical mountains with their sheer ravines and their limpid streams. He felt the cool damp of the coffee grove under the feathery shade of the guava tree. He talked with the plantation owners and found that only a tittle of his workmen were worth their salt, and that they were held on as laborers—with a wage pitifully low, it is true—because the owner hadn't the heart to turn his half-starved people off, sick as they were. He personally verified their ragged clothes, their lack of shoes, and their docile, animal-like constancy in the work of the *amo*, or master. He talked with the *jibaros* and found a man who had descended almost if not quite to the level of the beasts, stumbling about by day over the slippery mud of the coffee plantation, sleeping cold and wet at night without bed or bed covering, eating what he could get, a fare limited principally to a mess of rice and beans, with codfish and tubers—and procreating, with no thought of the morrow, no thought of the hereafter, no thought of the future of his sons and daughters, not even a thought of a freer, better life; only a monotonous repetition of today, yesterday, and of the other yesterdays before." [1]

Ashford wrote about conditions early in the century, shortly after the end of the Spanish regime. But in 1929

[1] From a Soldier in Science, by Bailey K. Ashford (New York: William Morrow and Company; 1934). Copyright 1934 by William Morrow and Company. Quoted with permission of the publisher.

Governor Theodore Roosevelt, Jr. described the island's country people in much the same language. The Puerto Ricans were truly a stricken people. As everywhere in Latin America, although those who worked for the absentee corporations were somewhat better off than the rest, there was still justice in charging the North American corporations with exploitative imperialism because they mixed in politics and did what they could to perpetuate the local feudalism under which they could thrive.

From the beginning of American rule until the grim 1930's Puerto Rico's official statistics showed steady gains in trade, education, public health, road construction, and virtually all other matters to which such figures are devoted. The external trade grew from $19,789,000 in 1899 to $183,285,000 in 1930. We began to point with pride to the fact that under the American flag Puerto Rico had acquired more telephones per inhabitant, more miles of roads, more seats in schools, more hospital beds, more of almost everything imaginable than many another country in the Americas—whichever happened to be convenient for comparison. There were more jobs than formerly, and certainly the per-capita income, calculated on the basis of total income divided by total population, was higher than it had even been before. Since 1903 there had been a University of Puerto Rico, and some of its graduates had been able to find jobs in the insular scheme of things—in government, in the professions, in public services, and the like.

The only difficulty about all that was that it didn't benefit the people. Writing in New York in 1929, Muñoz Marín called Puerto Rico "a land of flattering statistics and distressing realities."

The illness of the island's colonial economy became apparent during the late twenties, even before the onset of the depression, when the Brookings Institution published its survey and Bailey Diffie and his wife Justine produced their *Porto Rico, a Broken Pledge.*[2] The book was extremely important as the first passionate—though at times exaggerated—attack on the evils of Puerto Rico's colonial economy to be made by a non-Puerto Rican scholar. The Diffies pointed out that although Puerto Rico usually enjoyed a favorable balance of trade in which the value of exports exceeded that of imports by about $10,000,000 annually, the balance of payments was seldom, if ever, taken into account.

The profits drained from Puerto Rico by absentee investors, the freight paid on goods exported from Puerto Rico or imported to the island from the mainland, rents on absentee-owned properties, and various other items came, according to the Diffies and to Jack De Golia's later study of the tariff and trade situation, to somewhere around $20,000,000. That meant that the economy as a whole grew poorer by about $10,000,000 per year—except for federal expenditures and the new capital investments that stopped about the time the Diffies wrote their book.

Muñoz Marín pointed out in one of his articles that Puerto Rico's "favorable" balance of trade resembled that of a burglarized house, in which exports also exceed imports.

After 1930 Puerto Rico headed rapidly toward complete bankruptcy. Municipality after municipality could not pay its obligations in wages and salaries; the bonded indebtedness, as well as private mortgages, rose to unprecedented heights; personal suffering amounting to near starvation permeated the population.

Under the aegis of the United States and in line with a

[2] Note: The island's official name during the first three decades of American rule was Porto Rico, a matter which caused many Puerto Ricans to complain that we had robbed them even of the correct spelling of their name. It was changed to Puerto Rico during the early years of the Roosevelt regime.

common colonial phenomenon that demographers have never been able to explain satisfactorily, the birth rate also began to go up. Poverty and hunger are often themselves contributors to a downward social spiral, to which a high and growing birth rate is another contributor. In 1900 the population was about 900,000; by 1940 it had risen to nearly 2,000,000. To be sure, the economy expanded during the century's early decades, but it was an artificial economy as far as Puerto Rico was concerned, devoted in too great a measure to other people's enrichment. Moreover, it didn't expand as rapidly as did the population, and stopped expanding about 1929, when new capital stopped flowing into the island.

Throughout the first four decades under the United States, Puerto Rico remained a stricken land, disease-infested, hungry, beset by poverty, unable to help itself through political action, virtually without hope.

5

Colonialism Bankrupt

WITH the universal fertility of the poor the Puerto Ricans kept shooting children like cannon balls at the rigid walls of their economy. That the economy stopped expanding with the advent of the world depression and actually began to contract increased the emotional need for the bombardment. Children kept coming; the population continued to grow; the means for supporting the population diminished. Drawn into that vicious downward spiral, Puerto Rico began to reflect the general unrest that gripped the entire Caribbean area during the 1930's. Tensions mounted; anti-American feelings increased noticeably; the desire for independence spread far and wide, not always because national sovereignty was regarded as being in itself a good thing, but because to some almost anything looked better than the prevailing inexorable destruction of human life and values. Others yearned for independence and "freedom" as symbols of human dignity and pride.

As everywhere else, the world depression proved colonialism to be bankrupt. All Puerto Ricans knew that they had come to the ends of their ropes as colonial subjects, though the native tycoons, their bread buttered lavishly on the sugar side, either refrained from saying so or screamed for statehood—as the same people still do. But it was one thing to know that colonialism was bankrupt and finished; it was quite another to know what to do about the matter in a situation in which the ultimate political power for making changes rested with the federal government, and local leaders must be careful not to offend Washington lest they themselves be finished as leaders. The arts of temporizing with authority, of knuckling under, of seeking results only through sly political maneuvering may assure the survival of politicians, but they do not create revolutionists. They create demagogues instead—rural and urban ward heelers on large or small scales.

Toynbee has generalized on such situations, which have existed before in human history and which have usually led to eventual explosions. But Toynbee has pointed out that the explosion demands the leadership and unifying influence of "a powerful personality—a breaker of the cake of custom." That breaker of the cake was on the political scene during the depression and was very busy: shaping his own thinking, winning followers among the poor, among the *colonos*, and among a few dedicated intellectuals, but also making himself increasingly feared, first by the sugar interests and later by the federal government— through the men who had been appointed as local representatives of Roosevelt's liberal New Deal. However, he was not yet quite ready to break established traditions.

Meanwhile, the Puerto Rican people and voters flocked to hear the speeches made by their established leaders; that was one of their principal forms of entertainment. But, although they were "politically-minded" to a high degree, they were also cynical about politics as a means of solving their basic problems. They knew that their leaders were ultimately controlled by Washington and therefore lacked the personal power to carry out most of their promises.

Just as they had been excluded from high positions in
American firms as a matter of U.S. business policy, Puerto
Ricans were also excluded, during the first two decades of
our rule, from high positions in their own government. Not
until 1917 were they able to secure such positions, though
still for the purpose of carrying out policies that had been
formulated in Washington; not until 1952 were the island's
people entirely free to determine their own policies, within
the framework of the American Constitution as interpreted
by the U. S. Supreme Court, and to elect their own leaders
for the purpose of fulfilling those policies.

Puerto Rico's insular politics struggled always in the
black shadow of abject poverty, dominated by that poverty
and the resulting struggle for twelve cents. Men at the
bottom of the social scale voted as they were told because
they needed their mean wages; men and women higher up
found that the greatest single employer of white-collar
workers was the government. There were virtually no industries to absorb the energies of those the university was
turning out. When the economy stopped expanding in 1930,
government became almost the only possible employer of
the ever swelling stream of maturing, educated Puerto Ricans who had to make their livings in one way or another.

Hence, although it was always carried along by glowing
phrases devoted to high ideals, Puerto Rican politics became largely a partisan struggle for control of the budget
—and thus also of patronage. A man's living, his very life,
the living and the lives of his children, often depended on
whether or not his party came to power or at least won a
few crumbs of patronage. Neighbors were set against
neighbors, ostensibly over matters of principle, but, in reality, over the question of jobs. Tradesmen, druggists, and
haberdashers in the various towns were patronized or
shunned according to their political affiliations.

As politics was largely a struggle for bread and butter, it
also came to dominate the entire insular scene. Everybody

was politically-minded, down to the lowliest street sweeper, who, though he might have been all for Puerto Rico's independence, gladly proclaimed to his party boss his loyalty to the party, as well as his passionate love for the United States, in order to get and hold his job and to be able to recommend his friends for other jobs.

Under such circumstances, it is surprising to find that Puerto Rico's politicians have always been among the most honest to be found anywhere, as far as money is concerned. Virtually all of them, during and since the Spanish regime, maintained high moral standards in financial matters involving their personal integrity; every one of them died poor. The island has never experienced great scandals involving large-scale graft as opposed to petty pilfering; the Cuban and Mexican patterns of graft-ridden large or small government offices has never developed in Puerto Rico.

Nevertheless, before Muñoz Marín changed matters in 1940, elections were riotous displays of cynical dishonesty. Votes were bought openly and shamelessly and all the more easily because the men who sold them needed the money for their hungry families. All the tricks known to crooked politicians—false registration, the use of floaters, the enlistment of the dead—were employed by the various parties with enthusiasm. A friend of mine went to the polls rather late in the 1932 elections only to be told that he had already voted—no fewer than twenty times. As all the watchers there were his personal friends, they allowed him to cast the twenty-first vote. Another friend voted in eleven different polling places in the same election. In some towns, in several elections, the number of votes cast exceeded the total populations of men, women, and children.

There was the typical story of a group of political workers who had spent a day driving about in a car, distributing campaign literature. They were driving home late in the evening, with several hundred undistributed handbills still in their car. As they passed a cemetery one of them threw all these bills over the wall to the gravestones. A companion protested. "Stop that," he cried. "Paper and printing cost money."

"Why not?" was the answer. "Those fellows vote, don't they?"

Cultural anthropologists might well speculate on whether or not the Haitian institution of the Zombie had its origins in politics, where it has existed for a long time.

The one outstanding political issue to which all parties gave lip service was that of ultimate status. While the upper classes tended to advocate eventual statehood, the majority, for one reason or another, leaned toward independence. Both were known to be beset by perils, but no other emergence from colonialism was preached as an active political tenet. Other solutions to the status problem were advanced from time to time, but not by the island's politicians addressing their constituents. Even they, however, had to keep their eyes always on Washington.

During the early years of American rule the various Washington-appointed chief executives governed with the help of the island's Republican party, which, although for statehood and therefore undoubtedly loyal, was also by far the minority party. Then Wilson was elected President, and he appointed Arthur Yager governor of Puerto Rico. Yager was a liberal-minded man who showed great respect toward local feelings on political status and did not believe that the desire for independence amounted to disloyalty to the United States. Yager was the first to co-operate with the majority party—Muñoz Rivera's Unionist party—which had strong leanings toward independence and had actually been in power since 1903. He also began the practice of placing Puerto Ricans in important executive positions that had previously been filled almost exclusively by continental Americans. As a result, relations between Washington and the island showed marked improvement.

Governor Yager also endeavored to have the original organic act, the Foraker Act, replaced by a more liberal basic law. The resulting Jones Act was a marked step in advance, but did not, however, please all the Puerto Ricans. Some of those who advocated independence objected to the fact that this act offered U.S. citizenship to the Puerto Ricans, who had until then under the Foraker Act been citizens of Puerto Rico, but not of the United States. They felt that the issue of eventual status would be clouded by that citizenship. Others objected with good reason to the fact that the Jones Act, as had the Foraker Act, stipulated that the curricula and policies of the island's school system be shaped by a Washington-appointed Commissioner of Education responsible to Washington and devoting his efforts largely to something that was vaguely and erroneously called "Americanization." They wanted school curricula to be determined by a Puerto Rican Commissioner of Education responsible to the insular legislature and permitted to devote his efforts toward shaping an educational system designed to meet the needs and problems of Puerto Rico's people.

But the Jones Act was passed in 1917, despite such objections. Both it and Yager's liberal and enlightened rule strengthened good will toward the United States immeasurably—until Harding succeeded Wilson as President, and Yager was succeeded in Puerto Rico by a new governor of the go-getter type.

This was J. Montgomery Reily, apparently appointed by Harding to wave the flag, shout hurrah, and stand for no nonsense. His inaugural ceremony on July 30, 1921, was one of the most splendid and impressive the island had ever seen, being designed to show the Puerto Ricans who was boss, and to celebrate the return of Republican sanity to national affairs. At his first meeting with leaders of the Unionist party, which had helped Yager to govern, Reily delivered a blast against the idea of independence, which he regarded as amounting to disloyalty to the United States, and announced that he would govern only with the help of men who were its avowed enemies. He would appoint Unionists to office only if Antonio R. Barceló, the party's president, publicly renounced his earlier stand on political status. Then the governor went on a barnstorming tour to all parts of the island, in which, in town halls, schools, village greens, he violently denounced the idea of independence.

That kind of thing did nothing to endear the United States to the Puerto Ricans, or to give them faith in their own political power and stability. There could be little continuity in political development as long as the island was at the mercy of changing governors with varying sets of official and personal ideas. It was dangerous to be too close to *any* governor, even a good one, lest he be succeeded by somebody who might feel otherwise and practice recriminations.

Under these circumstances of uncertainty, which characterized the 1920's, a "leader" arose who won much attention, attracted large crowds to his speeches, for a time enjoyed enthusiastic popular applause, but fizzled out tragically because his thinking had been bankrupt and outmoded from the start.

The classical, dogmatic answer to colonialism is nationalism and national sovereignty, only too often defined as being synonymous with individual freedom. The classical means of achieving that sovereignty is through violence of one kind or another—be it via George Washington or Simón Bolívar. The classical patriotic attitude toward the ruling country is one of bitter hatred expressed through constant denunciation of the grasping tyrant.

Those were the emotional ingredients of the various American revolutions. In many parts of Latin America, where nations had emerged with Spanish, Catholic cultures and with oligarchic Spanish concepts of liberty, the United

States had come, during the nineteenth and twentieth centuries, to be the classical culture enemy—the materialistic, Protestant Colossus of the North.

Stir all those ingredients together in the person of a fiery orator, and you are likely to have an explosive mixture with a strong appeal to a certain number of poverty-stricken adolescents of various ages, bewildered and hurt by their second-class citizenship. Pedro Albizu Campos was the leader who for a time had an enormous appeal for that segment of the island's population. He used an emotional patriotism, coupled with fanatical hatred of the United States, almost as a smoke screen to hide the details and real nature of Puerto Rico's ills.

Nevertheless, at a critical time, though in a tragic, negative manner, he exercised a powerful influence on Puerto Rico's history. By exploding into terrorism, he and his followers focused attention on the fact that things were seriously wrong on the island; their very terrorism forced an earnest striving toward sane and effective means of righting those wrongs.

Pedro Albizu Campos was and is a bitter man who hates the United States venomously. That he was an illegitimate child and dark in skin are said to have added to his bitterness. Certainly in all his political speeches he ceaselessly and relentlessly attacked the United States on the one point in which we are weakest in human relations—the race issue.

He attended Harvard University and graduated in 1917 with a bachelor's degree in law. During World War 1 he registered for the draft in Cambridge, but was allowed to transfer to Puerto Rico, where he was sure that no color line would be drawn. He was wrong. The U.S. army had introduced the color line where it had not existed before. Today it no longer practices racial segregation, at least in Puerto Rico; in those days it did. Albizu was assigned to the 375th Regiment, a Negro regiment whose activities were

confined to doing degrading manual labor and garrison
duty in Puerto Rico and Panama. Later he was admitted to
an officers' training camp, came out with a commission,
and was a lieutenant in the 375th when he was discharged
in January 1919.

Acutely sensitive to the many snubs he had received as a
Negro, he now began to devote his life to the cause of Puerto
Rico's independence, in the beginning as a journalist. He
argued that the United States was a usurper with no legal
standing on the island, as the section of the Treaty of Paris
by which Puerto Rico was turned over to the United States
had never been ratified by the island's people. In 1927 and
1928 he visited eleven Latin-American countries, preaching Puerto Rico's right to be a republic and doing his best to
stimulate South American hatred and suspicion of *el coloso
del norte*. The South Americans of that era were inclined to
listen to him. He became widely known and respected as a
kind of Latin Gandhi. To some Latin Americans he is still
so regarded, though their number is decreasing rapidly.
Many groups of varying kinds gave him official support.
They included Catholics and Communists, as well as a wide
variety of revolutionists.

Albizu's idea in those days was to gain international support for his cause of independence by pleading before the
League of Nations, and his apparent success in South
America was encouraging. However, one thing was still
lacking to make his case complete: popular support from
Puerto Rico itself. He sought it through the election of
1932.

In 1930 he had been elected President of the Nationalist
party, and set about immediately to prepare for the voting.
People loved his fiery speeches, in which he attacked the
United States relentlessly as a ruthless enemy desirous only
of exterminating the Puerto Rican people by means of the
birth control that seemed so mandatory to many. At one
time he even claimed that he had discovered a diabolical

plot on the part of the United States to kill off all Puerto Ricans through the injection, in their veins, of the (probably nonexistent) cancer virus. But he offered no economic program through which existing evils were to be cured.

The enthusiasm with which he was greeted everywhere raised his hopes to high pitch. But when the election returns were in it was found that he had won only five per cent of the total vote in his personal race for the office of Senator-at-Large, and his party had polled less than two per cent. That killed the Nationalists as a political "party," as the law stipulated that they had to win a minimum of ten per cent in order to go to the next election without a preliminary petition inscription of the same size. Since then their membership has shrunk to a mere 300 or so, and only the future can reveal whether or not those few are still devoted to the terrorism to which their political rout had reduced them.

Some claimed that independence couldn't possibly win in a colonial polling because the weapons of economic terrorism would later be used against those who voted for it; but whatever the election's meaning, Albizu could not, with a two per cent vote for his platform, go before the League of Nations in Geneva to claim popular support for Puerto Rico's independence.

Defeated in their efforts to create a real Republic of Puerto Rico, the Nationalists now built a sham one in a play-acting fashion. Many of them, especially the younger ones, were deadly serious about it as within the existing climate of stagnation there were no other outlets for their creative, patriotic impulses. Albizu Campos was President, with a number of busy ministers to conduct the affairs of state, with the foreign representation he had built up in eleven Latin-American republics, with an "Army of Liberation" uniformed in white pants and black shirts and armed, if at all, largely with wooden guns.

Politically, the Nationalists seemed to content themselves with making speeches during the first few years after the disastrous 1932 election. They harangued the Puerto Rican people everywhere—on the streets, in the plazas, in halls, and over the radio—with a message of unceasing, bitter hatred for the United States and everything North American. President Roosevelt and Mrs. Roosevelt, Secretary Ickes, and other federal officials, the institution of colonialism, America's intentions toward Puerto Rico, the island's own officials and leaders, especially Muñoz Marín, the absentee ownership of land, and the morals of various prominent ladies—all these and many more things were blasted indiscriminately and venomously for years.

The students at the university canonized Albizu, but he came to talk himself out of that honor in several vituperative speeches in which he accused the university boys of effeminacy and lack of patriotism, and implied that the girls, because they were departing from traditional Spanish patterns of behavior and dress and were taking on freer American ways, were immoral. In 1935 many of the students therefore decided to defend themselves, and arranged for an assembly of censure to be held on October 24. Feeling ran so high that it was agreed that all students attending the meeting would have to check their revolvers at the door before entering. Determined to break up the meeting, armed Nationalists drove to the university in cars. They were stopped by the police, and in the ensuing exchange of shots a policeman was seriously wounded, a spectator and four Nationalists were killed, and one Nationalist was injured. That was the beginning of Puerto Rico's recurring bath of blood. Two days later, at the funeral of his four "martyrs," Albizu preached a violent sermon of hate against everything American and against the police as tools of Yankee imperialism, calling on his listeners to avenge the deaths of their four heroic comrades in arms.

Colonel E. Francis Riggs, the Washington-appointed chief of the island's police force, was the first to be singled out for that revenge. He was a decent man, tolerant, well-liked, liberal in his political views, who favored Puerto Rico's independence in the sense that he favored the principle of self-determination. He was also an ardent Catholic who went to Mass regularly. On Sunday, February 23, 1936, on his return from San Juan Cathedral, he was waylaid by two young Nationalists and shot to death. They were immediately arrested and taken to the police station, and there the police lost their heads. Behind the station's closed doors, their prisoners disarmed, they reached for their guns and riddled the two Nationalists with bullets.

The tragic chain of events set off by that senseless lynching is described in Chapter 6. Suffice it here to say that Albizu created a situation in which all the Puerto Ricans seemed officially to be blamed by Washington for the actions of a few fanatics, and all Puerto Rico was punished accordingly. He and seven of his associates were tried in the federal court, and sentenced to relatively brief terms in Atlanta Penitentiary. On his return to Puerto Rico in December 1947, he again began to urge his fanatical followers to commit murder in Puerto Rico's holy cause.

The Nationalists made news again in 1950, when they staged a widespread and bloody upheaval in many parts of Puerto Rico—while trying to assassinate President Truman in Washington and Governor Muñoz Marín in San Juan. On March 1, 1954, the day of the opening of the Tenth Conference on Inter-American Affairs in Caracas, four of them stood in the gallery of Washington's House of Representatives, uttered a cry for Puerto Rico's freedom, and sprayed the House with bullets, indiscriminately wounding five congressmen. They did it in an attempt to embarrass the United States at the Caracas conference. However, by the time of those two terroristic actions the government of the

United States, the press, the American people, had grown more realistic in their concepts of Puerto Rico and had begun to abandon the senseless former habit of lumping all Puerto Ricans under the vicious term "they." No longer were all the island's people blamed for the acts of a few crazy terrorists seeking martyrdom in a chimerical cause.

Two years before the 1950 outbreak the people of Puerto Rico had elected their own governor for the first time in their history. The island's colonialism had been modified drastically and Washington's officials no longer thought it necessary to take charge of every major move in its affairs. Albizu was this time tried in a Puerto Rican court, which convicted him of inciting to murder and sentenced him for eighty years. But again he managed to win a certain international audience, this time by inventing a fantastic martyrdom.

While in prison he complained ceaselessly and bitterly, writing letters to the Pan-American Union and to various Latin-American republics about the evil United States. Day and night he kept wet towels on his head, his chest, and his genitals—as protection against the atomic radiation with which, according to his claims, the United States was inefficiently trying to kill him. He accused Washington of keeping three machinery-laden ships anchored off Puerto Rico's coast to send a steady stream of radiations against his poor, frail body, and believed that those ships contained radar equipment to keep track of his precise whereabouts —just in case the Puerto Rican authorities tried to move him out of the bombardment's way.

Governor Muñoz Marín pardoned Albizu in 1953, one reason being that he was obviously a sick man, whose "martyrdom" won him a certain amount of sympathetic attention in non-Puerto Rican circles. One result of that official clemency was the shooting in Congress on March 1, 1954. Today Albizu is back in prison for life. He can receive visitors; he still complains of U.S. efforts to kill him with atomic radiations; but he receives the best care, medical and other, the Puerto Rican government can give him.

Governor Muñoz Marín spoke not only for himself, but expressed Puerto Rico's general view, when he told Congress, the President, Washington officialdom, and the press, immediately after the fateful shooting of March 1, 1954, that Pedro Albizu Campos is in fact a bitter enemy of the Puerto Rican people rather than of the United States. The governor is also known for the statement that "never in history has one leader exercised so strong an influence over so few people."

The Nationalists are today aging and rapidly diminishing in numbers. Nationalist cells may still exist, especially in New York and Chicago, where Puerto Ricans are widely regarded as an alien group, with second-class citizenship akin to that of Negroes. One thing, however, has been definitely established by the history of recent decades: the motivations of these terrorists must not be sought in the realm of reason, but in that of abnormal psychology.

While the Nationalists were coming to prominence during the depression, the U.S. government tried to face Puerto Rico's ills in its own way.

Throughout the first three decades of American rule virtually all the governors had filled their official reports and public statements with statistics on mounting trade, favorable balances, increasing numbers of schools, telephones, and miles of roads constructed; they waved the flag with varying degrees of enthusiasm and played with varying degrees of skill on the "here we are and watch us grow" theme. Hoover's governor, Theodore Roosevelt, Jr. was the first to look at people, instead of statistics, and to say: "This is awful." A decent man, profoundly shocked, he wrote articles in the U. S. Press about the conditions he saw, and did his best, as governor, to ease the people's misery. In 1929, in an article in the New York *Herald Tribune* called "Children of Famine," he wrote as follows about island conditions:

"Riding through the hills, I have stopped at farm after farm, where lean, underfed women and sickly men repeated again and again the same story—little food and no opportunity to get more. From these hills the people have streamed into the coastal towns, increasing the already severe unemployment situation there. Housing facilities, of course, are woefully inadequate. Besides, the lack of funds and the increased work have rendered it impossible for our Health Department to cope satisfactorily with our increasing problem."

This article was published before the stock-market crash. When the world depression finally became officially recognized as such, conditions in Puerto Rico were infinitely worse than anywhere in the United States. Slow, and sometimes rapid, starvation was found everywhere. Health conditions were awful: malaria, tuberculosis, and gastrointestinal diseases took a staggering toll. If one drove a car over the country roads, one was delayed again and again by sorrowing funeral processions carrying the caskets of dead infants.

Most of the cities were infested by "wolf gangs" of children ranging in ages from six to sixteen, many of whom had no idea of who their parents were. They pilfered and robbed; they "protected" parked automobiles, and if the drivers didn't want to pay for such protection, they siphoned gasoline out of tanks, stole hub caps, slashed tires. They slept where they could—in parks, in hallways, in alleys. The authorities could not cope with them. Not enough jails or other institutions were available, and if there had been, the children would have been only too delighted to go where they could obtain free board and lodging.

Teenagers were for a time successful in a special racket. They entered post offices and smashed boxes—always before witnesses. As mailboxes were federal property, they were then tried in the federal court and sentenced to the federal reform school in Chillicothe, Ohio. When one of them was sentenced, his family called in all the neighbors for a celebration that could not have been more joyful if he had won an appointment to West Point. The boy had made good! He was going to a place where, for a number of years, he would get an education, learn English, learn a trade, and enjoy free food, clothing, and housing. The crime wave stopped when the federal judge caught on to what was happening and stopped sending Puerto Rican boys to Chillicothe.

Grown men, workers in the cane fields, committed honorable crimes to be able to hold their jobs. Many of them became so weak and emaciated during the seven months' "dead season" between harvests that they were in danger of not being able to bring in the harvest at all. A month before the cane-cutting season began they stole things out of stores —again always before witnesses—in order to be sent to prison, where society would build up their strength with adequate food and treatment for malaria and other wasting diseases.

Colonialism's bankruptcy was piled on top of the world depression. Early in the New Deal days, in August 1933, Washington sent its Emergency Relief Administration to Puerto Rico, where it became known first as the Puerto Rico Relief Administration, or PRERA, and later as the Federal Relief Administration, or FERA. Headed locally by James Bourne, now of Rhinebeck, New York, and his wife, Dorothy Bourne, an able social worker who is now Dean of Bard College, it became a tremendous, organized effort to spend a million dollars a month where the money would do the most good, in accordance with the rules that had been formulated in Washington. Its primary purpose was to keep people alive by providing millions of meals to the starving.

The need for relief was even greater in Puerto Rico than

on the mainland. It was increased considerably in 1934, when the Costigan-Jones Act put sugar production on a quota basis, reduced the island's production of sugar, paid bonuses to the proprietors for *not* growing cane, but made no provision for the thousands of agricultural workers who were thereby deprived of their jobs.

The PRERA was a vast, sprawling organization, harassed by Washington's rules, according to which relief was to remain essentially relief and not a plan for changing the basic economy. The organization frantically trained social workers to tackle the insuperable job of evaluating the human needs that were only too devastatingly obvious. It began its enormous task with direct relief, but soon branched into work relief, bending its efforts toward economic reconstruction and developing plans for future steps in that direction. White-collar projects included research, investigation, and planning in many branches of the island's life. Those activities were to prove invaluable; they focused attention on the detailed nature of prevailing ills as nothing before them had ever done. Many a Puerto Rican who was later, after the election of 1940, to play a role in his country's reshaping had his or her first stimulation in that direction from James and Dorothy Bourne; it was their activities, too, that were responsible for the first rough draft of the program that was to be carried out after the people of Puerto Rico had gained control of their own destiny.

There were, of course, thousands of dole payments in money, meals, clothing, and other necessities. A program of public works created badly needed new schools, hospitals, bridges, and the like. In its agricultural program the PRERA fostered home truck gardens, provided seed beds and nurseries for the coffee belt—which couldn't sell its crop in any event—and gave facilities and instruction for the establishment of canning centers in which women could preserve their crops. The co-operative movement

that is today beginning to gather real strength had some of
its earliest beginnings in the PRERA co-operatives for bar-
ter and exchange, and for the production and marketing of
hand-made arts and crafts. There were projects in fisheries
and shoemaking, and 5,000 women were kept reasonably
"busy" in needlework shops where they were constantly
cautioned to slow down because Washington, instigated by
private industry, had issued a fiat on the total expenditures
that must go, relatively, for wages and for materials.

The PRERA instituted and maintained many public-wel-
fare activities, among the most famous of which was the
maternal-health program. This was Puerto Rico's first organized public attempt at birth control. In a number of free
clinics women for whom it was mortally dangerous to have
more children obtained advice and contraceptives. The
clinics were swamped with clients. Later, when the relief
organization was replaced by the Puerto Rico Reconstruction Administration, the maternal-health clinics were
taken over by the latter as being among the most important
federal activities on the island. Just before the election of
1936, however, they were closed on peremptory orders
from Washington, resulting from political pressure on
Roosevelt.

The Catholic women in a Catholic society avidly accepted help for the limitation of their families. It was not
they who objected to the dissemination of birth-control information; it was politicians in the Protestant ruling country!

All that and much more amounted to the ruling country's
declaration of colonialism's bankruptcy. It was an anguished time, but also—though few realized it—a time of
creation. The Relief Administration demonstrated the need
for some kind of economic reshaping to eliminate some of
the basic causes of suffering. Out of relief, by tortuous
means, was to come the Reconstruction Administration;
emerging from that, again with much friction and agony,

was the modern, progressive Puerto Rico. That did not happen gradually through the slow processes of evolution. It happened suddenly, explosively, between the elections of 1936 and 1940.

6

The Breaker of the Cake

ALBIZU CAMPOS and the fanatics among his followers were and are dogmatically "Latin American" in thought and orientations. The troubles they caused, once widely applauded throughout Latin America, are symptomatic of the gulf that still exists between the Latin-American and Anglo-American cultures. That the gulf is narrowing rapidly in Puerto Rico is not a unique phenomenon; it is narrowing, though too slowly, everywhere down to Cape Horn. However, Puerto Rico could not play an important role had not its modern leader, Muñoz Marín, first bridged the gulf between the two cultures in his own person, his own thinking and orientations. His followers call him "our first twentieth-century leader."

At the beginning of the century the cultural gulf between the two Americas—and also between Puerto Rico and the United States—was far wider than it is today. The ceding of their island to the United States demanded a traumatic readjustment of the Puerto Ricans. Descent from the feudal conquistadors—four centuries of living in and with a Spanish cultural environment while virtually isolated from the rest of the world—could hardly prepare these people to deal successfully as colonial subjects with those who had descended from the freedom-seeking Pilgrims, from Roger Williams and Calvin. In those days, moreover, the United States, just beginning to emerge from its own classic isolation, was even more lusty and all-knowing than it is today, cocky about its sudden assumption of a new role as a world power, sure of itself, not given to philosophic speculations.

Puerto Rico's political leaders during the island's first three decades under American rule were essentially Spanish in their philosophy and orientations. Their language, their thinking, their sense of social values and of human dignity often clashed with the American go-getter spirit. Their traditional, oligarchic sense of liberty and justice and their cultural demand for intellectual and philosophical consistency were often sharply at variance with America's exuberant, youthful faith in the superiority of everything American.

Even Luis Muñoz Rivera, one of the greatest of them all, found it difficult to cope with the American Congress after he had coped successfully with the Spanish Cortes. When he first went to Washington as the island's Resident Commissioner, he knew almost no English; it is said of him with admiration that he became eloquent in the language through only one year of hard study. Nevertheless, his language differed radically from that of Congress. He could hardly be expected to grasp the semantics involved in the sudden, overwhelming outrush of American corporate enterprise, with all its political ramifications, with its smug assumption that Puerto Ricans of all classes stood to gain most from the maximum gains of those branches of American business which had early established themselves on the island.

Known as Puerto Rico's George Washington, Muñoz Rivera was the man who had obtained from Spain the short-lived charter of home rule which had been set aside when the United States stepped in. He was the founder and editor-owner of *La Democracia*, a crusading newspaper, and was one of the group of men who, during the nineteenth century strove to awaken Puerto Rico's people to their own dignity, problems, and powers. The idol of the island's country people, he stood politically for Puerto Rico's autonomy.

His son, Luis Muñoz Marín, was born in San Juan in 1898, but was reared mostly in New York and in Washington. For some years his father published a crusading magazine in New York, exposing Puerto Rico's woes as a colony. Later he became the island's Resident Commissioner in Washington. The son early became acclimatized to U.S. ways of thinking, and came to be intimately acquainted with the workings and psychology of the American government. The great problem of adjustment the century presented to his people was and is no personal problem to Muñoz Marín. Not only is he a master of English and a brilliant conversationalist in either English or Spanish, but he seems never to have been torn between the Latin and Anglo cultures; he is as much at home in the one as in the other.

Like many Latins, young Muñoz was greatly—and in his case bilingually—interested in poetry. He didn't write much, but what he did produce showed a deep identification with Puerto Rico's poor, whose idol he was to become later in life. One fragment—about the submerged sugar laborers—is worth repeating here. Its English version is from the poem "Pamphlet," found in the *Anthology of Contemporary Latin-American Poetry*, edited by Dudley Fitts.

> *I have drowned my dreams*
> *in order to glut the dreams that sleep for me in*
> *the veins*
> *of men who sweated and wept and raged*
> *to season my coffee. . . .*

The dream that sleeps in breasts stifled by tubercu-
losis
   (*A little air, a little sunshine*)
the dreams that dream in stomachs strangled by
hunger
   (*A bit of bread a bit of white bread*)
the dream of bare feet
   (*Fewer stones on the road, Lord, fewer broken*
   bottles)
the dream of calloused hands
   (*Moss . . . clean cambric . . . things smooth,*
   soft, soothing!
the dream of trampled hearts
   (*Love . . . life . . . life!*)

In 1919 Luis married Muna Lee, originally from Mississippi. For a time they lived on Staten Island, as friends and neighbors of Edwin Markham. There young Muñoz wrote a famous and still standard Spanish translation of "The Man with the Hoe." Earlier he had read a book on socialism and had come to regard himself as a Socialist. In 1920 he went to Puerto Rico, became associated with the island's Socialist party, made speeches for the party, and had his first taste of active political campaigning. Though Muñoz Rivera had died in 1917, many people were shocked that the son should depart from his father's Union party and associate with the political Left. Despite its name, however, the Socialist party was not particularly radical; in effect, it was a labor party identified with the A. F. of L. on the mainland. Nevertheless, his open associations with it indicated young Muñoz's political leanings; they also showed that he had no intention of riding into politics on the coattails of his famous father: he intended to make his own way in his own manner.

Returning to New York, he resumed the life that Rexford Tugwell in his *The Art of Politics* describes as a wastrel's dilettante existence, as aimless loafing. But Tugwell was wrong. In terms of wordage Muñoz's literary output was small; in terms of content it was enormous. As a freelancer, he began to write articles on Puerto Rico for such periodicals as *The Nation, The New Republic,* and H. L. Mencken's *The American Mercury.* By far the most brilliant and daring analyses ever written of Puerto Rico's ills and its relations with the United States, they created a sensation on the island, though they were also resented by the superpatriots as being radical and even revolutionary in nature. As a New York writer, Muñoz became a new voice in Puerto Rican affairs; he set new patterns of thought and captured a small but important following of intellectuals.

Through and with Muna Lee, Muñoz came to have close contacts with a number of outstanding American intellectuals, with prominent Latin Americans, and with young and ardent Americans—Anglo as well as Latin—who were later to become prominent. Composed of poets, singers, novelists, engineers, journalists, philosophers, politicians, that heterogeneous group met at his home every Sunday evening for the sole purpose of stimulating each other. The "Sunday evenings at home" became a famous New York institution. There almost any week one was likely to meet such people as Edward Arlington Robinson, Sara Teasdale, William Rose Benét, Vilhjalmur Stefansson, George Hubert (later Sir Hubert) Wilkins, Horace and Marya Gregory, Constance Lindsay Skinner, and many others of New York's famous, near-famous, or about-to-be famous.

In midsummer 1926 Luis and Muna and their two children, Luisito and Munita, moved to San Juan, where he became editor of his father's old newspaper, *La Democracia.* The paper was financially in bad straits. Getting it out was a daily struggle and problem, but editing it gave Muñoz another platform from which to talk to his people. He talked plainly and bluntly, and often he was every bit as embarrassing to the cautious politicians on one side as on the other. He pounded away at Puerto Rico's ills, called on both U.S. and Puerto Rican leaders to do something about them, strengthened his hold on the island's intellectuals, frightened the politicians, and was written off by the blasé and respectable as a mere dilettante and an incurable Bohemian.

In 1928 the island politicians got together to get him out of the way. They sent him on an "industrial mission" to New York, charged with finding capital for new Puerto Rican industries. But in those days there was hardly a chance of finding such capital; Muñoz must have known it, and the politicians also. The aim of sending him on that wild goose chase could have been only his removal from the Puerto Rican scene.

It was undoubtedly during this time that Muñoz's political thinking began to jell. Up to this point he had analyzed his country's ills and had repeatedly made passionate appeals to Puerto Rico's political leaders, as well as to the United States' authorities, to do something about those ills. Except for his own exile to New York, the results of those efforts were hardly spectacular. The two sides in the political lineup were stalemated, politically bankrupt. It must have been increasingly evident to Muñoz in those days that if ever anything was to be done to save Puerto Rico from destruction, the people of Puerto Rico would themselves have to take the initiative. The psychologically devastating institution of colonialism stood in the way of such action; salvation from colonialism was deterred by the lethargy it created. Statehood was no possible way out; among other things, it could well result in more, rather than less, domination by corporate United States interests, as well as in the kind of destructive cultural humiliation that had been suffered by the once proud Latin Americans in Texas, New Mexico, and California.

No political solution seemed possible except Puerto Rico's eventual independence. In 1931 in San Juan I once ar-

gued the question with him, pointing out the economic and
other dangers involved in a struggle for sovereignty.
"Damn it," he answered, "we are the ones who have to save
ourselves, and we can't do it under the present system. Our
hands are tied. And besides, I want my people to *want* independence. It is degrading for a lot of colonial subjects not
to want to be free. They don't assert themselves. They can't.
Let them once want independence, and they will begin to
assert themselves. Then we can cross the next bridge when
we come to it. Let them once assert themselves, and they
may not need independence. Perhaps we can then find
something better. But, as of now, independence is the only
solution."

The money for his "industrial mission" soon ran out.
While Muna Lee worked for the University of Puerto Rico
and later for the National Women's Party in Washington,
Muñoz wandered about the United States in an old car he
had acquired for the purpose, writing weekly articles for the
Baltimore *Sun,* occasional articles at space rates for other
papers, and living as best he could—largely on bananas and
hamburgers. Some years later, when *Fortune* interviewed
him about his dramatic victory in the 1940 election, he
mentioned that foot-loose period and said: "When I found
I could do that, I knew I was a free man." Wherever he was,
however, all the time he was roaming he kept writing ardent letters to his friends in Puerto Rico and to Puerto Rican political leaders who may or may not have been his
friends, trying to arouse them to action, pounding away at
the one central message: "independence is the only possible solution."

Those years were in no way a wastrel's "loafing." As I
look back on my own contacts with him in those days, and
as I read the bits of history and memory others have written since, it seems clear that he was driven by one force,
and one only: a profound, if at times unrecognized, sense

of destiny, of complete personal identification with Puerto Rico's future.

For some years he was bracketed with the fanatical Albizu Campos as one of the island's two outstanding leaders for national sovereignty; in the thinking of many super-patriotic Puerto Ricans and of some continental Americans he was therefore branded as an enemy of the United States. Today, at a time when his island has found a new way of living and working with the United States for the benefit of both countries, his political opposition still points out that he started his political life as such an "enemy." The opposition uses the argument to cast doubt on the integrity of his current leadership.

But, while it was true that Muñoz and Albizu were for a time the two outstanding strivers for their island's independence, their basic motivations were poles apart. The one hated the United States bitterly; the other cherished it. "I want independence," Muñoz said, "as a matter of mutual convenience to the people of Puerto Rico and those of the United States." The one advocated violence and death as a means for achieving his end; the other insisted on working out differences by friendly and peaceful means. In later years, when he was heckled by a congressional committee for his views on independence—and the terroristic actions of the Nationalist had by that time succeeded in identifying a desire for independence with hatred and murder—he startled the congressmen by saying: "Gentlemen, without in the least wanting to belittle the memory of George Washington, I must still say that I am unalterably opposed to the achievement of independence by force of arms."

Albizu had no economic program, he stood for "dignity" and "patriotism" and avoided the word "starvation." During the depression years, when Muñoz saw a liberal Uncle Sam pouring many millions of dollars of relief money into his island, he said: "Puerto Rico is a lean and hungry cow, which must be fed by the American taxpayers, only to be milked by four great sugar corporations."

The structure of his thinking on independence came to have a complex base of apparently solid practicality. Puerto Rico needed to enforce the federal Five-Hundred-Acre Law; apparently that could not be done under either statehood or colonialism. Independence seemed the only answer. The Puerto Ricans needed to create and protect the infant industries that were impossible in those days in part because of the constant threat of dumping from the mainland. Under statehood, such protection was impossible. Independence seemed the only answer. They needed low-cost shipping. Under colonialism, as well as statehood, they would be tied to the U. S. Coastwise Shipping Law and to U.S. shipping, which is the world's most expensive. To be sure, they enjoyed a free market within the structure of the U.S. tariff. But within that structure they also had to buy in the U.S. market—the world's most expensive. Under independence they would be able to buy in low-priced markets —meat in the Dominican Republic, rice in Brazil, instead of codfish in Gloucester and rice in Louisiana.

To Muñoz, independence was not a mere emotional, patriotic matter, but a means toward the dignified survival of people and the human spirit. The "solution" was the poet's solution, in the sense in which a poet is one who at all times identifies with people rather than with established dogmas —with the problems, fears, and aspirations of live human beings—instead of with life's ideological distillates.

For these reasons and others, including the fact that he had a deep affection for the United States, there was nothing in his thinking to preclude his working *with* Washington's more liberal elements toward ultimate solutions to Puerto Rico's more pressing problems. Moreover, regardless of whether or not he realized the fact, his task of educating Washington and the American people was every bit as great as was that of educating the San Juan politicians and the people of Puerto Rico.

During the terrible depression year of 1931 he felt ready to return to his country and get back into political life. He drove his rattling old automobile to New York, gave it to a friend—a famous, embattled leader for women's suffrage —and spent the better part of a night drinking innumerable cups of coffee with a struggling Latin-American novelist. This was Rómulo Gallegos, who was soon, through his *Doña Bárbara,* to become world-famous as one of South America's greatest writers, Later, in 1948, Gallegos became Venezuela's first democratically elected President, only to be deposed after a few months by the reactionary military junta that was to lead to General Pérez Jiménez's unspeakably despotic rule.

The next day Muñoz sailed for Puerto Rico. The son of the beloved Muñoz Rivera, a brilliant speaker in his own right, a man with independent ideas and unassailable intellectual integrity, he had no trouble in establishing himself as a person to be reckoned with politically. His ability to attract votes was undeniable. The question of which party would get the benefit of those votes remained to be answered.

The Socialists with whom he had once worked were now out of the question. For the 1932 election they had entered into an alliance that seems fantastic to North Americans, but was understandable in Puerto Rico's atmosphere of political expediency. By way of making a united front against the powerful Liberal party, the Socialists had entered into a coalition with the reactionary Republican party, which stood for statehood and "Americanism" of the 200 per cent kind. The Liberal party, which had been getting the majority of votes, had strong leanings toward independence, and was the lineal descendant of Muñoz Rivera's former Union party with its dedication to "autonomy."

Muñoz Marín joined the Liberal party, ran for Senator-at-Large, and came to office in the same electoral upheaval that brought Franklin D. Roosevelt to the Presidency in the United States. The Liberal party did not "win" that election. It polled more votes than did any other, but not more than did the Coalition of Republicans and Socialists, which gained official control of the insular government. At the Liberal party's convention, Muñoz had forced it to come out officially on the question of political status, with independence the most important single plank in its platform. The party's head, Antonio Barceló, lived to regret having taken in the stormy young man whose subsequent career was to destroy the party. Washington was suddenly to find a new kind of Puerto Rican on its doorsteps and in its offices, one who worked toward a new kind of psychological relationship between the federal government and the island, an earnest, persuasive young man who nevertheless had a tremendous lust for life, was a trencherman of the first order, and spent long nights on end in the various hotel taprooms, in brilliant conversation with a wide variety of friends.

Going to Washington was not his business. His business was to prepare and vote on local legislation, within the local, colonial scheme of things. Relations with Washington were officially in the hands of the Resident Commissioner, Muñoz's former friend, Santiago Iglesias, founder and head of Puerto Rico's Socialist party. Nevertheless, after succeeding in putting through legislation by which slot machines are still barred in Puerto Rico, the young senator transferred most of his activities to the national capital, where his successes were to drive the Coalition politicians wild with anger, frustration, and apprehension. Indeed, those successes were eventually to spell the death, also, of the Socialist party in that they led to entirely new political lineups in Puerto Rico, based on new sets of ideas.

A considerable part of his success as a lobbyist and of his strength as a leader on the island owed to his resuming the editorship of *La Democracia,* which gave him a newspaper platform, and to his arranging for the services of a remarkable woman as the paper's Washington correspondent. She was an old friend of Muna Lee, named Ruby Black. Ruby was intensely interested in Puerto Rico's cause, ran a news agency of her own, and was one of those several women journalists who were friends of Mrs. Roosevelt and at times enjoyed almost a family relationship with both her and the President.

Ruby came to be Muñoz's indefatigable co-worker in Washington during the four years following his election. As a journalist she had access to much information and gossip, which she passed on in a steady stream of letters. In part through her, whether he was in Washington or in San Juan, Muñoz seemed to know much more about what was going on in the capital than did the official Resident Commissioner. When he was in San Juan and wanted to send confidential messages to various people in Washington, he could rely on her to do the job. When he wanted information, she got it for him—at times through discreet snooping, at others by interviewing people. *La Democracia* came to have much better coverage of the Washington scene, under Ruby's by-line, than did any of the more powerful and successful papers.

Muñoz's political enemies, of course, unused to that kind of relationship, accused her variously of being his mistress, his half-sister, or a nonexistent figment of his diabolical imagination. But his Puerto Rican friends came to know her well. Ruby's Alexandria home became a salon for any and all Muñocistas who came to Washington, and the latter talked jokingly about hauling down the statue of Columbus in San Juan and putting Ruby Black in his place as a twentieth-century discoverer of Puerto Rico.

The case of Robert H. Gore was Muñoz's first dramatic political triumph, as well as his first resounding victory against the hocus-pocus of colonialism.

Precisely as Puerto Rico had long been a dumping ground for shoddy American goods, so it was also at times convenient as a dumping ground for shoddy, third-rate politicians for whom the powers in Washington could find no other place. Now, after Roosevelt's election the Democratic party demanded its pound of flesh. Gore, a Florida politician with money, who had helped to start and finance the Roosevelt boom, wanted his just reward, and the President thoughtlessly appointed him Governor of Puerto Rico. In 1953 José Padín, then and now the island's honored Elder Statesman, wrote me: "Gore defeated himself through his own appalling incompetence. I believe that the appointment of this man as governor . . . is the most disgraceful act committed by any President against Puerto Rico. . . . Roosevelt was a very irresponsible man at times. Of course, he corrected his error, because he was a great man."

Getting Gore in was Jim Farley's doing; getting him out again was Muñoz's.

Shortly after the new governor's arrival in San Juan, Muñoz and Barceló called on him as representatives of the party that had polled the most votes, bringing with them a list of the Liberal party members whom they wanted Gore to appoint to various positions. They soon discovered that (1) the governor was going to work with the Coalition and intended to give nothing at all to the Liberals, whom he regarded as being anti-American because of their stand for independence; (2) he made it a condition of appointment that the incumbent give the governor his resignation, with date left blank, on the day he took office. They hastily withdrew their entire list and were in the happy position of having the Republicans and Socialists almost as indignant against the governor (over the insult of the undated resignations) as they were themselves.

In *La Democracia* Muñoz now began to publish a series of fiery editorials attacking Gore, who foolishly denied that he had ever demanded the resignations as conditions for appointment to office. The most famous of them appeared under the English headline. GOVERNOR GORE, YOU ARE A DAMN LIAR and dared the island's chief executive to sue the editor. The latter didn't, but Puerto Rico had the example of a leader who dared to stand up openly against the representative of the United States.

Gore regarded the university as a hotbed of anti-Americanism, principally because the majority of its students were for Puerto Rico's independence. To its Board of Trustees he appointed a man whose Americanism was unquestioned, but who was otherwise all but illiterate. The students went on strike against the appointment. Tensions mounted throughout the island. A small, harmless bomb—perhaps a stick of dynamite, perhaps a firecracker—made a noise and thus created newspaper copy when it exploded harmlessly at Jajome Alto, the governor's official country residence. Muñoz Marín caught the first steamer for the continent. In Washington Ruby Black arranged for him an unofficial appointment with Roosevelt, over a cup of tea.

Muñoz complained to the President about the mess that Gore had made in Puerto Rico, the tensions he had created, the unnecessary but dangerous resentments against the United States that he was stirring up. But Roosevelt was thinking of the students' strike, being perhaps apprehensively aware of the bloody role that Cuban university students had a little earlier played in the ABC uprisings that had brought the army sergeant Fulgencio Batista to power as President of Cuba. He objected to students, "immature children," mixing into political matters. "They ought to be spanked," he said, wishing that they would stick to sports and studies.

"Mr. President," Muñoz, answered, "I mentioned the student strike only to show that the opposition to Gore is nonpartisan. The students belong to all parties. Besides, the alumni passed a resolution backing up the students, and you must admit that most of *them* are probably over twenty-one."

The President admitted that they probably were.

"Not only that, but the parents passed a resolution backing up their striking sons and daughters—which almost never happens when our students go on a rampage."

With that Roosevelt let out one of his characteristic guffaws. "I'll admit that *they* are over twenty-one. They must be over twenty-one."

Alike in many ways, the two men understood each other at their first meeting. Later Roosevelt was to become increasingly annoyed with Muñoz, but at that meeting he gave his promise that Gore would resign. There was some delay because Roosevelt didn't like to withdraw one of his appointees under fire. Muñoz sent a "cease fire" cable to San Juan, and the storm abated. But he waited in Washington, getting acquainted with various New Deal officials, until the resignation was announced. Then he took the first steamer home.

When he landed, he found thousands of people waiting to welcome him at the dock, as the triumphant conqueror. The spontaneous parade they gave him was one of the most enthusiastic in the city's history; it was all the more dramatic because Gore had himself returned a few weeks before and had been met by a crowd that had gathered to boo and hiss him.

Muñoz was definitely established as a popular leader. The only fly that was to appear in the ointment was that Gore's successor, though not appointed for the cynical purpose of repaying a political debt, was even more inept than Gore had been.

General Blanton Winship was a handsome, correct, southern gentleman who had formerly been the army's Judge Advocate General and had once gone to Liberia on a legal mission. He didn't look offensive and he didn't say much, partly because he didn't have much to say, partly because he was elderly and tired, and said openly that he wanted no headaches and planned to devote his governorship to resting amid pleasant surroundings. They were to become less pleasant as time went on; the uproar against him was to grow even greater than had been that against Gore; but Roosevelt was tired of sending governors to Puerto Rico only to have their recall demanded almost immediately.

What was only vaguely apparent was that in those days the institution of colonialism had itself already run its full course and was due to be scrapped, along with the device of a Washington-appointed governor—regardless of whether he happened to be a good governor or a bad one.

Sometime after the Gore affair, Mrs. Roosevelt and Rexford Tugwell, then Washington's Undersecretary of Agriculture, visited Puerto Rico. Muñoz had meanwhile organized a discussion group, which met on occasional Sundays in the home of Dr. Carlos Chardón, chancellor of the university, to discuss the island's plight and its possible remedies. He invited the two distinguished visitors to meet with this group; they were so impressed that Chardón and two others, Rafael Fernández García, a professor at the university, and Menendez Ramos, the island's Commissioner of Agriculture, were eventually invited to Washington as a commission to draft a comprehensive, workable plan for the island's economic reconstruction. Muñoz was asked to go along as an unofficial member.

Unprecedented in the island's history, this step stirred high hopes and higher enthusiasm. Not only was the commission a sign that Washington really cared about the plight of the Puerto Ricans, but it was also the first group of Puerto Rican technicians ever to be called in officially to advise the ruling country on the island's problems and their possible solutions. Previously virtually all the wisdom for

managing Puerto Rican affairs had come from Washington, from the office of the War Department, and, directly or
indirectly, from the mouths of congressmen.

Hastily drafted, and at times almost naïve by modern
standards, the report of the Chardón commission recommended a number of steps and programs through which
Puerto Rico's economy was to be reshaped to function more
effectively than previously for the benefit of the Puerto Rican people. It called for the enforcement of the Five-Hundred-Acre Law, for the redistribution of land, for rural re-
settlement, for the governmental purchase and operation
of at least one sugar mill to be operated as a yardstick for
regulating future relations between grinders and growers,
for certain kinds of relief (including hurricane insurance)
in the coffee regions, for a program of co-operatives, for the
extension of rural electrification, for the beginnings of
Puerto Rican industrialization through the construction of
a local cement plant, and for the construction of various
university laboratories to aid in the training of Puerto Rican technicians.

The plan included a number of matters which had long
been considered essential for Puerto Rico's salvation, but
had come to be regarded as impossible as long as Puerto
Rico was a colony. By the same token, many regarded its
adoption by the federal government as an obvious step toward independence. In part because of Muñoz's energetic
lobbying, the plan was accepted by Washington and became
the basic program of a new federal agency, the Puerto Rico
Reconstruction Administration, which was to replace the
existing Relief Administration at the earliest possible time.

The agency was provided with a "revolving" operating
fund of $40,000,000, set up in such a way that there would
be no need to ask for more money every fiscal year. Puerto
Rico was transferred from the War Department to the Department of the Interior because the latter could be better
trusted to do a good job of social and economic reform

than could the army. Dr. Ernest Gruening was appointed
Director of Territories and Administrator of the PRRA. His
record as a crusading liberal, an ardent anti-imperialist
and a friend of Latin America, was well known in Puerto
Rico, where his appointment was hailed with jubilation.
Dr. Carlos Chardón took leave of absence as chancellor of
the university, and accepted the post of Regional Administrator to take charge of the PRRA work in Puerto Rico under
the general direction of Gruening. Those two and Muñoz,
who refused to take a job in the PRRA, were regarded on the
island as a triumvirate of saviors, as the true heroes of the
Puerto Rican people.

The sugar interests, however were deeply apprehensive,
and in the ensuing years they hired publicists to brand the
entire PRRA effort as creeping socialism and worse. Inevitably, the Chardón plan and the creation of the PRRA had
powerful political repercussions in Puerto Rico. The Coalition, which held the government, played the sugar game
and opposed the entire matter violently, thus putting itself
in the position of opposing the federal government, which
it had once set out to defend against dangerous radicals
like Muñoz. The Coalition didn't help itself when the Puerto
Rican legislature in 1935 passed a resolution that roundly
attacked the Chardón plan and presented a hastily drafted,
"respectable" alternative to the President and Congress.
Such antics lost the insular government much popular support, which at best had always been tenuous.

With the creation of the PRRA, which came to be a kind
of government within the government, probably as dis-
tasteful to the appointed governor as to the Coalition, the
Liberal party had stolen a march on its opponents in the
matter of patronage. Muñoz had worked hard to keep politics out of the PRRA operations, but he could not stem the
tide in job-starved Puerto Rico with its job-slanted politics.
More and more the PRRA came to be infested with members of the Liberal party; their appointments were some-

what condoned by the fact that the Coalition had come out openly against the Chardón plan and therefore could not be trusted to carry it out.

The defeat of 1932, the setback of the Liberals when Gore had refused them any part of the patronage, had now been transformed into a resounding victory. Despite himself Muñoz was regarded as a political wizard who produced jobs and political plums for his party where none had existed before. He and the Liberal party seemed invincible, and unmistakably had the election of 1936 in their pockets. However, they, like everybody else, reckoned without the terrible chain reaction that was to be set off by the shots that killed Colonel Riggs in February of that year.

After a stormy but effective start, backed by popular enthusiasm, the PRRA settled down to a long existence as a federal agency for spending federal funds. In 1954 it was liquidated as such. It accomplished much, but it failed to fulfill its great promise largely because it was at best another phase of imperialism. Nevertheless, it was tremendously important. Enlightened imperialism is better than unenlightened, and very surely, though by anguished and tortuous routes, the PRRA paved the way for Muñoz's later triumphs and for modern Puerto Rico's emergence from despair.

7

Climax and Disintegration

LIKE the New Deal in the States, the Reconstruction Administration started as a crusade on behalf of the common man. Muñoz refused to accept an official post in it, but he became its unofficial representative in the political field. He kept in close touch with the administration's officers, ceaselessly trying to shape policies in the manner he considered best. He also waged an unending campaign to arouse and maintain his people's enthusiastic support for the great effort. His message was that the PRRA, though a federal effort in the administrative sense, was actually a Puerto Rican effort, designed and carried on by Puerto Ricans for the benefit of Puerto Rico. He did not see it as deterring the independence that was his ultimate goal; on the contrary, he regarded the PRRA as a preparation for independence, reshaping the economy in such a manner that an eventual Republic of Puerto Rico could survive.

As part of the federal program a new attorney general was appointed, with instructions to begin legal actions toward enforcement of the Five-Hundred-Acre Law. This was Benigno Fernández García, brother of the Rafael who had collaborated in drafting the basic Chardón plan. He was locally famous—or notorious—as a labor leader who had been active in strikes aimed at improving the terrible lot of the agricultural workers. As was to be expected, the ruling Coalition opposed both his appointment and his program vehemently. In Puerto Rico one saw the curious spectacle of one branch of the federal government upholding the reactionary Coalition by means of its governor, and another branch fighting it tooth and nail by means of the Department of the Interior and the PRRA.

On January 28, 1936, Fernández García filed a complaint in the Puerto Rican Supreme Court against the Puerto Rican firm of Rubert Hermanos, Inc., charging that this corporation held approximately 12,000 acres of land in violation of its charter and of the organic act, and asking the court to impose a fine and order the corporation's dissolution. All the sugar interests rallied to the firm's defense; all of Puerto Rico's liberal elements rallied behind their attorney general. The sugar lawyers claimed that the Five-Hundred-Acre Law, having no teeth for enforcement, was never meant to be enforced; having been ignored for decades, was a dead letter. Nevertheless, on July 30, 1938, the Puerto Rican Supreme Court ruled in favor of the insular government.

But sugar kept up the fight. On September 27, 1939, the District Court of Appeals in Boston set aside the Puerto Rican decision. The insular government, in league with the federal, also kept up the fight, On March 25, 1940, the Supreme Court of the United States upheld Puerto Rico and irrevocably gave the insular government the right to enforce the Five-Hundred-Acre Law. That same year was to be the "year of revolution," the great turning point in Puerto Rico's history, the year when Muñoz Marín won the election with and for his newly founded Popular Democratic party. The legally established right to enforce the Five-Hundred-Acre Law was to become a powerful weapon in the arsenal with which he fought the old order of things.

While the legal battle was being prepared and fought, the Reconstruction Administration began its important work with programs of aid to Puerto Rican farmers—in coffee, tobacco, cattle, coconuts, sugar, and all other branches of the stricken agriculture. The aid was never enough to meet the existing desperate needs, but it was still sufficient for gaining experience, making mistakes, and building up a body of knowledge. The PRRA program of low-cost housing greatly stimulated the slum-clearance effort for which Puerto Rico is today world-famous. Its financial aid to various branches of the insular government—as in education and public health—helped the virtually bankrupt government to keep functioning in some of its important activities.

The PRRA bought land in several parts of the island, divided it into homestead plots, built houses, stores, hospitals, and research stations, settled indigent farmers on the land against long-term repayments, organized them into co-operatives, and thus gave further impetus—beyond that of the PRERA and the FERA in earlier years—to Puerto Rico's co-operative movement.

In southern Puerto Rico the PRRA bought a sugar mill and its plantation of 10,000 acres. This was the French-owned Central Lafayette. The farmers who were settled on the land were given the opportunity to buy their farms as well as the mill, out of future earnings. Later the PRRA bought another mill and plantation, Los Caños, on the north coast. The two mills are today famous as the two best-managed sugar co-operatives to be found anywhere; their debts to the federal government have been paid long ago, their operations have served as a yardstick by which relations between other mills and the independent planters can be regulated.

The PRRA formed a Self-Help Corporation to organize

and finance co-operatives. It did valiant work, and some of its co-operatives have since those years grown powerful while others died in the natural course of events. The PRRA gave assistance to the insular government toward the creation of more hydroelectric facilities for providing low-cost power and spreading the benefits of rural electrification. It started Puerto Rico's industrialization program by building a cement plant with federal funds. This was later turned over to the Puerto Rican government, which paid for it very soon out of profits and in turn sold it to a private operator in 1948.

I became identified with the Reconstruction Administration as a consultant on planning, loaned to Puerto Rico by the National Resources Committee. We organized a Planning Division within the PRRA, with Rafael González as chairman and myself as secretary. We raided the university for young economists and others to give us their spare time, preparing reports, and planning future economic action. Two of them told me that they liked the work, but that I was crazy just the same. They said that it was impossible to plan in a capitalistic society, and especially in a colony. My stand was that they were the ones who were crazy; they were not talking about planning, which could be done anywhere, at any time, in any society, and was at the very least a good way of evaluating problems. They were merely afraid that their plans could not be *carried out* under capitalism and colonialism. The two worked well with us despite their misgivings. Their names are Rafael Picó and Sol Luis Descartes, and both of them are today famous in the world's planning circles.

In a sense, however, they were right in that the plans we drafted could not then be carried out. In any event, most of them *were* not carried out, and some, with their somewhat devastating reports on conditions in Puerto Rico, were eventually suppressed by federal officials who had been frightened into conservatism by the shots that killed Colonel Riggs. But in those days nobody could know that Muñoz would capture the Puerto Rican government in 1940 and would embark on a Puerto Rican, as opposed to federal, program of reconstruction. Then the men who had worked in the PRRA, in the planning division and elsewhere, became the principal organizers and administrators of Muñoz's daring new program. A number of the specific plans drafted within the PRRA under federal aegis were taken off the shelves, dusted off, and used to buttress the new program. The planning we had begun as a federal activity was revived in 1942 by Governor Tugwell as an integral activity of the Puerto Rican government. The Planning Board today plays a major role in the Commonwealth's work; it advises the governor and the legislature, shapes efforts and policies for the future, guides urban development, and integrates the activities of the government's many branches.

Sugar and its friends were not idle while all that and much more was going on. The sugar interests hired public-relations men—and at one time two reputable economists —to defend them against so radical a movement. The sugar corporations also began an unofficial though powerful line of talk, an obvious threat, to the effect that they were on the verge of withdrawing from Puerto Rico entirely. Such talk, plus the campaign against the sugar monopoly, plus the depression, sent the value of sugar stocks tumbling. A number of Puerto Ricans, apparently not intimidated, then bought thousands of shares of those stocks as investments, which they have never since regretted. Absentee ownership in sugar came in such fashion to be reduced materially.

Attacks from sugar did the PRRA no great harm. They were expected, and Washington officials recognized their source and meaning. Internally, however, the PRRA had serious weaknesses, which were to contribute heavily to its collapse as the embodiment of a great Puerto Rican ideal and effort. Those weaknesses stemmed from the rigid control that was exercised by Washington over all its activities and policies and that convinced its Puerto Rican officials that they were merely hired men.

The agency was dominated by a corps of eager young lawyers shipped down by Washington. All of them were graduates of Felix Frankfurter's Harvard Law School, and were convinced that one could not be a socially conscious lawyer *unless* one had graduated from that school. They were crusaders for social welfare, but nevertheless were ignorant of the Puerto Rico whose welfare they had set out to improve. The continental lawyers were everywhere; they mixed into every operation, large or small; they altered policies and contracts at will; they overrode high Puerto Rican officials again and again. In a great new organization dedicated to the pious principle of giving all positions of responsibility to Puerto Ricans, the young lawyers held all the ultimate power as Washington's representatives on the PRRA's administrative scene.

That situation contributed materially to the debacle of 1936, which changed the PRRA back to being a mere federal money-spending agency, without intellectual appeal to the Puerto Ricans. There can be no doubt, either, that it greatly strengthened Muñoz Marín's conviction that *only* the Puerto Ricans, acting as such, could save Puerto Rico. The lawyers may well, also, have contributed to the resurgence, in 1936, of the demand for independence as presumably the *only* status under which the Puerto Ricans could do things for themselves without interference from a lot of idealistic but meddlesome continental Americans.

The break between the federal government, as represented by the PRRA, and the Puerto Rican people, as represented by that vague thing called public opinion, was precipitated by the Nationalists' assassination of Colonel Riggs. A wild, irresponsible act, that killing had offended most Puerto Ricans, who regardless of whether they were for or against their island's independence, were decidedly against murder. In the chain of events that followed, the people and their leaders became utterly bewildered by a federal course of action that was apparently designed to punish all Puerto Ricans for the fanatical action of a few misguided terrorists.

In the prevailing tense atmosphere the senseless police action of lynching the assassins of Riggs did much to widen the rift between Puerto Ricans and the United States.

Muñoz Marín was in Washington at the time, and Dr. Gruening asked him to make a public statement condemning the Riggs assassination in order to show that the Puerto Ricans as a whole were not behind it. Muñoz refused to make such a statement on the ground that he would also have to condemn the lynching of the two Nationalists, and such condemnation would, in effect, be an attack on the federal government. He did not believe that any purpose could at the time be served by attacking Washington. Gruening accused him of putting his own political destiny ahead of his people's welfare. Muñoz is reported to have answered that his personal destiny *was* that of his people. Quite probably Gruening regarded the answer as arrogant and egotistical. At any rate, there was a violent quarrel.

One of the side results of that quarrel and the ensuing, widening rift between the two men was that Muñoz began to lose his influence with President Roosevelt, who was a friend and a staunch supporter of Gruening. Secretary Ickes followed Roosevelt. From the day of that one quarrel with Gruening, Muñoz began to lose his personal power as a Washington lobbyist. In Puerto Rico, too, he began slowly but surely, to lose influence. His hold on the Puerto Rican people, on the *jíbaros*, the poor, was undeniable. But the San Juan intelligentsia were not at all sure that it was wise to go along with a man who was *persona non grata* in the ruling capital.

Now, on April 23, 1936, news came like a thunderclap from Washington that Senator Millard Tydings of Maryland had introduced a bill in Congress providing for the island's independence. Locally it was regarded as an administration bill. That was denied by administration spokesmen, but confirmed years later when Secretary Ickes' diaries were published. Gruening and Ickes had conceived of it and planned it; Gruening had taken charge of drafting it; Roosevelt had suggested that Tydings be asked to introduce it. Its aim had been to scare the Puerto Ricans out of all desire for independence. Ickes wrote in his diary that "such agitation as has been going on in Puerto Rico recently would be put to an end for probably twenty years." He was due for a series of major surprises.

To be sure, the bill was nicely worded as a liberal document in that it provided for a plebiscite by which the people of Puerto Rico should be permitted to vote on whether or not they wanted independence. It added a joker, however, by defining the kind of independence on which they would be allowed to vote in such a manner as to spell certain starvation for the island if achieved. The bill gave the island almost no time in which to readjust its economy from the colonial to the independent. It threatened, within a few short years, to turn Puerto Rico out from behind the American tariff structure, without providing sufficient time or means for creating an economy that could function outside of that structure. Muñoz summarized the resulting indignation when he said that the bill was a return to the old Mexican *ley de fuga,* or law of flight, under which the Mexican police used to arrest people, then tell them magnanimously to run away, and then shoot them in the back for trying to escape.

At best, the bill was regarded as an insult to Puerto Rican *dignidad,* intelligence, and integrity. At worst, it clouded and confused the issue of status by wilfully defining independence in the worst possible terms. The enlightened and liberal Washington administration, which more than any other had repeatedly assured the Puerto Ricans of their right to independence if they wanted it, seemed now to be showing its hand by ill-naturedly telling the island that it could damn well starve, too, if it did happen to want it.

The result was electrifying. In Puerto Rico one began to hear even ardent Republicans, advocates of statehood, 150 per cent Americans, say: "If that is the best we can expect from Washington, we have no choice but to be for independence at any cost!" The newspaper *La Correspondencia* accurately expressed public sentiment when it said: ". . . if the American government is in an angry mood and imposed it as an act of vengeance, let independence come, even if it costs our lives." *El País* editorialized: "The displacing of the American flag ought not to be a disorderly act, but should be done respectfully and following a friendly understanding."

Why, the question was widely asked, had no Puerto Rican been consulted on the terms of a bill that so vitally affected the island's destiny?

In Washington the Resident Commissioner, Santiago Iglesias, attacked the bill bitterly on the floor of the House of Representatives. The Tydings bill failed to pass, but it did much to undermine Puerto Rican faith in the United States. Several subsequent bills providing for statehood, and one aimed at making Puerto Rico an incorporated territory of the United States, failed equally to pass. All that undoubtedly served as a valuable political education for Muñoz Marín, modifying his stand on independence.

About this time Dr. Gruening became concerned with political activities within the PRRA, which were forbidden to federal employees under the Hatch Act. He instigated a series of rather high-handed inquiries into such alleged activities, some of which he headed himself. As a result, some of the outstanding Puerto Ricans in the organization —all of them supporters of Muñoz Marín—were separated from the federal payroll; one of them, Rafael Fernández

García, one of the three drafters of the original Chardón plan, was discharged *with prejudice*.

Late in 1936 the situation flared into violent explosion. Dr. Carlos Chardón, one of Puerto Rico's heroes, resigned as regional administrator, unable to function any longer in his impossible position between Puerto Rico and the federal government. A group of us sent a cable to Gruening, signed by fifty respected men, urging the doctor not to accept Chardón's resignation, but to come to Puerto Rico to discover the real grievances that had prompted it. Instead, he sent a pair of lawyers and a small-time politician, apparently instructed "to break up the Puerto Rican conspiracy," which I, as a "renegade American," was accused of having organized.

A stench of fear arose within the PRRA and smothered all enthusiasm and creative effort. Many employees whose bread and butter depended on Gruening were afraid to be seen with Muñoz. If for one reason or another they felt impelled to discuss something with him, they parked their cars blocks from his house and sneaked in the back way. A number of Puerto Rican officials who had been indignant until that moment now changed their tunes and began to sing the praises of Gruening, who controlled the jobs. Several dozen others resigned in a body, in sympathy with Chardón, even though most of them had no other jobs to turn to. Some of them moved to New York; some found whatever they could in Puerto Rico; some managed to return to their old jobs in the university. But all who stayed went underground in the sense of thereafter keeping quiet about Washington, until Muñoz won the 1940 election and pulled them out of hiding again.

While all that was going on, Albizu Campos and a number of his followers were arrested and brought to trial on charges of conspiring against the United States. On those charges they had to be tried in the federal court, under a federal judge, and again there was much indignation.

Many Puerto Ricans felt that the Nationalists should have been tried on murder charges in a Puerto Rican court, and that their trial in the federal court not only showed an insulting lack of confidence in Puerto Rican justice, but also injected serious language difficulties. There were also many who wholeheartedly condemned murder, but could not understand how and why the striving for independence, no matter what the means, could be fairly construed and punished as conspiracy in a situation in which Puerto Rico had repeatedly been told by Washington that it was entitled to independence if it wanted it.

The Nationalists had two trials. The first resulted in a hung jury, composed largely of Puerto Ricans. The second, before a jury composed of two Puerto Ricans and ten Americans—several of whom knew virtually no Spanish—resulted in the conviction of Albizu and seven others. The leader and one other, Luis Velázquez, were sentenced to six years in Atlanta Penitentiary, to be followed by four years of probation. The rest were sentenced to four—and in one case five—years in Atlanta, also followed by four years of probation. The trials created a certain amount of public sympathy for the Nationalists as martyrs and patriotic Puerto Ricans which they would not have enjoyed as murderers. That, however, was blown away the following year when two Nationalists tried unsuccessfully to assassinate Governor Winship and thus established the "party" as being definitely dedicated to a program of terrorism.

Governor Blanton Winship, a correct and gracious southern gentleman who was bewildered by the New Deal and all it stood for, handled popular unrest in true military manner by enlarging the police force, buying it tear gas, machine guns, cars, and sending it to summer camps for intensive training. Whatever his reasons, he came to be widely accused of militarizing and brutalizing the force and turning it from an arm of the insular government into a tool of the federal government's most reactionary officials.

Because tensions were mounting, people everywhere wanted to meet and discuss the situation. On several occasions groups in various towns—not Nationalists, but ordinary, peaceful Puerto Ricans—asked permission to hold meetings; the permission was granted by the local mayors whose business it was, but eventually it was rescinded by the governor, who sent his police to enforce his decree.

The net result of such bungling was that the United States was accused of running a police-state government in Puerto Rico; in turn, the desire for independence spread far and wide. A people who have painfully throughout four centuries labored and struggled for civil rights, for a measure of self-government, for the right of free speech and free assembly, are bound to be sensitive in such matters and to be indignant about apparent infringements by the ranking representative of the ruling country.

A number of incidents fed that sense of indignation and lowered the United States's prestige still more. Fear, resentment, and indignation came to a head as a result of the shameful Palm Sunday affair of 1937. The Nationalists requested *and received* official permission to hold a parade in Ponce on that day. They began flocking to the city from all parts of the island, but so did the police, heavily armed with revolvers, tear gas, and machine guns.

About a hundred Nationalists, with their wives and sweethearts in the Women's Auxiliary, assembled for the parade, surrounded by the police and watched by a large group of curious spectators. At the last minute, after they had assembled for the start, they were told that permission for the parade had been revoked.

They started marching despite the police order, and immediately a fusillade of shots rang out, which kept on, according to the testimony of conflicting witnesses, for a period of up to half an hour. In the melee, fifteen Nationalists, one bystander, and two policemen were killed, the latter probably by their own cross fire. Fifty-five people were wounded.

Governor Winship immediately ordered a government investigation, but there was little popular faith in it, not only because the government itself, which would do the investigating, was considered by many as being one of the parties responsible for the shootings, but also because the governor had already made a public statement in which he definitely justified the conduct of all the police and other government officials who had been involved. As expected, the governor's investigation disclosed that the Nationalists had fired the first shot and all others thereafter that had hit policemen, and cleared the police of all blame in the matter —lauding them, in fact, for their excellent behavior.

But then the American Civil Liberties Union of New York was persuaded to send Arthur Garfield Hays to Puerto Rico to organize a commission of inquiry into the Ponce affair and into the question of civil liberties in general. The commission held extensive hearings and announced its findings in a public meeting in San Juan, permission for which had been granted only after Hays's defiant insistence. These findings were that despite the governor's public statement that the Nationalists had fired the first shot, there was no evidence that any of them had been armed; the police had undoubtedly fired first and killed each other with their own cross fire, and the whole thing amounted to a brutal, bloody, and unpardonable massacre, even though it was recognized that the Nationalist party contained the elements of fanatical Fascist gangsterism.

It was further concluded by the Hays committee that civil liberties had been seriously and arbitrarily curtailed in Puerto Rico during the preceding year.

The Inés Mendoza affair was a by-product of the Hays investigation. Miss Mendoza had for years been a capable teacher in the island's high schools; she now appeared voluntarily before the commission to testify that in her opinion the old Washington-initiated custom of doing all the teaching in English was bad because it served mainly to confuse the children. Virtually all Puerto Rican teachers felt that way, but she was the only one who had the courage to testify in public. When her contract was thereafter not renewed and she was thrown out of the public-school system, there was again much indignation. Apparently, Puerto Rican professionals were not permitted to criticize policies that had been arbitrarily handed down from Washington.

Some years after the 1940 elections, when Puerto Rico had a new lease on life and started energetically to set its own house in order, all the island's teachers openly condemned the old attitudes toward English as the language of instruction, and the educational system was changed to correspond. By that time Inés Mendoza was the wife of Muñoz Marín. Today she is highly respected as the first lady of Puerto Rico, but largely forgotten as one of the island's earlier fearless fighters for civil rights.

The Tydings bill had given rise to the United Front, a group of earnest intellectuals who held meetings in all parts of the island to explain to the people that independence was not necessarily as terrible as the Maryland senator had pictured it, and that the issue must under no circumstances be discarded.

Muñoz went to Washington late in 1936, where he drafted what he considered a workable independence bill. He wanted first to have the people of Puerto Rico vote on the idea of independence; then, if the vote were favorable, to have the terms worked out jointly by Puerto Rican and federal leaders, and then to have another plebiscite on the specific independence developed. In effect, he proposd the development of a political compact between Puerto Rico and the United States. His object was to educate Congress in the meanings of various kinds of independence—to teach Congress that political sovereignty need not mean economic ruin, either for sugar or for the Puerto Rican people. He persuaded a congressman to introduce the bill, but it never got out of committee. However, it did result in further political education for Muñoz. It started the thought processes that eventually led to his disavowal of the "separate-independence" formula for political freedom. It began to dawn on him that Puerto Rico's possibility for economic well-being depended solidly on the continuance of free markets within the American tariff structure; that no Congress, no matter how well disposed, could possibly grant anything better than most-favored-nations status to an independent Puerto Rico; that Puerto Rican sugar could not possibly compete with Cuban if it had to pay duty in the American market; that the collapse of the sugar industry, with nothing on hand to take its place, would mean ruin for the island.

But it was to take time and much effective effort before these suspicions grew to the full convictions the governor of Puerto Rico displays today. The postwar granting of independence to the Philippines seems to have been the clinching argument. Muñoz realized that Puerto Rico, having no geographic frontier, no industries except sugar, no natural resources to speak of except limited areas of land, climate, and too many people, would be ruined by the kind of independence that had been granted to the Philippines. He began to think of something new—of political freedom within the American economic and political structure.

In Puerto Rico in 1936 and 1937 Muñoz precipitated a bitter political struggle within his own Liberal party. He wanted the party to boycott the 1936 election on the ground that the Tydings bill had clouded the independence issue. Antonio Barceló, the party's president, objected. He felt sure of victory because the *Liberales* had, after all, brought the PRRA to Puerto Rico. The party went to the election, and was again defeated by the Coalition. Barceló blamed Muñoz.

The latter organized a splinter group, called the "Authentic Liberal party," tried to use it for capturing control, and demanded that Barceló resign and hand over to him the insignia of his leadership. Barceló wrote him a long and sorrowful public letter, addressed to "My Young Fellow Patriot," advising him that if he wanted to be a real political leader he ought to go out and scratch for followers as others had done before him, accusing him of having been a disruptive influence—and expelling him.

There were rumors—how correct they were I have no way of judging—of a private deal between Barceló and Washington, in which the Puerto Rican had been promised much federal patronage for his organization, despite its defeat, if he ousted Muñoz, but had also been told that no Liberal could get a federal job if the stormy senator stayed in the party.

Whatever the truth of those rumors, it is true that Muñoz's political fortunes had hit rock bottom. The rocket that had soared so brilliantly was now a dead stick in the opinion of the political analysts, who had no inkling of the enormous prestige the son of Muñoz Rivera still enjoyed among the *jíbaros*. The *jíbaros* didn't count politically in any event. Their votes were bought, and Muñoz had no money—no matter what his prestige. The consensus, both in San Juan and in Washington circles interested in Puerto Rico, was: "Muñoz is through. No respectable party will take him now, and there is nothing left for him except to join the Nationalists and try to take control of them while Albizu is in jail. And that—definitely—is political suicide!"

Arturo Morales Carrión, writing in the present tense about the events of 1936-7, expressed himself as follows: "The island now suffers days of intense political reaction. Albizu's extremism not only prejudices the evolution of the independence thesis, but also confuses and disperses the groups devoted to economic and social reforms. Without the energetic popular support which Muñoz had aroused in the beginning, federal aid degenerates into a bureaucratic activity with sparse results. Psychological fatigue, disillusionment, and disorientation spread in the urban centers. Muñoz, who for a moment had been the great promise, disappears from the urban scene. His star is in deep eclipse, and he is now seen only as the leader of a routed faction, a political bohemian who had pilfered the treasure of a name and an illustrious tradition."

8

Faith in Ourselves

REGARDLESS of circumstances, it was probably inevitable that Muñoz should eventually be ousted by any party that had taken him in—no matter how brilliant his record. Political parties need money to survive, and in the Puerto Rico of those days money came largely, directly or indirectly, from the sugar interests, which didn't mind a man talking about enforcement of the Five-Hundred-Acre law and other reforms as long as he could be trusted to do nothing realistic about the matter. But Muñoz was a dangerous man in that he was no lip-service politician. He meant what he said.

In 1936, when the present governor was still a senator, I talked to his chauffeur. "Señor," he said, "I have driven for nearly all the big political figures on the island, but I never again want to drive for anybody but Muñoz Marín. He is the only political leader here who always says exactly the same things to people who ride in his car with him that he says in his public speeches." Such a man, who made no private political deals of any kind, could not stay long in an organized political party that depended for its survival on the generosity of the sugar interests and the good will of the federal government.

It was, of course, known that Muñoz enjoyed great popularity among the hill people, who could numerically swing an election. But it was also a truism that they would not vote unless they were paid. Some would vote as directed, in return for two dollars; some would accept money only from the party of their choice and allegiance; most would refrain from voting unless they received their money. That attitude was an integral, firmly established part of the Puerto Rican way of life, a deep-rooted culture trait that could not (as people then thought) be eradicated in one campaign by a discredited, penniless politician.

Rejected by Washington and his own party, written off by the politically wise as being politically dead beyond hope of resurrection, without a cent for purchasing votes, with hardly a dollar with which to support himself and his family, Muñoz now addressed himself to the submerged rural poor. Crisis had narrowed down his open friends to a small nucleus of those who were held to him by the qualities of integrity and personal dedication which are the essence of leadership, as well as to a few who in one way or another felt that they could afford to continue working with him. Among them were a few fanatics who valued integrity above financial security, a handful of men who were financially more or less secure, and some who had previously worked with Albizu Campos, had no jobs to speak of or to lose, and were captured by Muñoz's ideas. He was also backed by a few *colonos*—independent sugar growers who sold their cane to the mills, were squeezed by the big corporations, and saw in Muñoz some hope for emancipation.

These men and women now organized the new Popular Democratic party. Their official slogan was "Bread, Land, and Liberty," and their emblem was the profile of a countryman wearing the traditional Puerto Rican straw hat, the

pava. In the beginning they were derided by the sophisticated; the Popular Democratic party was considered a bit
of political play-acting, almost as foolish and unrealistic as
Albizu's Army of Liberation had been. Most of the island's
newspapers, with the exception of Muñoz's *La Democracia,*
referred to it, if at all, with quotation marks around the
word "party."

The platform of the Popular Democratic party was unique
in that it said nothing about ultimate political status. Indeed, it was stressed throughout the campaign that status—
independence, statehood, or dominion status—was in no way
a campaign issue. The *Partido Popular* bid for the vote entirely on the issues of such social-economic reforms as could
be endorsed by anybody who was hungry enough to see the
need for them, regardless of his ideas on ultimate political
status. Muñoz and his followers campaigned for the enforcement of the Five-Hundred-Acre Law, for legislative steps
toward making sugar a public utility and thereby assuring
independent cane growers fair prices for their crops, for the
improvement of the banking system to liberalize credits to
farmers and businessmen, for land to be given free to landless agricultural workers, for the promotion of local industries, for social legislation to protect the island's workers, for
slum clearance, for reforms in the school system and the
extension of education.

Other parties, to be sure, also advocated social reform and
improved social justice, but it was widely recognized that the
only party that was in a position to carry out its promises
when and if elected was the one that had no commitments
to the enemies of social reform, no financial ties of any
kind, and was indebted to nobody except the people who
voted for it. Its only great difficulty seemed to be that it had
no chance whatever—for precisely those reasons—of being
voted into power.

The Popular Democratic party's small group of loyal workers labored feverishly, reproducing its symbol as often and

as widely as their small means permitted, and running off thousands of petition forms on the presses of *La Democracia*.

Meanwhile, in the hills, in the small towns, in the village meeting places, in small meetings in private homes, Muñoz began his tremendous work of campaigning, talking to the peasants, appealing to their natural common sense, winning friends and followers. Finally, on July 22, 1938, he was able to announce that sufficient signatures had been obtained in Barranquitas and Luquillo to register the party in those two municipalities. Barranquitas had been his father's birthplace and is still revered as his shrine; it was a dramatic place in which to begin.

Eventually the party obtained twice as many signatures on its registration petitions as it needed to function as a party on an island-wide basis. But still it was not considered as having a chance in the election. In 1932 Albizu Campos had also received many registration signatures, but had failed miserably when it came to getting the vote. Besides, it was known or suspected that the other three parties actually urged their constituents to sign Muñoz's petitions. As he couldn't win, it could do no harm to see to it that he went to the elections; every old-line rural ward heeler felt so sure of his personal following that he thought that any votes Muñoz might win must necessarily be taken from the ranks of the opposing old-line rural ward heelers; the *Liberales* felt that he could take votes away only from the Socialists and Republicans, and vice versa. Most of them, while laughing at him, therefore also welcomed him in the field and did what they could to assure his actually going to the election.

Not being able to pay the driver who had served him so faithfully in his more prosperous days, Muñoz had lost him. But he had to have a driver, and when he asked his friends to find him one, he gave these specifications: a man who needed no salary, didn't have to eat, and could drive a car without gasoline. Somehow, he seems to have found such a paragon.

He had made a speech and was due for another in another part of the island. He said to his driver: "How much money do you have?"

"I have seventeen cents."

"Good. I have nine cents. Get all the gasoline the money will buy and drive as far as it will take us. Maybe somebody will help us at the other end."

The driver said: "When do we eat? And on what?"

His employer, who is famous as a trencherman, answered: "Somebody will feed us."

In various parts of the island friends and admirers with modest homes gave food and lodging to Muñoz and his driver. He took up collections among the poverty-stricken country people—five cents here, a few pennies there, a quarter from some particularly rich *jíbaro*—but the money received was never used for his own expenses. It was a contribution to the party treasury, however small. He wanted to establish the principle that the *Partido Popular* was the people's own party, to be supported by them, and not the usual organization of questionable largesse that came out of the cities at every election to distribute political bribes.

Starting with countless meetings and discussions with the *jíbaros*, in their little homes and on village greens, with small groups and in an informal, nonoratorical manner, and building up to larger and larger audiences as he came back again and again to every corner of the island's mountains, by car, or horseback, on foot, Muñoz received attention from the beginning, not only because of his reputation, not only because he was the son of Muñoz Rivera, not only because of his clear and simple logic, but also because his naturalness set him off from other political leaders and their *dignidad*.

At one political meeting when he felt thirsty, he reached for a bottle of Coca-Cola and began to drink. A man said: "This man is different. Another politician would be wearing a coat, necktie, and hat, and would try to impress us by having the Coca-Cola brought to him on a tray, with a glass, and by drinking from the glass. This man leaves off the coat, hat, and necktie; his clothes are wrinkled and full of sweat because he has come far and worked hard; he drinks his Coca-Cola from the bottle. He acts like one of us, and I am for him."

But Muñoz said: "Just a minute. I appreciate your support, but I happen to drink out of a bottle only because it is convenient and there doesn't seem to be a glass around here. But if you people supported me for that reason, if you voted for candidates because they drink out of bottles instead of glasses, every political son of a bitch on the island would run around sucking on a bottle all the time. But that is not the way you vote. You vote for principles that I will explain to you, and that is why we will win this election."

Beginning with all the small towns and settlements in the island's interior and descending to the coastal cities only near the end of his long campaign when he felt fairly sure of the mountain areas, he explained Puerto Rico's plight in simple, intelligent terms. He talked about his party's determination to redistribute the lands of the sugar estates by legal means under the Five-Hundred-Acre Law. He talked about the need for social reform to protect the workers' interests, for minimum-wage laws, for slum clearance and low-cost housing. He wrote and distributed a pamphlet, now famous—*El Catecismo del Pueblo, The People's Catechism* —explaining not only the issues at stake, but also the power of the vote when used correctly for the improvement of one's personal life. Again and again at meetings he would pick out an older man and ask him: "How many times have you voted?"

"Eight times, Don Luis."

"Did you ever see any change in your life as a result?"

"Never, except that things grew worse."

"Then, for heaven's sake, give us a chance. Lend me your

vote, just once. You can take it back later and give it to your old party if you don't like what we do with it."

"Give us a chance—just one chance to show what we can do!" became almost a campaign slogan, repeated in hundreds upon hundreds of meetings, to tens of thousands of men and women, in private and in public, verbally and in print, in homes, town squares, and village greens. "All we ask is this one chance!"

He talked at great length about the practice of selling votes. "Nobody can really blame you for selling your vote," he told his listeners. "Two dollars is extraordinarily hard to come by and will buy a lot of beans and rice for yourselves and your starving families. Who can blame you for wanting to provide for your children? But, you must look at this thing clearly. Do you want two dollars or do you want justice? You can't have two dollars *and* justice, and this time you have to make a choice. Forego the two dollars and vote for us, just this once, and see what happens!"

"If you sell your votes," he explained, "somebody has to put up the money with which to buy them. After that, whoever wins the election is tied to the fellows who gave him the money to buy your votes. That is why you have seen many political parties win while you have never won. The only way in which your votes can count to diminish your hardships is by not being sold, so that the party that triumphs shall not owe anyone except you."

"You can't have two dollars and justice!" was repeated again and again to all who would listen and some who would not, to those who nodded their heads in solemn agreement as well as those who sneered. Throughout his campaign Muñoz pounded away at complete honesty; he also continued to preach against taking two dollars from sugar and then voting for him anyway. It is not known today how many, when the voting took place in November 1940, followed his advice in that matter. What is known is that votes are no longer bought in Puerto Rico today simply because the poor have discovered their dignity and political power and now refuse to sell their votes with the same tenacity with which they once refused to vote without pay.

The results of the 1940 election were to prove so over-whelmingly beneficial that by the next election of 1944, vote selling had become almost universally recognized as a social evil, to be suppressed, if it appeared at all, by community disapproval.

There are those who say that Muñoz's greatest political achievement was the education of his people in the matter of vote selling. It was to have far-reaching results, not only in the general field of democracy, but also in Puerto Rico's entire politico-economic structure. One of many explanations for the island's famous successes since 1940 is the fact that the political power has been taken away from the great monied interests and has been given to the people, the voters, where it belonged in the first place. That shift was made through the simplest means imaginable—by merely convincing the voters that they couldn't have two dollars *and* justice, and had to choose between the two. Had the shift not been made, however, Operation Bootstrap could today not exist; the program of industrialization would be impossible; Puerto Rico would still be a run-down sugar colony.

Carefully, in meeting after meeting, in village after village, Muñoz explained the meanings of politics to his people. He told them that they had heard politicians talk before, year after year, in campaign after campaign, and that it never meant anything real. "Don't ever trust a politician," he said. "Not even me. How do you know that I won't swindle you out of taking somebody else's two dollars and then saddle you with just another gang sold out against you? You don't, and there is nothing that I can say to convince you. Nevertheless, if you give us the one chance that I ask for, if you now throw out the rascals in San Juan and vote us in, and if we then prove to be every bit as great a set of rascals,

you will have learned how to use your vote for the purpose
of tossing rascals out of office, and you can toss us out in
turn in the next election. Can you sell such power for two
dollars?

"Always politicians have made you vague promises—as I
do here when I talk about justice. What do they mean? This
time we want you to know what they mean. We are not campaigning for a set of loose and rattling planks in a platform.
We are campaigning for specific things, even for specific
bills. We have drafted our bills for land reform and other
things even before you elect us. Read them, discuss them,
amend them by writing to us—now, before you vote us into
power. They are your personal bills, designed to change your
personal lives. You are entitled to know exactly what you are
voting for."

Muñoz was getting results in that he was being talked
about—in the hills, where it counted. But one man couldn't
work fast enough; the island's radio facilities were not available to him; he had to devise other ways of spreading his
voice. Somehow he acquired a recording machine. Whenever
he made a speech thereafter, it was recorded, and thirty or
more records were hurriedly pressed from the master and
played in thirty or more villages throughout the island.

He founded a rural newspaper, *El Batey*, published for
free distribution whenever he had the time to write an issue.
In this he hammered away incessantly at the issue involved
—land reform, social legislation, industrialization, health
and education—preaching incessantly, too, against the old
vice of selling the vote. There was so great a demand for the
paper that it soon grew from a two-page affair to one of four
pages; the demand and the consequent circulation grew dramatically until there was one issue with a million copies.
That was more than the circulation of all the other Puerto
Rican papers combined. The island's ultraconservative businessmen, who knew well that Muñoz had no chance of winning the election, and who would have shivered in their

boots had they for a moment thought that there might be
such a chance after all, knew a good advertising medium
when they saw it. In no time at all *El Batey* was amply supported, through advertising, by the political enemies of the
Popular Democratic party.

All this time, too, Muñoz was perforce also building up a
political machine. The old leaders, the Creole *caciques*, the
rural ward heelers, numbered about 400—belonging to all
the parties. Before he was through, Muñoz had a machine
composed of nearly 4,000 local leaders, men whom he had
picked in all the small and large places, men who had caught
his ideas and whom he could lead by those ideas, unpur-
chasable men who could not purchase anybody else either,
jíbaros themselves who could work among their fellows as
jíbaros.

Revolutionary in the sense of promising to do things that
were administratively in Washington's hands and not in
Puerto Rico's at all, Muñoz's campaign was by the same
token also a great and adventurous gamble. How could he
know that if he won the election and came to control the insular legislature, his enemies in Washington would not send
him another reactionary Governor Winship who would play
the sugar game and veto the bills as fast as the legislature
passed them?

On September 15, therefore, the party held a mass meeting in Santurce, a borough of San Juan, at which were approved all the bills to be passed in case the party won at the
polls. Before a crowd of more than 15,000 persons, each
Popular candidate for the insular legislature took an oath to
vote for the bills, regardless of what the federal government
might say.

When election time came, Muñoz was helped immeasurably by the new election law that had perforce been passed
by the Coalition in 1936—as a result of popular insistence
arising from recurring scandals. Under that law, first tested
in 1940, there is now one polling place for approximately

every 150 voters. These may assemble at the school, or whatever building serves for the purpose, at any time before two
o'clock; after that time no others are admitted, and the
voting begins. The names of the registered voters are read off
in alphabetical order, and they go one by one to the curtained
booth to cast their secret ballots. Each man or woman steps
out of the assembled group in full sight of all the rest, in a
situation in which everybody watches everybody else. People
may leave after they have voted, but nobody may enter the
polling place until all the voting is over. By that system all
floaters, repeaters, and ghosts are rigidly excluded.

On election night, November 5, 1940, Muñoz sat at home
with his old friend and loyal supporter, Jorge Font Saldaña.
The latter had been one of those who had resigned their
PRRA jobs in 1936 in indignation and in support of Muñoz.
Since then he had had four terrible years, at times barely
eking out an existence for himself and his family, but never
for an instant diminishing his support of the leader. Now the
two were waiting for the returns to come in. They came first
from Bayamón, which was traditionally Republican. But this
time the Republican vote had been reduced considerably,
while the *Populares* had made a real showing.

"They are doing it!" cried Muñoz. "They are doing it! They
have refused to sell their votes!"

Returns came in from one of the mountain districts. The
Popular Democratic party had won there.

Profoundly moved, Muñoz began to cry. "They are doing
it, Jorge! Those wonderful people. They are starving and
they haven't let me down. They haven't sold their votes!"

A few more returns came in. "We needn't wait for the
whole picture. We're in! We've won! The *jíbaros* aren't selling their votes, and there is not a chance in the world of our
not winning the election."

That, of course, called for celebration, but Muñoz had
only a very little wine in the house and no money with which
to buy more.

"Listen, Jorge. Do you have any whisky at home?"

"I have about half a bottle."

"Go get it. Telephone your house and ask your wife to bring it. Tell her to hurry. We have to celebrate."

Jorge telephoned his home and got the cook. "Please ask Doña Carmen to come down here and bring that half-bottle of whisky that's in the pantry!"

"The whisky! The whisky! Praise be to God!" The cook knew immediately what the order meant. "We've won!" She ran to the window. "Listen, everybody out in the street. We've won. The *Populares* have won the election."

Long before all the returns were in, there was jubilation in all parts of the island. "The *jíbaros* didn't sell their vote! We have won the election. Don Luis has won!"

When the final count was completed, it was found that the *Populares* had received ten of the nineteen Senate seats, a majority of one. They received eighteen seats in the House, as against another eighteen that went to the Coalition. But there was another group, the *Unificación*, which had won three seats in the House. With some judicious trading to line up this group on his side, and with constant use of the caucus to make sure that all his party members voted as a bloc, Muñoz, who became President of the Senate and the island's political leader, could expect to swing the legislature.

It was no overwhelming victory; the *Populares* had won thirty-eight per cent of the total vote and had barely managed to gain control of the legislature. But it paved the way for future overwhelming victories; in 1944 they were to receive sixty-four per cent of the total vote, and their strong hold on the island's electorate has never diminished. The victory of 1940 also paved the way for future reforms and programs so drastic that today's Puerto Rico bears only slight resemblance to that of twenty years ago.

The 1940 campaign, when political status was not a party issue, intensified Muñoz's serious questioning of his former ideas on Puerto Rico's independence. Whatever one said about ultimate political arrangements, it was clear that the poor would be at the receiving end of whatever status might emerge from Puerto Rico's turmoil. Muñoz now discovered that the various ideas about status that had been so ardently discussed for so many years by the intellectuals meant little to the rural poor except as something the politicians talked about. What was it these people wanted? They wanted the same things that all other people want the world over. They were hungry and they wanted food. They were sick and they wanted medical care. They wanted education and opportunity for their children. They wanted the human dignity that was too often denied them. Most of them would be content to take such things from any government that would provide them, no matter where it might be centered.

Muñoz discovered that there was among the *jíbaros* very little of the hatred for the United States which had been preached by Albizu. Those people might hate their boss at the sugar mill if he was a son of a bitch, but they hated him for that reason and not because he was an American or drew his power from the American regime. In fact, they were often, and simply, proud of their American citizenship, of the fact that they could go to the States without passport whenever they wanted and had the means, that they were, through that citizenship, one with the world's most powerful democracy. Moreover, even though the sugar boss might be a scoundrel (more often a Puerto Rican than a continental), they sensed that most Americans were not scoundrels. If they had a real complaint against the sugar boss, they might even go to court and win the case; and what poor man could do a thing like that, for instance, in the sovereign Dominican Republic? They knew that the United States had given them roads, schools, hospitals, and health programs—not enough, to be sure, but certainly more than Spain had given them during four centuries. The United States had given them the PRERA, the FERA, and the PRRA in their hour of greatest need—which were again not enough, but were far more than they could expect, under independence, from their own politicians.

Muñoz also began to realize that in the event that he did achieve the island's independence, well over half of Puerto Rico's men and women might easily want to retain their U.S. citizenship—of which nobody would be able to rob them. What would he do with that tremendous body of "foreigners"?

So, slowly began the mental process that eventually led to the new idea of a permanent tie with the United States as defined by existing realities, rather than by any political doctrine. Ten years later, still led by Muñoz, the Puerto Rican people were to vote in a plebiscite for a compact with the United States whereby they would become self-governing under a constitution written by themselves and for a form of political relationship (devised in the colony) that was unprecedented in world affairs, unheard of and undreamed of by political scientists.

The deep love between Muñoz Marín and the *jíbaros,* which began to manifest itself during the 1940 campaign, has never diminished. In 1948, when Muñoz ran for the office of the first governor ever to be elected, there was an old *jíbaro* in the Isabela region who promised the Virgin that if Don Luis was elected, he would make a pilgrimage to kneel at his feet. Don Luis *was* elected, overwhelmingly. Then for a time, and because the politicians in San Juan were driving him mad, he retreated to Ellsworth's Treasure Island resort in the mountains, where he gave instructions to his guards that they were to admit nobody except members of his family —*and any jíbaro who might want to see him.*

The old *jíbaro* at Isabela sold his last two chickens to raise forty-five cents for bus fare. He arrived at Treasure Island barefoot. When he told the governor-elect about his promise to the Virgin, Muñoz said: "A man must keep his promises, and you must kneel. But I have made no promises one way or the other, and there is no reason why I should not kneel, too. Let us both kneel."

And then after the poet had knelt with the peasant and when the latter was ready to leave, Muñoz's family told him about the chickens and the forty-five cents.

"He sold his last two chickens," they said. "He doesn't have return fare. The least you can do is to give him ninety cents for his transportation."

But Muñoz's answer was: "When a man offers you his soul, do you give him change?" He refused to give him money, but there was no reason why he shouldn't give him transportation. He sent the old man home in his own car.

In 1951 I attended a political rally and stood at the edge of the crowd while Muñoz talked. Next to me stood a *jíbaro*, a fine old man, in worn but immaculate blue denims, a *pava* on his head, a snow-white, bushy mustache adorning his weatherbeaten, seamed face.

"Eso es," he said repeatedly as the governor addressed the crowd. *"Eso es,"* he said, nodding his head. "That's it."

When the meeting was over, he turned to me and said: "Do you know why we love that man? It is because he has given us faith in ourselves."

And with those few words he revealed the secret, not only of Muñoz's outstanding political success in Puerto Rico, but also of his present growing world reputation.

9

Tugwell

THE audacity with which Puerto Rico's colonial voters had handed the ruling capital a package program for their own salvation—carefully worked out, widely discussed, sworn to by all the winning party's candidates, voted upon by the people in what could be interpreted only as a mandate to Muñoz —is probably unparalleled in modern colonial history.

In effect, the 1940 election had informed Washington that the Puerto Ricans were now ready and determined to take matters into their own hands, to create for themselves the reforms for which they had in vain begged the United States during the preceding decades, and to do this even as colonial subjects. There must have been men in Washington in those days to whom the entire matter proved again that Muñoz was essentially an irresponsible political adventurer.

Muñoz's first gesture toward the federal government was to write Roosevelt a letter of congratulations on his third election to the Presidency, in which he also mentioned his own victory and outlined the aims and policies of the Popular Democratic party.

Roosevelt answered in part: "The purposes of the Popular

Democratic Party as you have outlined them are highly praiseworthy and should result in vastly improved social and economic conditions for the island. I particularly appreciate your pledge of co-operation and assure you that this administration stands ready to do all in its power to assist in finding a solution for the problems of Puerto Rico."

Secretary of the Interior Ickes, however, was the man to do the assisting pledged by Roosevelt; the extent of his happiness is not known. The stubborn, autocratic curmudgeon was a decent and honest man who had Puerto Rico's wellbeing at heart and had to endorse the Popular Democratic party's platform in principle. Nevertheless, whatever Muñoz might say or do, Ickes still had the ultimate responsibility for Puerto Rico's well-being. He could in no way wash his hands of that responsibility.

The Secretary was acutely aware of Puerto Rico's political tensions, though far from understanding them. The troubles and violence of the preceding four years had convinced him largely that the Puerto Ricans were a volatile lot, undependable, ungrateful for the blessings Ickes's Reconstruction Administration had brought them. He sensed a rising wave of anti-Americanism in the island that had been placed in his care, and did not want it to grow stronger. If he now appeared to oppose the New Deal program that had been handed to him on the silver platter of a successful election, he might well increase the anti-American feelings by convincing Muñoz's followers that Washington did not, after all —despite the fine talk—have their well-being at heart.

But Ickes was also a bureaucrat who liked to keep power in his own hands. What had Muñoz meant by making campaign promises without first clearing with the man in Washington who had the responsibility? What had he meant when he promised things to his people, his voters—things he lacked the power to deliver under the prevailing colonial system? Who was to carry out the land reforms that had been promised so freely in the campaign speeches? The reforms in education? The regulation of the sugar companies? The industrialization program? Such matters were the federal government's job, to be handled by the Interior Department. After the PRRA's moral fiasco, would Muñoz Marín, as President of the Senate and as Puerto Rico's undisputed political leader, be willing to give his program back to the federal government, where, by all the game's rules, it belonged?

Whatever Ickes may at one time have thought of Muñoz's brilliance and integrity, it now seems clear from his posthumously published diaries that the Secretary of the Interior had come to write him off—if only because his ideas on independence "proved" him to be against the United States.

Specifically, Ickes's immediate problem boiled down to the question of whether the governor of Puerto Rico—by this time Admiral Leahy had succeeded Winship, and Guy J. Swope had succeeded Leahy—should sign Muñoz's drastic bills or veto them. If he did veto them, what would happen to American prestige on the island? Who could draft a federal alternative to Muñoz's program, which had raised such hopes? Would such an alternative, originating in Washington, be accepted by the Puerto Rican voters after their experiences with the PRRA?

Moreover, Ickes no longer had Dr. Gruening, who had resigned as Director of Territories and had become Governor of Alaska on Roosevelt's insistence.

The Secretary therefore borrowed Rexford Tugwell from New York, where the latter had been engaged in city planning, and sent him to Puerto Rico to investigate the entire business and advise the United States on what to do—especially about the land law, which provided for the breaking up of the great corporate sugar estates. A political scientist, a brilliant and distinguished academician in his field, Tugwell had previously, until 1937, been one of the outstanding New Deal leaders and intellectuals. As Assistant Secretary, and later Undersecretary of Agriculture, he had had much to do with problems of land tenure. He was known to be friendly to Puerto Rico's aspirations, had indeed been the one federal official who had in 1934 made it possible for the Chardón commission to go to Washington. As a man of firm and even arrogant convictions, however, as one of the most irreconcilable New Deal philosophers, he was cordially hated by a great many men in the government.

Tugwell's reaction to Muñoz's land law was curiously revealing. He seemed astonished that the law's main features showed signs of real intelligence. He seems to have regarded the law as a sudden flash of inspiration on Muñoz's part, not as something with which the latter had lived through twenty years of struggle and thought. He disliked certain other features, but could do little about them in dealing with a bill which had in toto been submitted to the electorate even before the election, and which every incumbent of the Popular party had sworn publicly to uphold if voted into office. To his credit be it said that he recommended that the governor sign the bill. Swope did sign it and several others; the great Puerto Rican revolution was legally under way.

Tugwell had gone to Puerto Rico as an investigator. Eventually he was made chancellor of the university; a little later he became the island's last continental American governor. In San Juan he is today regarded almost universally as by far the greatest non-Puerto Rican governor in the island's history. His regime was one of great turmoil, great tensions, but still greater achievements. If the latter were primarily those of Muñoz and his followers, Tugwell nevertheless backed to the hilt a program that was in those days revolutionary. No governor before had ever given so much of himself, so freely, for the furtherance of a great idea.

Nevertheless, judging from his writings during and immediately after his governorship, Tugwell seems not to have realized that he was not the designer of Puerto Rico's new program, was *not* the great leader whose task it was to define, explore, and chart new paths for the island's salvation. Formulation of the program had been begun by Muñoz

Marín in 1920, when he was a free-lance journalist in New York. It had been buffeted, shaped, and reshaped during the succeeding two decades, through the lessons taught by the PRERA, the FERA, and the PRRA. Puerto Rican professionals and intellectuals, trained analysts, had modified it through careful studies. It had been further modified again and again for reasons of expediency. Now, no matter how he saw himself, Tugwell was in the governor's mansion primarily to lend his sturdy help and administrative experience to the task of following paths that had long since been charted by others.

Outside of the strong moral backing that he gave Muñoz, Tugwell's really great personal contribution to Puerto Rico's reshaping was that of the political scientist who could take a revolutionary philosophy and program and translate them into definite government structures and actions. He knew how to create and run a government machine to accomplish great things. Muñoz and his followers did not—until Tugwell taught them.

Who were these men whom Muñoz now pulled out of their various exiles and entrusted with the job of forming a new government? They were eager, incorruptible young men dedicated to a great idea, but they were also poets like their leader. They may never have written verse, but they were poets, nevertheless, in their various fields of economics, law, sociology, and geography. They could make their way through scholarly essays peppered with footnotes and graphs, but what did such men know about creating and running a stable and effective government? Tugwell taught them. He could not teach them anything about decency and honesty in government: those things were already inherent in the quality of the officials themselves. But the complex and yet efficient working structure of Puerto Rico's present government, one of the most socially beneficial found anywhere on earth, is Rexford Tugwell's great achievement.

One of his greatest mistakes was to write a book while he

was fighting his battle. The book was published shortly after his departure from Puerto Rico, under the title *The Stricken Land;* with some justice, a number of Puerto Ricans said that it should have been called *The Stricken Rexford.* The book indicates his discovery of what many a continental had discovered before him: that the Puerto Rican road is rough for the non-Puerto Rican Man of Destiny. Throughout some 700 pages it records less the struggle of Puerto Rico than the minutiae of the struggles, the agonies, the rationalizations of Rexford Tugwell, and the clashes between Tugwell, the highly trained political scientist, and Muñoz, the poet, both of whom were driving at exactly the same goal.

The war created tremendous problems for the island, which was of special interest to the enemy because of its strategic location. Submarines sank dozens of ships loaded with the necessities of life. The importation of foods was drastically curtailed, and prices rose sharply. The ghastly spectacle of air-raid alarms—and in one case of hurricane warning—dispersing long bread lines as was all too common. On the mainland the war created conditions of unprecedented employment and prosperity for the civilian population; in Puerto Rico, lacking industries and partly isolated by the submarine campaign, it did the opposite. The needlework industry collapsed because of transportation difficulties, as did the citrus-fruit industry, while most of the other branches of the economy were seriously impaired. Unemployment rose even higher than it had during the depression; mounting relief was an imperative necessity.

At the same time, however, the island's rum industry enjoyed a prosperity it has never even approached since V-J Day. On the mainland the production of whisky and other liquors was cut down because the alcohol was needed for the war effort; Puerto Rican rum—the manufacture of which had got under way about 1936—came largely to take their places.

The excise taxes on rum soared; Puerto Rico's budget, which before 1940 had been around $22 million, shot up to as high as $150 million. With such funds the government could build factories, purchase lands held in excess of five hundred acres by the sugar corporations, provide machinery for the working and distribution of those lands, stimulate its public-health service, implement its new social legislation, foster co-operatives, and engage in all the multiple activities of a stricken society reshaping itself, while also contributing to wartime relief. The war and the resulting prosperity of the rum industry got Puerto Rico's "Operation Bootstrap" off to a flying start during those first four turbulent years of the Tugwell regime.

Morally, too, the war contributed to Muñoz's great effort. Whatever was said—and plenty was—about the socialistic and un-American nature of his program, military men knew that a large unemployed, discontented civilian population is a serious military problem in a location of strategic importance. Muñoz's leadership and his effective program of reform and economic improvement held the island's people together despite their wartime hardships, and greatly strengthened their loyalty to the ruling country.

In his inaugural address Tugwell had expressed his basic philosophy as governor, which differed in no respect from that of Muñoz as political leader, in the following words: "In bettering public health, in educating children, in bringing power, light, sanitation into people's homes, in building more homes for the underprivileged, in providing all kinds of needed work, in the conservation of soil and other resources, in the use and tenure of the land, in the search for higher wages and greater social security—in all these we shall find work enough crowding in upon us in the years to come."

The Planning Board was created for the purpose of charting the island's progress and of integrating all government functions. That organization is today becoming world-famous for the effectiveness of its operations, which, among many other things, prevent wasteful duplication.

The task of carrying out the new land policies, arising from the enforcement of the Five-Hundred-Acre Law, was entrusted to the newly created Land Authority. As funds became available, the government now began to condemn lands held in excess of the legal limit, to purchase them from the sugar companies, and to work them in such a way that the companies could stay in the manufacturing business of operating mills. The administration of those holdings, their partial redistribution to small farmers, planters, and squatters, the active program of social services and community improvement which is carried on as part of the Land Authority's work, are the fruits of a social inventiveness that today promises to have its repercussions in India, Pakistan, Indonesia, Africa, and the Latin-American republics—in all the lands that are sending observers to Puerto Rico.

Muñoz knew well that industrialization was essential to Puerto Rico's continued growth and development, yet apparently was impossible under existing conditions, as it required the investment of large sums of private capital, which were not forthcoming. Puerto Rico's economic climate was not conducive to investment. Nevertheless, factories *had* to be built if the society were to survive. Hence, the government created the Development Company, modeled after Chile's *Corporación de Fomento,* and the Development Bank for the purpose of making industrial credit available. The government's aim in creating those institutions were similar to those of the Chilean organization. Knowing that industrialization was essential, the government took the stand that private capital should at all times be favored, but that when and where private capital did not come forward for building and operating factories, government would do the job. The government, too, would pave the way for private enterprise, would make investigations through which private industry might be encouraged; under certain circumstances it would give various kinds of direct and indirect financial aid to potential private investors.

From the PRRA the insular government had already acquired the cement plant that was to provide the building materials so badly needed for all kinds of constructions, and a private company in Ponce had built another cement plant. Now, under the leadership of Teodoro Moscoso, the Development Company, constantly hampered by the fact that machinery and materials were hard to obtain during the war, enlarged the cement plant and set out to create more industries.

The rum industry needed bottles; the government built and managed a glass factory, which started operations in January 1945, two and a half years after the creation of the Development Company.

A factory for the manufacture of pulp board and paper from waste paper and begasse (the fibrous end product of sugar-cane grinding) was built adjacent to the glass factory —justified for construction during the war because its operation would cut down considerably the amount of shipping needed for supplying Puerto Rico with essential materials.

A clay-products factory was built, turning out glazed tiles in the beginning, but later producing washbowls and toilet bowls for the government's enormous program of slum clearance and low-cost housing.

Because it was evident that the tourist industry could someday be built up to contribute materially to the island's economy, the Development Company participated in the founding of the Puerto Rico Travel Association to promote the interests of *turismo*.

A shoe factory was built by the government in the southern part of the island.

Meanwhile, the government collaborated with the university in arranging for research toward further industrialization, especially in the utilization of the sugar industry's by-products, while the Development Company also promoted the training of Puerto Rican technicians in such mainland institutions as M.I.T. The improvement of labor relations, through the education of both labor and management, became a special concern of the Development Company; it was discovered early that government-operated enterprises in a democracy in which a number of legislators may well be labor leaders on the side are particularly vulnerable to strikes and feather-bedding demands.

Although not created during Tugwell's administration, the Water Resources Authority completed its final organization during that period. Its purpose was to provide cheaper electricity, hydrogenerated wherever possible to reduce the importation of fuels. It flung a single great network of distribution lines over all the island. In T.V.A. style that agency, by means of its low-cost power, has by now become effective in attracting a number of privately financed industries to Puerto Rico. It is also, however, intimately concerned with the conservation of water and soil resources, having been created for the purposes of "conserving, developing, and utilizing, and aiding in the conservation, development, and utilization of water and energy resources of Puerto Rico, for the purpose of making available to the inhabitants of the island, in the widest economic manner, the benefits thereof, and by this means to promote the general welfare and increase commerce and prosperity. . . ."

A Transportation Authority and a Housing Authority to work toward the substitution of decent dwellings for the evil, unsanitary slums were among the other government agencies set up by Tugwell and Muñoz for the purpose of carrying out the mandate of the people for an improved life.

The United States was by then becoming accustomed to such innovations. In Puerto Rico, where the most reactionary elements had held the government for eighteen years before 1940, they seemed revolutionary. Charges of statism and socialism were made unceasingly for the purpose of em-

barrassing Tugwell and Muñoz, and were echoed by reactionary elements in the States. Muñoz's often repeated
answer to those charges was: "We are neither radical nor
conservative. We are merely realistic." Puerto Rico discovered what Chile had discovered earlier and what many
emerging societies such as India and Pakistan are discovering today—that a modern, underdeveloped society cannot
find salvation by following doctrinaire patterns.

Through four centuries the Puerto Ricans had been a
stricken people—starving, disorganized, not permitted by the
rulers to take effective steps toward the improvement of their
lives, lethargic and fatalistic as a result. Now in 1941 they
resolutely set out on new paths of achievement; during the
eight ensuing short years they laid the solid foundation for
the great effort that is today attracting visitors and students
by the hundreds from all parts of the world; their greatest
gain during those years was, however, psychological. New
energies were released for new creative enterprises; the former lethargy gave way to new hopes for some two million
men, women, and children; the exhilaration of a hard uphill
struggle with great rewards in sight took hold of the island's
people; Muñoz and the Popular Democratic party gained
daily in popularity bordering on adulation—among the lower
classes, that is, which comprised well over eighty per cent
of the population.

The upper classes—the wealthy landowners, the ultraconservative businessmen were in a turmoil of fear and tried
their best, supported by the Coalition, to hamper the Puerto
Rican government at every turn. At one point they sent a
delegation to Washington, composed of the island's most
powerful businessmen, to demand that Puerto Rico be given
a strong military government because, as they claimed, the
island was being led straight into un-American socialism.

In the 1940 election the Coalition had won the office of
Resident Commissioner, Puerto Rico's official representative
in Congress. That man was Bolívar Pagán, and he did every-

thing in his power to hinder Muñoz and discredit him in the eyes of Congress. At one congressional hearing in Washington he tried to embarrass Muñoz by asking him, before a number of congressmen, if his program did not amount to socialism and thus was against the American way of life. Muñoz answered that he didn't know whether or not it was socialism; he did know that it was badly needed and was proving effective for dealing with Puerto Rico's ills. As for socialism, however, he wanted to refer the assembled congressmen to the Honorable Bolívar Pagán himself, to the man who had asked him the question, because the Resident Commissioner was *the head of Puerto Rico's Socialist party.*

The embattled 150 per cent Americans also used the F.B.I. for the purpose of confusing and hindering the government program. Agents of that organization were, of course, everywhere, investigating everything constantly. When they asked questions about a candidate for some job, they usually went first to the superpatriots of whose loyalty and respectability they were certain. These superpatriots then told them that the candidate was, or had been, an advocate of Puerto Rico's eventual independence and must therefore be regarded as being un-American and a poor security risk. As a large percentage of Muñoz's following at the upper level was, or had once been, in favor of independence, as the F.B.I. investigators could not be expected to understand that such sentiments did not necessarily mean that the people who held them were anti-American, and as it did not seem to be clearly recognized that a large number of independent countries and peoples were wholeheartedly on the side of the United States during the war, that practice gave rise to a number of irritations. At the lowest political level such use of the F.B.I. seemed a device for having Republicans appointed to jobs in a government devoted to carrying out tasks and programs that were anathema to the Republicans.

Shortly before the 1944 election, which was to test Muñoz's popular strength after four years of political domination, the island's Republican opposition made its prize mistake, which proved also to be its dying gasp as a political force. Stocks of food had run perilously low; people were starving, and continued government relief was imperative. However, the funds designated for relief were running out; new funds were delayed by the opposition's political tricks. Confronted by that dilemma and feeling that it could not stand idly by while people starved, the government began to use other funds, which, according to the Republicans, could not legally be used for the purpose. In a grandiose gesture of righteous indignation, a Republican judge then ordered Tugwell's entire Executive Council, his cabinet, to be arrested and put into jail for contempt.

One suspects that the Puerto Rican people took the gesture with a hearty laugh; certainly the cabinet members did not seem perturbed over their sudden acquisition of jail records. They telephoned their wives and asked them to come to the jail with playing cards, pajamas, possibly a spot or two of liquor, and, above all, photographers. Certainly with photographers!

In commenting on the incident, Tugwell wrote: "Never in all my political experience have I seen a campaign document so effective as the picture of those commissioners looking out deteminedly from behind the bars of La Princessa. To the *jíbaro* and *obrero* (worker) it was plain that the members of his government, all *Populares* but one, had suffered the humiliations of prison in order to protect his right to an income during unemployment. The whole effort of the *Populares* to redistribute social benefits in Puerto Rico was thus symbolized. It seemed not unlikely, after this incident, that the *Popular* victory might be so great as to be embarrassing. It was difficult to see how the *Coalición* could win anywhere at all."

As predicted, the election proved a clean sweep for Muñoz's party. In Tugwell's words, the Coalitionists "ended not only with an infinitesimal representation in the legislature but also without any adequate explanation of their political insanity. They were completely bankrupt."

There is room for doubt, however, whether, as Tugwell seemed to think, the foolish action of a judge and the picture of a cabinet in jail had much to do with the landslide. In 1940 Muñoz had said to the electorate: "Lend me your votes —only once, unless you like what we do with them." During the succeeding four years he had done many dramatic things with those votes and for the voters. Every election since then has been a landslide for him and his party. The Puerto Ricans have loaned him their votes again and again, in ever increasing numbers. Evidently they did and do like what he has done with them. In view of that tremendous and deep-rooted human reality, shallow, mechanistic interpretations of election results seem out of place.

Incidentally, the judge who in 1944 gave his party's election prospects the *coup de grâce,* was the same Marcelino Romany who was later, in 1952, to win momentary international fame by breaking the tensions of the Republican convention in Chicago with his earnest parliamentary efforts. Today, however, he is a staunch supporter of Muñoz Marín and the Popular Democratic party.

Tugwell's book is full of accounts of how his enemies in Congress, encouraged by Puerto Rico's reactionaries, tried their best at all times to attack him by hindering and embarrassing the Puerto Rican program. That was important then; it is no longer important now, when Congress has co-operated wholeheartedly in the program's political evolution. Indeed, the opposition of those days by a congressional minority, seems on the whole to have benefitted Puerto Rico in that it served to bring the island's plight to the attention of congressmen. Two congressional committees visited Puerto Rico in a spirit of bitter hostility to Tugwell; once there, their members were awed by the spectacle of all but universal poverty—sick, hungry people and reeking slums. Muñoz gave them eloquent expositions on the problems to be solved, the many difficulties encountered, and the goals to be achieved.

One letter, which is today a historic document in Puerto Rico, attests to the congressional education regarding the island. Senator Robert A. Taft had gone to the island as a member of a committee presumably hostile to Tugwell. As a man of real integrity, he eventually gave the Puerto Rican program what was—considering its source—its greatest boost.

The glass factory, designed, financed, and owned by the Puerto Rican government, was being built during Taft's visit, but was having trouble under wartime regulations in obtaining machinery from the continent. The island's superpatriotic Republicans pointed it out to him as one more instance of state socialism, of government going into the manufacturing business. So well had he come to realize Puerto Rico's desperate needs, however, that he surprised everybody by coming out strongly in favor of the project. On his return to Washington, on March 12, 1943, he wrote a letter to Donald M. Nelson, Chairman of the War Production Board.

> Dear Mr. Nelson:
>
> I understand that the Puerto Rico Glass Corporation, in part financed by the government-owned Puerto Rico Development Company, has applied for priorities on glassmaking machinery.
>
> I have just been in Puerto Rico with the Subcommittee of the Senate Territories Committee, investigating social and economic conditions there. In view of the number of people crowded into a small island, I believe that the only possibility of a decent standard of living lies in the industrialization of the island. The construction of a glass factory will not only give employment, but it will make it possible to continue other industries now shut down for lack of glass containers and cans.

The rum industry and the canning industry must have some assistance, and glass containers can no longer be shipped from the United States because of the shortage of shipping.

The situation in Puerto Rico is not like that in the United States because there is no war work to which the employees of these industries can turn. Furthermore, in view of the shortage of food, canning is essential to provide more food for the people themselves. I have never been very strong for government-supported industry, but the situation in Puerto Rico is such that I believe the government has a proper function in promoting the development of new industry.

I hope that every consideration will be given to the application of the Puerto Rico Glass Corporation.

Sincerely yours,
ROBERT A. TAFT

Tugwell resigned in 1946, one reason being that his continued presence as governor in the face of the bitter congressional opposition to him proved embarrassing and harmful to Puerto Rico. It had been his hope to have Congress pass a bill under which the people of Puerto Rico could thereafter elect their own governor instead of having to put up with any more in the long line of appointed executives from beyond the island. The bill, however, had no chance of passing at that time. Tugwell did persuade Truman to appoint a Puerto Rican as his successor. Jesús Piñero, a sugar planter who had been an ardent supporter of Muñoz, became the island's first native governor.

Piñero had been Resident Commissioner in Washington, elected in 1944 to replace Bolívar Pagán. On his appointment to the governorship, he was replaced in Congress by the able, astute, and energetic Antonio Fernós Isern, who had during the preceding four years done wonders as Puerto Rico's Commissioner of Health. Fernós managed to get a bill through Congress providing for the popular election of future governors.

In the election of 1948 Muñoz ran for the governorship. He promised no wonders in his campaign; he promised his people only increasing opportunity to struggle the long, stony, difficult uphill road on which they had started in 1941. Four other candidates ran against him; the island's entire press was solidly against him; his own *La Democracia* was long since dead, and he had no newspapers until the last few weeks of the campaign, when one was started by his friends. The opposition controlled the entire press and made full use of the radio facilities for a ceaseless, vituperative campaign, some of it slanderous and aimed directly at Muñoz in person. When the returns were in, it was found that he had won over sixty per cent of the total vote. Unmistakably he had another mandate from the people.

His inaugural parade and ceremony on January 2, 1949, was the greatest, most enthusiastic celebration in Puerto Rico's history.

10

Neither Radical nor Conservative

DURING the Tugwell regime Puerto Rico's leaders often groped fearfully in the dark. They had a job to do—in a hurry—and a long-range program to get under way, and they discovered early that they could do neither by following doctrinaire patterns. Four centuries of Puerto Rico's past, while resulting in traditions and culture patterns that could not be brushed aside, offered few positive precedents and taught largely how the pressing tasks could *not* be accomplished. The present was clamorous in its urgent demands, the future clouded by fearful uncertainties. Everything that was done in those days would itself eventually become a precedent that might either strengthen or wreck the program's future.

Technically Puerto Rico was still a colony, and Tugwell's unpopularity in Congress was a terrifying threat. What if Washington sent down a successor who, partly in retaliation against Tugwell, set out to undo the entire program by reshaping it along authoritarian lines dictated and controlled by Washington? The legal power to do so obviously existed, and called for an active political program designed to increase and strengthen Puerto Rico's autonomy in the matter of making decisions and shaping internal policies. Such political evolution—visible, vital, and effective—was needed to nourish the nascent flame of self-confidence which energized the entire transformation. However, Puerto Rico could expect little help from private investors unless its great effort led to continuity and was not subject, as had been the island's past life, to sudden changes as governor succeeded governor on the island and political administrations replaced each other in Washington.

However, while the march toward political emancipation had got an excellent start in 1940, the details of its route could not be announced, if only because an announcement could strengthen the hands of its enemies and might well lead it into the morass of mere acrimonious debate. In his book *The Art of Politics* Tugwell repeatedly complains that as governor he didn't know what Muñoz as political leader was driving at. Of course he didn't. As governor—good, bad, or indifferent—he represented Washington, and Muñoz was much too astute a leader to tip his hand in advance, to move in any manner except step by step, taken when and if—and *only* when and if—Congress and the Washington authorities seemed ready for that particular step.

The appointment of Jesús Piñero as Puerto Rico's first Puerto Rican governor was a decided step in advance, even though as a federal appointee he was still administratively responsible to Washington. But he had been the first of the *colono* class to back Muñoz and was one of the founders of the Popular Democratic party. He had lived with the program from its earliest beginnings, and could be expected not to oppose any parts of it on doctrinaire grounds. The interim of his regime, from 1946 to 1948—when the island was at long last able to elect its own governor and chose Muñoz Marín—was devoted in part to the task of revising old policies and shaping new ones for the long pull of the future. It was now necessary to take stock, to develop a basic social, political, and economic philosophy, a creed to live by that would be no less American for being essentially Puerto Rican, growing out of the island's needs.

The present "Commonwealth" status was achieved in 1952. In agreeing to that status, Congress ceded to Puerto Rico most of its power over the island's internal affairs. Only the U.S. Supreme Court—only on grounds of constitutionality—can today revoke laws passed by the Puerto Rican legislature. No longer can an appointed governor, whose appointment must be confirmed by the Senate, veto such laws.

The evolution of political thought which led to the establishment of Commonwealth status was a part of the general shaping of new creeds and new policies, which had so great an impulse during the Piñero regime. Then it was also possible to go ahead with some of the things Tugwell had previously blocked through his veto power, one of which was the use of tax exemption to stimulate industrial growth.

The first "Socialist" stage of industrialization by means of government investment and management could not long endure within the American scheme of things. Not only was it counter to American *mores*, but it tended to cut the island off from many financial resources that might otherwise be available. It was plainly evident, moreover, that the Puerto Rican government would not be able, through socialism, to keep pace with the rising tide of demands made upon it. Budgets were higher than ever before, but the demands on those budgets grew more rapidly than did the monies available. More money than had ever been imagined during the days of sugar colonialism was needed for education, public health, public works, communications, and the like. The growth of population alone made it apparent that a government that created new industries out of its own limited funds would never have sufficient capital available to come anywhere near the mounting need for more new industries.

Puerto Rico, therefore, wanted its share of private capital that was piling up in the United States, ready and eager to invest itself in productive American enterprises. Much of the former indignant preoccupation against the absentee ownership of means of production began to give way to the realization that absentee *monopoly*, rather than absentee ownership, had been the great curse ten years previously.

The island's leaders began to realize that with expansion, diversification, and adequate government control to assure optimum social benefits the new economy could be healthy even though financed largely, in the beginning, by absentee capital—as the early development of the United States had been financed largely by British capital and guided in its technical phases by British skills. The development of such an economy would undoubtedly raise wages and therefore the standard of living, which was the first goal of the Puerto Rican government.

A new policy was therefore adopted in 1948, by which the government could offer certain inducements to attract new capital for investment in the Puerto Rican effort, including tax exemption for some years and various kinds of technical and social co-operation and help. This worked so well and was so much more effective than the former industrialization program under government ownership and management that the government eventually in 1950 sold its own factories for $10,000,000 to the island's leading industrialist. He was Luis Ferré, whose family had long managed a large iron works in Ponce, making and repairing machinery for the sugar industry. Active in the Republican party, he was, and is, moreover, one of Muñoz Marín's strongest and most outspoken political enemies. For those reasons the sale naturally stirred up a certain amount of local criticism. The governor, however, said that the plants had been sold to Ferré because the latter's record proved him to have much more sense as an industrialist capable of managing important enterprises than as a politician.

In the midst of shifts and changes, progress and setbacks, the task of providing a badly needed, integrated philosoph-

ical framework for the guidance and unification of the island's many new departures in its life, for the information
and guidance of continental congressmen, editors, and potential investors in the Puerto Rican effort, naturally fell to
Muñoz Marín. As a result, he is becoming much better
known throughout the world as a vocal philosopher with
something important to say to today's bewildered people,
than as an able administrator, the leader of a party, and an
astute political maneuverer able to win elections and achieve
results between them.

In the course of years the famous slogan "We are neither
radical nor conservative, we are merely realistic" had to be
interpreted, translated, and transmuted into many specific
forms, all of which added up to the truism that if a people
wish to be saved they must save themselves according to
their own *mores* and realities. For instance, in addressing
the American Legion Convention in Chicago, September 4,
1958, Muñoz said: "The U.S. did not insist that Puerto
Ricans become carbon copies of people in the States." That
was, of course, part of the constant struggle to maintain cultural integrity, to remain Puerto Ricans with a Puerto Rican
cultural heritage that must be honored and respected as a
source of pride and strength, though it is constantly shaped,
reshaped, and strengthened by culture borrowings from elsewhere.

For such sentiments, those of his political enemies who
clamor for statehood often accuse him of nationalism, while
those who want independence accuse him of precisely the
opposite. He takes pains to be clear on that point. On October
14, 1958, at the opening session of the important international Conference on the Inter-American Exchange of Persons, held in San Juan, he described "extreme nationalism"
as "fertile soil for the harvest of prejudices, distorted images,
myths about peoples and cultures." He said that nationalism
is not "in harmony with man's deepest and noblest aspirations" and that it "cannot contribute much to the future, if

the future is to be a good one." He went on to say that "of nationalism only cultures will remain—not the static but the dynamic aspects of cultures—their diversity, their creative powers, their profound sources of individual expression, languages, arts, concepts of good and evil, manners of expressing beauty and unraveling mysteries." Full recognition of and respect for such cultural autonomy, he said, can lead to "a crusade of understanding, a crusade against the false collective image that we often have of each other, against resistance to the adoption of good ideas and the valuable techniques which we can share, a crusade, in other words, through which every one can, without losing his identity, without denying his tradition or language, enrich himself from what his neighbor can offer, and exchange with that neighbor the fruits of his labor and his thought."

All that, of course, implies freedom of every people to choose the specific paths and policies for its own salvation. In his American Legion speech he referred to the new Puerto Rico's early days of government ownership of industries. "I suppose," he said, "that's socialism, although we didn't care much what tag was on it, so long as it was carried out in terms of freedom and unfaltering respect for the dignity of the individual." In tribute to the United States he added that "Nobody in the United States denounced us for it. Nobody chose to ostracize us and by so doing create confusion and bewilderment as to the meaning of free, democratic choice."

Again and again Muñoz has talked, and continues to talk, against the widespread attitude that demands that those whom capitalism helps in their emergence from poverty and in capitalism's battle against communism must accept capitalism's purest doctrines, must avoid whatever may be tagged "socialism." Referring to Puerto Rico on September 23, 1954, in a speech to the annual convention of the A. F. of L., he said: "We do not worship either public ownership or private enterprise. We believe that each in its place—and every people will have different places for them—are good and useful tools of the democratic way of life. So long as you don't hold either of them sacrosanct, they can both be very respectable means to the ends of economic freedom. It's a dangerous thing to be religious about anything except religion."

On March 10, 1958, he urged the United States, through the Senate Foreign Relations Committee, to incorporate a similar tolerance of varying economic philosophies into its official policies toward Latin America. Drawing on Puerto Rico for examples, he said: ". . . We did not make private enterprise a sacred cow, but a productive and contented one."

In his first inaugural speech, on January 2, 1949, he dealt at some length with the problem of Puerto Rico's ultimate political status. But, as always, he came back to the place of status in the general scheme of things. "A political status, of course, does not exist in an economic vacuum. Thinking on a political status cannot be developed in a vacuum of economic or cultural thought. Ways of living and working; the forward-looking habits in a community; the religious vision; the land and its crops, and the factories, and the tools, and the techniques, and the raising of children, and the cultivation of the understanding, and science, and art, and recreation, and health habits, and sustenance, and clothes, and sheltering roof, and justice, and light, and generosity, and serenity, all these together, and their political status, and more, are the life of a people. The manner of expressing all these together in harmony is the ideal of life of a people. And the spontaneity and dynamism with which they are expressed constitute the people's integral liberty.

"Of course, certain aspects of integral liberty are closely related to the possibility or impossibility of other aspects. If a community does not develop an economy which is founded, or has hopes of being founded, on a victorious productive effort, it will see other forms of its life and liberty impeded, or decayed, or destroyed. From this comes our great dedication, which we should further strengthen on this day, to the task of constantly increasing production in Puerto Rico—more rapidly than the growth of population; more rapidly still to absorb unemployment; more rapidly still to go on raising the standard of living and security; and more rapidly still so that the present imperative need for aid shall not become permanent."

Through the years he has become increasingly preoccupied with the social and individual evils of too great a dedication to mere acquisition, to the frenetic American demand for a new and better car every year, new and "improved" goods of all kinds acquired through installment buying, more and more material things as marks of social distinction. In his legislative message of 1949 he called for "more of the good life within reach of more people every day, and education as to what is meant by the good life. Good living does not always mean the good life. Frequently it is far from being so. And the evil life of misery and insecurity is never the good life, although many good people live that life. Bent as we are on production, we must ask ourselves: production for what? Economic production for its own sake, without a life objective to guide it, only leads modern man to gluttony for worldly goods and to spiritual confusion. We produce so that people will have more of the good life, and here it is well to make clear whether we understand by this the mere multiplication in the consumption of trivial objects which titillate our appetite for acquisition, or whether we are to apply this term to the creative ideal of abolishing extreme poverty and broadening security and liberty in the lives of all men. I believe that in an economy based on high production there can be a good minimum standard of living for all, as well as a high level for those who can legitimately attain it."

On June 16, 1955, at Harvard University and on the occasion of receiving an honorary degree, he asked: "Are the attitudes and habits that are associated with modern high productivity inexorably interwoven with the attitudes and manners of relentless material consumption? Can a culture be efficient in production and at the same time wise and modest in consumption? Can it be feverish in output and serene in intake? I say we are getting to the time in which it must—and if it must, it probably can. Economists could tell us that a higher rate of multiple consumption is necessary to a high rate of production, and therefore of employment and of income, and that what I am talking about would bring economies tumbling down on our heads. It need not be so, because of the evident possibility of re-gearing high productivity to higher ends. If it were so it would most certainly be time to ponder what to do about a situation in which serenity could bring about catastrophe.

"In the Declaration of Independence of the United States the young republic was dedicated to the rights of life, liberty and the pursuit of happiness. In Puerto Rico we are trying in our modest setting to bring to a harmonious success, for the good of our souls and bodies and for the observation of our fellow citizens and of such parts of the world as may care to look, Operation Bootstrap—the right to life; Operation Commonwealth—the right of liberty; and Operation Serenity—the pursuit of happiness with some hope of really catching up with her."

While talking in that vein, Muñoz also set himself the task of teaching his administrators and politicians the meaning of true democracy. It is no easy matter to teach a ward heeler to give up demagogy, or an employee to put the common good ahead of his own. On many occasions the task has required the exercise of firm, disciplinary control, and Muñoz has often been accused—by his political opposition in Puerto Rico, and especially in the ceaseless stream of vituperative propaganda that emanates from the offices of Dictator Trujillo of the Dominican Republic—of being a dictator.

In his first legislative message as governor, on February 23, 1949, he referred to the momentous political and economic implications of the island's new directions toward a more abundant life, and of the new demands the island's people made, not only on the conscience of all branches of the government, but on the "conscience which is well informed." "This country," he informed his legislators, his politicians, "does not need a government which is merely less bad than another; what it needs, and what from the eloquence of its action it has shown itself to deserve, is a government that is a good government. It does not expect perfection, for that is not a human possibility, but it does expect devotion. . . .

"The people expect of you and me at this propitious moment the ultimate degree of the most enlightened good faith. The first condition of this good faith is the absence of personal motives in public life, arising as they may from greed or pride, ambition or vanity. . . . There is nothing more censurable in the eyes of the people than to take a public action or to assume a public attitude because of motives connected with careers or ambition or personal position. That is the great sin against the spirit of the people. This is true because it leads irrevocably to demagogy, which in its turn arouses irrational passions of group against group, be they economic, or racial, or religious, or groups which contribute one type of knowledge necessary to the work of government against groups which contribute another type. . . . Certain it is that the votes of the people do not authorize this, nor will they authorize it at any time the people be consulted. You know that personal interests play absolutely no part in my public life. And I can tell you that my life would be of no use to our people if day after day I were forced to be on the watch for demagogy."

Such affirmations as this draw charges of dictatorship. At the same time, however, they have by now made Puerto Rico famous in many Latin-American circles as by far the most democratic and vital of all Latin-American societies.

In the governor's preoccupation with a "conscience which

is well informed," in his constant, restless demand for information lies one explanation for an outstanding characteristic of modern Puerto Rican life.

The systematic investigation of the island's social and economic problems is, of course, not new in Puerto Rico. It began during the nineteenth century with the establishment of the island's several cultural societies. However, during the Tugwell regime, and especially since the beginning of Muñoz's governorship, Puerto Rico has become a veritable researcher's paradise. The Planning Board carries on a large number of projects designed as guidance for specific actions; the university's Social Science Research Center and other units delve with varying degrees of judgment and success into a number of aspects and problems of the island's life; the Economic Development Administration employs a staff of research experts to probe special economic problems.

In that feverish activity continental Americans have begun to play a new role. Where they had once assumed most or all of the high policy-making positions in government and private enterprise, they are now hired by the Puerto Ricans— whenever their specialized and technical qualifications for a given task seem better than those of available Puerto Ricans —for the purposes of research and fact-finding.

The American consultants receive salaries somewhat commensurate with those they would have earned on the mainland, which are higher than those paid to Puerto Ricans. But many of them stay on the island, identified with its affairs, year after year, doing excellent work and making valuable contributions, while wondering increasingly as time passes why they can never achieve true integration into the Puerto Rican society and government to which they are devoting a large part of their lives and energies. Whether they like it or not, nearly all of them remain "consultants," which means that they have only temporary status in the government.

"We are mistresses," said one such consultant who had

done invaluable work for the Commonwealth and was prepared to spend his life in Puerto Rico. "We enjoy good pay
and much affection, but we can never hope to be fully accepted in the official family."

The government's various guiding policies, discussed in
succeeding chapters, have been formulated and enunciated
by Muñoz Marín again and again. For instance, it is *not*
Puerto Rico's policy to industrialize on an economic foundation of permanent cheap labor, to subscribe to the long-established, though usually unspoken, doctrine that "wealth
must paradoxically be founded on hunger." The policy is to
raise wages, and with them standards of living, as rapidly
as circumstances permit, and to aim at 1975 as the year
when the latter will correspond to those that prevailed in the
United States in 1955. It is *not* Puerto Rico's policy to open
new factories at the expense of old ones in the States, to de-
prive U.S. workers of jobs in order to create payrolls for
Puerto Ricans. In his legislative message of 1952 he said:
"The economy of the United States generates more than
twenty-five billion dollars of new capital each year. Out of
this new and enormous capital wealth Puerto Rico is legitimately seeking an investment of thirty or forty million dollars of new capital a year—I repeat, of *new* capital, not
transferred capital. The American citizens living in Puerto
Rico comprise one and one-half per cent of the population of
the United States. And our industrial plan calls for less than
one fifth of one per cent of the new capital generated, not
without the modest collaboration of Puerto Rico, by the
American economic system every year. It would seem clear
that, as good citizens, we need have no fear that the industrial system of the United States is in danger of destruction
at the hands of Puerto Rico."

Addressing himself to those who maintain that Puerto
Rico's current successes are due solely to unprecedented
showers of federal gold and to the system under which the

island makes no financial contributions to the federal treasury, he said in 1952 that federal grants in aid on the island are relatively small and are not "the decisive factor in the economic struggle of our people." In the same speech he began to discuss the possibility of soon contributing more than formerly to the treasury of the United States. "A large factor [in the economic struggle] is that Puerto Rico is a part of the American Union and does not contribute to the Federal Treasury and to the running expenses of the Union. Obviously the right to be a part of a union of peoples and states without paying a proportionate share of the common expenses involved cannot be maintained as a principle. The respectable principle is that those who can pay should pay their share into the common treasury. There is also the principle that great associations help, during the period when help is required, those members of the association that cannot at the time pay their proportionate share. This is a great principle, a profoundly Christian and civilized principle, which in our case is based on common citizenship. There is another great principle that no taxes should be collected from people who do not have adequate representation in the bodies levying the taxes.

"If we take these three principles together, the possible future development of our people emerges rather clearly. Puerto Rico ought to pay its share into the Federal Treasury as soon as it is in an economic position to do so, in the same way that it is now contributing morally to the good democratic reputation of the Union. It would, however, be un-Christian, uneconomic, un-American, and extremely foolish to exact such a contribution to the Federal Treasury if that were to mean aggravating instead of ameliorating poverty, surrendering health to disease, closing instead of opening schools, lowering instead of improving standards of living, increasing instead of decreasing unemployment, and abandoning hope to desperation. But a day will come when this will not be so. And when that day arrives we ought not to wait until we are asked to share in the expense; we should rather be the ones to propose the sharing and to pay for it ourselves in the exercise of our own democratic authority and our own great responsibility as members, in a new way, of a great Union."

Such statements and sentiments form the guiding philosophy of a society that is now becoming so famous throughout Latin America that President Prado of Peru, when I introduced myself to him in 1958 as having come from Puerto Rico, exclaimed almost involuntarily: *"Qué país de maravillas! What a land of wonders!"* But it is in the political field that Muñoz is today becoming even better known everywhere south of the Rio Grande. He is widely regarded, and often acts as the head of a Latin-American state, rather than as the governor of a part of the North American Union, which is insignificant in area as well as population. While many Latin Americans still cling doggedly to the old idea that Puerto Rico, not being a sovereign nation, must still be an exploited colony, the significance of the island's present relationship with Washington has begun to dawn on an increasing number. Indeed, more and more Latin Americans are coming to recognize the governor of Puerto Rico as a truly Latin-American leader and as one of the three outstanding such leaders for a democratic, prosperous future Hemisphere. The others are Romulo Betancourt, Venezuela's present President, and José Figueres, former President of Costa Rica, both of whom are close friends of Muñoz.

United States policy in Latin America is now beginning to show Puerto Rico's influence. On March 10, 1958, in response to an official invitation, Muñoz Marín addressed the Senate Foreign Relations Committee. He mentioned the fact that extreme nationalism is today waning in Latin America, though also kept alive by the dictators. ". . . The more authoritarian the government," he said, "the more nationalistic its behavior." He talked about the "natural spirit of democracy and freedom that all Hispanic and Iberian people possess," lamented the fact that too often "it is throttled into temporary voicelessness by ambitious and unscrupulous leaders," and rejoiced that "recently it has been very much in the ascendancy." He urged the United States "to encourage this inherent will toward free institutions" and to become cooler than they were formerly toward dictators, and warmer than they were formerly toward the Latin peoples' current titanic struggle for democracy. "I do not mean," he said, "that the United States should intervene in the internal affairs of any Latin-American country, or that it should decide for its neighbors what form of government they shall have. This, of course, would not be proper, nor be to the best interests of the United States. It is a matter of degree, and the degree is most important. Nobody can deny this country the right to exercise its own freedom to determine and demonstrate what neighbors it feels enthusiastic about and what neighbors are subject to a minimum amenity. When you give equal consideration to dictators and tyrants as to proven democrats you cannot help but discourage democracy."

In the same talk he urged a stepping up of economic aid in the Hemisphere for the purpose of "reasonably diminishing the tremendous gap between the standards of living in the United States and those prevailing over enormous areas of Latin America." Such a program, he said, would be important even if the Soviet Union did not exist. He pointed out the dangers in taking Latin America so for granted that much more United States aid is given to countries near the Soviet Union than to those near the United States. He urged the further lowering of trade barriers within the Western Hemisphere, and said that "the great and difficult idea of a Latin-American common market or of regional common markets leaping as many political boundaries as possible deserves and needs greater support from the United States."

He also urged the United States not to tie too many strings on the economic aid it may give others, not to insist too strongly that the development resulting from such aid follow doctrinaire capitalistic patterns. "Don't declare either public or private initiative sacred, but only freedom. Every society has its own convictions, conditions, prejudices and conclusions about what type of development belongs in each sphere, or what individual undertakings belong in each. . . . It is of paramount importance that the United States or the developed Western powers avoid seeming to try to ram a doctrine down the throats of those who wish to receive their aid."

Similar sentiments, especially the one about being cooler to dictators and friendlier to democracy, were voiced in 1958 by Vice-President Nixon on his return from his all but disastrous tour of South America, and by Dr. Milton Eisenhower after his fact-finding tour of Central America. It was no mere accident, however, that after he left Venezuela and before he returned to Washington, Nixon spent the better part of a night talking to Governor Muñoz Marín in San Juan. Nor can the fact that Milton Eisenhower's official recommendations closely paralleled Muñoz's expressed thoughts be dissociated entirely from the fact that the President's brother, before returning to the States from his Central American tour, was an honored guest of the Commonwealth of Puerto Rico at the July 25 celebration of 1958, and spent some days as a house guest in San Juan's executive mansion.

It would be too much to claim that Muñoz Marín and Puerto Rico are actually "leading" Latin America in the present struggle for democracy, a better material life, and closer hemispheral unity. That struggle is a regional part of the entire world's momentous modern renaissance, and would take place even if Puerto Rico had never existed. What *is* true is that Puerto Rico's current transformation is part and symptom of that struggle, that an understanding of Puerto

Rico leads to an understanding of the aspirations of people everywhere, including Latin America, and that Puerto Rico has a leader and a governor who, as a literate, vocal, sensitive poet, expresses those aspirations perhaps as well as any man in today's world.

11

Agriculture

THE problem of latifundia, too much land in the hands of too few people, has played a powerful role in most modern revolutions. Henry VIII faced the problem in his own way, as did Mexico's Juarez. Latifundia was the basic motivation for the uprisings of Haitian slaves and Irish rebels, and for Denmark's social reconstruction of a century ago. It eased the way of the Chinese Communists when they finally took over their country, and is today one of Fidel Castro's pressing problems in Cuba.

Puerto Rico's agrarian problem of large, absentee-owned sugar estates was in 1940 regarded as the most urgent faced by the Popular Democratic party, and the enforcement of the Five-Hundred-Acre Law was said to be the *sine qua non* for effective social reform.

Forty years after the passage of that federal law, fifty-one corporations were operating 249,000 acres of the island's best lands—an average of 5,000 acres each. One corporation, the Eastern Puerto Rico Sugar Company, held almost 55,000 acres, or more than a hundred times its legal limits.

Congress had added the Five-Hundred-Acre Law to the

first organic act to the tune of oratory, expressing the fear that U.S. corporations might otherwise come to own all the valuable land on our newly acquired island, reducing the condition of the population to one of "absolute servitude." It seems, however, as stated in Chapter 13, that the farm lobby also had something to do with the matter, hoping that the Five-Hundred-Acre Law would protect the American beet-sugar industry against the rise of a new cane-sugar rival in Puerto Rico. Whatever its real aims, the law failed to achieve them. Having no teeth, providing no penalties for infractions, it was ignored for four decades. A powerful cane-sugar business *did* grow up in Puerto Rico; the island's population *was* reduced to absolute servitude; the first job of the Popular Democratic party after achieving power was to remedy that condition by breaking up the large estates. More difficult, however, was the task of deciding what to do with the land after that.

The modern dilemma in land tenure—encountered especially in sugar—is this: social justice may seem to demand that the available land be divided as equitably as possible, among as many people as possible—which means in small lots. Industrial efficiency, however, the use of heavy machinery and of expensive mills, demands that it be worked in large parcels. That, in a nutshell, is the basic agricultural problem of all "crowded" countries. A landed peasantry with small holdings, smaller capital resources, and no credit at the bank might for a time be able to eke out a bare subsistence, but this "Haitianization" would degenerate into utter misery as the population grew, the land became poorer, and the peasants, at the mercy of more powerful economic forces, eventually again lost even what little land they had.

A co-operative movement similar to those in Denmark and Mexico would seem to be the answer. But the creation of a strong, smoothly running co-operative movement requires years of hard and patient work, with many dangerous setbacks. In 1941 the co-operative idea had not yet been sufficiently entrenched in Puerto Rico to be trusted with the task of taking over an important share of the main branch of the island's economy. The failure of only one crop would have spelled disaster. Hence Muñoz's ingenious land law provided for acquisition of land by the government itself, to be used in various ways. Some of the land was to be incorporated in proportional profit farms owned and worked by the government to produce sugar cane and perhaps other cash crops; some was to be sold to small farmers in lots of up to twenty-five acres; more, while owned by the government, was to be given in usufruct, in small home parcels, to landless agricultural laborers who might, as a result, become identified with the soil. Areas that were relatively useless for other purposes were to be turned over to the insular forestry or conservation services. In addition, the Land Authority was given the power to acquire swampy and barren lands and to engage in reclamation projects for the purpose of adding to the island's arable areas.

At present (1959) the Land Authority holds 86,000 acres of land, of which about 9,000 are, for topographic and other reasons, not suited for cultivation, and of which 50,000 are under intense cultivation, largely in sugar cane. The government also operates two sugar mills. There has been no pressing need to condemn and buy all the sugar lands held in violation of the Five-Hundred-Acre Law. The fact that the government has demonstrated its power to acquire such land when necessary, and to work it efficiently, is enough to assure both workers and planters a fair deal in the industry and to keep the sugar industry out of Puerto Rican politics. Under those conditions the government can use its available funds for purposes other, and more pressing, than that of acquiring more land.

There are today seventy-one government farms, operated on a profit-sharing basis. Their managers share in the profits and also receive wages. The thousands of workers receive basic wages as prescribed by law, plus shares of the profits, distributed in proportion to the hours worked during any one season; at times and on some farms, these profit bonuses have amounted to more than 15 per cent of the wages earned. But the scheme has not always worked in a utopian fashion.

The Land Authority, for instance, has never had an easy time in its labor relations. Its system of sharing profits is just and is socially advanced, but the fact remains that government-operated enterprises are peculiarly susceptible to labor troubles. Moreover, the Authority was plagued from the start by the modern dilemma between creating more jobs and achieving the kind of efficiency that results in technological unemployment. In the social revolution's early days labor regarded the proportional profit farms as a means for taking up the unemployment slack; all steps toward the mechanization that is essential if Puerto Rico's sugar industry is to survive in competition with the world's were resented bitterly and were often fought by strikes in the fields or in the mills. There are indications that some of those strikes were financed by the private sugar interests, whose mills were sure to get the business when the government's were idle.

The situation will be eased as Puerto Rico succeeds in creating more jobs in all the branches of its economy. Meanwhile, labor education is being pushed as rapidly as possible, and Puerto Rico has attracted world attention for its efforts to create a body of agrarian workers, rooted to the soil and replacing the former landless, sporadic day laborers.

Since the program's inception, under Title VI of the land law, over 900 farms have been sold on easy terms for a total of $1,500,000 to small farmers who receive help from various insular agencies for the purpose of getting on their feet as independent agricultural producers. At the same time, under Title V no fewer than 50,000 small parcels of land, now used by a total population of more than 300,000, have been given in usufruct as home plots to formerly landless agricultural wage earners; the former company towns are being replaced as rapidly as possible by communities of rooted home owners. These are the famous *agregados*—squatters. They own their houses—indeed, they must have such houses and live in them within four months after acquiring the plots—but title to the land is retained by the government in order to prevent the program's defeat through a wave of real-estate speculation.

The settlers are grouped in well-planned villages to facilitate the provision of electricity, water, and education, and the fostering, by means of co-operatives and community programs, of an integrated community spirit. Once the village has been laid out and planned, the land being divided into parcels of about half an acre, with plenty of room for recreation grounds, churches (both Catholic and Protestant), a school, a co-operative store, and the like, all those eligible to receive lots acquire their specific plots of ground by drawing numbers out of a hat, after listening for some hours to justified and extremely convincing speeches about what a fine government they have. What happens next, however, is often the creation of a new rural slum, as the poor don't have money for building good houses.

However, after the slum has existed long enough for its inhabitants to have shaken together for group decisions and group action, the government, by means of Agriculture's "Social Programs Administration," proposes that it rebuild itself through the famous program of aided-self-help housing, which creates new rural homes of concrete—attractive, hurricane-proof, fire-proof, vermin-proof, and speculator-proof—at a cost of about $300 each. Other communities, not created by the government, can also at their request receive aid toward the construction of such houses. The government provides construction materials at cost, plus forms, plans, cement mixers, and technical supervision. The future owner, his family, his neighbors, and their families—and sometimes even neighbors who are themselves not eligible for such housing, but who want the right to use the new house as a shelter in case of hurricane—then build the house themselves at no pay.

An example of this group action is the "William Fuertes" community on the north coast, which was inaugurated April 10, 1959. It was the 130th such community to be created through the aided-self-help program, and brought the total number of houses up to 4,593, with 1,566 still under construction. The cost per house in that community was $348.24; the home owners paid down $20 each and are paying off the remainder without interest at the rate of $2.74 monthly.

After the new settlers have moved into their homes, the Social Programs Administration works with them constantly to foster mutual aid and self-help.

Co-operative stores spring up, replacing the company stores at which the sugar workers had formerly done most of their trading; credit unions provide lasting power over the dead season; where formerly the sugar companies had discharged workers for daring to plant even a few miserable stalks of corn in their front yards, individual or community subsistence gardens are encouraged, planned, planted, and worked with the best technical help available from the Department of Agriculture. Home handicrafts are fostered, for extra income, often in collaboration with continental industries. If the community lacks a road, it is encouraged to build one by community action and with government help. Some of these new settlements have built community centers, school lunchrooms for their children, milk stations, and rural libraries.

The Social Programs Administration of the Department of Agriculture and Commerce, and the Division of Community Education of the Department of Education, described in Chapter 15, are among the most vital and important new agencies created by the government. The hundreds of Point IV visitors who go to the island annually, from coun-

tries that have Puerto Rico's basic problem of small income
with which to meet large needs for social improvement, are
almost invariably impressed by their work and carry their
lessons back to such places as India, Indonesia, and various
parts of Africa and Latin America. A number of Caribbean
countries have adopted Puerto Rico's program of aided-self-
help housing and have at times borrowed Puerto Rican technicians for the purpose.

While the Land Authority got under way because co-
operatives in the early years could not be trusted to keep the
sugar industry going efficiently, the co-operative movement
itself, fostered by government action, has now also matured
to a point of real significance in the island's life and economy. In the early days everybody with a good idea and some
energy began to organize co-operatives. The federal relief
organization and its succeeding PRRA gave much thought,
effort, and money to fostering the movement. In 1935 and
1936 I was myself quite busy, with microphone and type-
writer, pounding away at the Rochedale idea and its social
significance; and also gaining a reputation—in some circles
—as a dangerous radical. In 1936 a few of us obtained
$100,000 from the federal government and used it to found
a "self-help-corporation" to organize, finance, and guide co-
operatives. To my delighted surprise I found it still in existence in 1959, still doing business, though with capital resources that are somewhat shrunken.

Today the Commonwealth government is furthering the
movement as energetically as possible through one organization—the Co-operative Development Administration
—which is backed financially by the autonomous Co-operative Development Bank. While the university, in its agricultural extension service, also has a section devoted to
co-operatives, it works closely with the Development Administration.

Some figures released by that administration suffice to
show the movement's growth. In 1949 there were 119 co-

operatives in the island, with 42,014 members, doing a total business of $23,128,400 annually. In 1958, 312 organizations, with 113,883 members, did a business of $55,254,900. These are divided into five general classes, viz: agricultural co-operatives to give farmers group strength in such things as purchasing and marketing; consumers' co-operatives; credit unions; housing co-operatives; and industrial and other organizations. The growth of the credit-union idea is significant in Puerto Rico's financial life; it indicates the growth of savings, which is in turn an index of the increase in capital available for development. In 1949, 33 credit unions had 5,000 members and did a business of $403,400; 1958 saw 172 credit unions, with 58,184 members, doing a business of more than $15,000,000.

Again and again I have had the stimulating experience of taking foreign visitors—from Ethiopia, Ghana, Jordan, etc.—to a newly created settlement of $300 houses and of being welcomed with an abiding pride by the inhabitants, who not only insisted on showing the visitors through their new homes, but also talked with deep satisfaction about having not only their own store, but even their own "bank."

The consumers' co-operatives, of which there were 54 in 1949, with 6,900 members, numbered 96 in 1958, with 13,097 members, doing an annual business of $7,807,500. In 1952 they began to be organized into a federation for group strength in buying, etc. In 1958, 73 of them belonged to the federation, which in that year did a business of nearly $4,000,000. Several co-operative supermarkets have in recent years been established in various cities, and more are being planned.

All that is encouraging, but still not enough. There are still too many people, in the government and in private life, who actively resist the co-operative movement as a kind of "creeping socialism" that must be fought or impeded on doctrinaire grounds. But Puerto Rico is a small, poor country. There are signs, at least in its agricultural life, that it will not reach the full flowering of its development unless it also absorbs the lesson once learned by the small and formerly poor Scandinavian countries: co-operation, however it may be borrowed from socialism's bag of techniques, must become a very way of life, integrated in the national *mores* as one of several essential means by which capitalism can and must save itself in small, poor countries.

The spread of supermarkets is a new phenomenon of the new Puerto Rico and may eventually have important influences on the island's agriculture by providing large, businesslike markets for agricultural products. But the farmers will themselves have to learn much before many of them can take advantage of such markets. The supermarkets demand *dependable* sources of food products, delivered on time and in the quantities needed, graded as to quality and packaged according to modern standards. An occasional Puerto Rican farmer has been sufficiently alert to meet those requirements; many lack the needed capital and means of transportation; others merely complain that the supermarkets import too many of their purchases from the continent.

Although good progress has been made in land distribution, Puerto Rico's agriculture has lagged far behind other branches of the economy in the kind of modernization that spells maximum or optimum production. The island's leaders realize that the land is a productive machine that must be put to its most efficient use if it is to serve well the society depending on it, but it is far easier to start from scratch in manufacturing—build factories and train people to run them well—than to unscramble the heritage of centuries in agriculture, the heritage of scrambled tenure, inefficient marketing, undue profiteering, wasteful farming methods. Writing in *American Forests,* October 1958, Monroe Bush says: "Puerto Rico's two million acres have been so mismanaged through 300 years of desperate subsistence agriculture that today only 300,000 acres are undamaged by erosion."

The U. S. Soil Conservation Service, according to Harvey Perloff in his book *Puerto Rico's Economic Future,* has pointed out that "only some 845,000 acres out of the island's total of about 2,103,000 acres of soil areas are well adapted to a permanent agriculture and that most of this land requires complex or intensive soil conservation practices if production is to be sustained." Perloff goes on to say that as of 1949 about 1,000,000 acres were actually in crops, and therefore Puerto Rico in mid-1949 had 2.2 persons for every acre of tillable soil. "This compares with about three acres *per person* in the United States—a highly industrialized country with much less dependence on agriculture."

The statement, however, is apt to be misleadingly pessimistic unless, as Puerto Rico's planners are now doing, one substitutes in one's thinking the term "productive use" for "permanent agriculture." Pastures, orchards, and forests are also productive and can, in one way or another, be made profitable for their owners and the society. The urgent task is to improve drastically the agricultural productivity of every square foot of land that is not needed for cities, roads, factories, and the like. But that requires a hard new look at existing government policies, tacit or expressed. Always the natural urge to get people "back to the land," to create a class of noble peasants, to use the rural land areas as reservoirs for surplus labor and as means for sustaining the otherwise unemployed, is in conflict with the inexorable need for modernizing agricultural production, for raising the rural population's living standard, for reducing the island's present enormous imports of foods from countries with more efficient agricultural and distribution plants.

The South American nations that are emerging today are in that respect better off. The six Amazonian nations, for instance, are discovering that they own among them a vast, rich frontier region which is almost as large as the United States and which has throughout the centuries been left as a kind of social-economic vacuum in the heart of the continent. They have physical room for expansion, and today they are energetically building roads into it and planning projects to expand their economies and absorb "surplus" populations. Puerto Rico's frontier lies in the realm of technology; its pioneering consists of making every bit of available land produce its maximum.

While there is a never ending effort toward diversification, sugar is still the island's predominant crop and even its one outstanding industry, producing for the United States market under quota regulations. The season of 1958 saw 30 mills grinding cane, employing 7,000 workers, and producing a total of 922,908 tons of raw sugar and 229,154 tons of refined. More than 300,000 acres were harvested to cane, and 55,000 workers were employed as field hands. Sugar is an industrialized crop and, in effect, a weed that requires little care and needs to be replanted only every five years or so. It yields a relatively high return per acre. Financial credit is available to sugar planters because they have mills standing by to receive their harvests, and an assured market within the quota system.

One of Puerto Rico's main agricultural problems is that of industrializing other crops, of building canneries and other processing plants plus distribution systems for them which assure markets both at home and abroad. Much of the long-established, crude subsistence agriculture still exists, but is doomed because it cannot compete with more efficient production elsewhere.

But now, suddenly, sugar has itself suffered a slump and seems well on the way to being another "sick" crop that in recent years has failed to produce the maximum tonnages established by federal quotas. Not only have there been some climatic afflictions—a hurricane, a year of drought, a year of floods—but it is also increasingly evident that Puerto Rico's sugar industry must again "modernize" if it is to regain its economic health. It must become more efficient, cut costs, make every acre produce more than formerly, improve its milling and hauling.

The first drastic change was from bag-shipping to bulk. Until very recently the shippers bought jute bags and sent their loads to the general cargo piers to be handled by stevedores. Then four bulk-loading piers were built at convenient locations, while the mills erected great warehouses in which to pile their raw sugar while waiting for the trucks to haul it away. Today the sugar is handled like sand; conveyor belts carry it onto the trucks, into the warehouses at the piers, from the warehouses into the ships. The system effects great savings, but also much apprehension among the managers of sea ports that had been built in large part for handling bagged sugar and suddenly saw their trade dwindling down to nothing in that important category. Naturally it also results in much restlessness among the stevedores who are thrown out of work.

Technology demands that the cane be ground within twenty-four hours after being cut, lest it lose an undue amount of its sugar content. Traditionally, therefore, the Puerto Rican crop has been shipped in a semi-refined condition, to be refined on the mainland. When a Puerto Rican producer some twenty-five years ago built a modern refinery, the howl from mainland refiners was considerable. Washington then made a ruling that only a small part of the island's sugar quota, 126,033 tons out of a total that was set at 910,000 tons in 1934 (and increased to 136,113 tons for sale in the States, in 1958) could be shipped in a refined state; the rest must be shipped in the crude state for the purpose of protecting established mainland refineries. That remnant of economic colonialism irked the Puerto Ricans. They claimed that if all the sugar produced on the island could be refined there, the Puerto Rican economy would gain by about $12,000,000 annually, and about 8,000 men would find new employment in the refining alone. Pleas and lawsuits did no good; the limitations on local refining were upheld. But in 1958 one began to hear disturbing talk from the industry that local refining has become uneconomic and that all refining may soon be moved to the mainland, thus throwing more workers out of jobs.

Meanwhile, it is also becoming evident that the entire business of planting and harvesting cane must be overhauled for greater efficiency, must be mechanized. That means eliminating the hillside plantings and bringing all the cane down to the coastal plains, where machinery can be effective, and planting new kinds of cane which give a higher yield.

Pineapples were a minor Puerto Rican crop twenty years ago. They were excellent—large, juicy, and sweet—but were not suited for canning. They had to be shipped raw, which meant that they were picked green, lost quality enroute, and were marketed in New York in a precarious fashion. But it was obvious that if properly handled, pineapples could become a major item in the island's agriculture. Without competing with sugar for the same land, they yield a return per acre comparable to that of sugar, while employing more men. Hence the Land Authority, some years ago, sent to Hawaii for the types of pineapples best suited for canning. When the Hawaiian interests refused to help, Puerto Rico turned to Mexico and obtained enough pineapples for an acre or two. Agronomists devised a method whereby each fruit could be made to produce eight or nine new plants, instead of the two that result from the methods of propagation used formerly. The pineapples were planted on government land, nursed along, multiplied, replanted, until there were enough to support a small cannery.

The canned products of the government's first pilot plant were so excellent that they commanded top prices in New York. The work of propagating pineapples on government land was pushed at top speed, while cuttings also began to be distributed to a large number of individual farmers who could now, with a cannery near to absorb their crops, afford to produce the fruit. The Land Authority abandoned its first cannery and built a new one at a cost of more than $4,000,-000—the world's largest. It is today operated by the government. Under contracts with private distributors, it produces a number of commercial brands of canned pineapples which compete in the market, though they all come from the same fields and are cooked in the same vats. As yet, the plant is far from operating at capacity. However, the work of propagating pineapples, of increasing the acreages devoted to them, goes forward energetically, and more are available for canning every year. The government's policy in a case of that kind is that it is at any time willing to sell the cannery to private interests after it has begun to show a profit and a customer comes forward.

Dairy farming, which hardly existed in Puerto Rico before 1940, now ranks second to sugar in economic importance. Plants for treating and bottling milk have been built in recent decades; breeds of cows new to Puerto Rico have been and are being imported; new grasses are tested, propagated, and disseminated. The spread of dairying is eloquent testimony to the rising standard of living. In 1940, when the island's per-capita average annual income was $121, few people could afford to buy fresh milk; today, with a per-capita income of nearly $500, local demands and purchasing power, plus the fact that many thousands of consumers now have refrigerators, provide incentives for the investment of millions of dollars in dairy farms and dairies.

Nevertheless, dairy farming still leaves much to be desired. Denmark is a dairy state in which a good economic herd, capable of yielding its owner a good living, consists of about a dozen cows. Puerto Rico's basic economic unit is closer to a hundred cows; dairying is there the game of well-to-do people who have much land and capital.

The two countries differ in climate and soils, though the Danes, having been longer in the business than have the

Puerto Ricans, also understand dairying better. The real secret of Denmark's success, however, is found in the outstanding success of that country's co-operative movement.

For example, Denmark has more than 1,000 modern
plants, co-operatively owned, for making world-famous but-
ters and cheeses. In Puerto Rico, where there is a seasonal
"surplus" of milk that cannot be sold fresh in bottles, dairy-
men have so far failed in their efforts to organize a co-
operative for the purpose of building and managing just one
such plant—and a small one at that. Evidently they would
rather pour their surplus milk away than accept the prices
at which a plant for making butter and cheese can make
a profit. While the dairy farmers insist on receiving prices
that are higher than the United States's average, wasting
their milk in the effort to sustain those prices, Puerto Rico
must import millions of dollars worth of butter and cheese
annually from the mainland United States.

At present, too, $30,000,000 worth of meat and meat
products are imported annually, draining the economy. One
of several reasons is that there is no modern slaughter house
on the island. Only now, in 1959, is such a slaughter house
being built by the government, to be operated, under contract by a private concern. While reducing the export of
monies for imported meats, it will also spur the dairy and
beef-cattle industries and put to productive use many hilltop
lands that are now being eroded, but will soon be covered
with forage grasses. The Water Resources Authority, whose
hydroelectric reservoirs are now filling with silt, washed
down from the hills, has a direct interest in the establishment of a modern abattoir. Until recently, however, it was
an economic impossibility. Not only were the island's people
too poor to buy fresh meat, but most of them had no refrigerators, while the rural poor lacked even electricity. Today, with the purchasing power rising steadily, the Water
Resources Authority is making so much progress with its
program of rural electrification that it will not be long be-

fore every home in Puerto Rico has electricity at low cost.

Before deciding to build and operate the government-owned slaughter house, the Puerto Ricans looked far and wide for private capital for the venture. But the vicious circle that is so often encountered in developing societies, demanding "socialist" action, and that forced the construction of the pineapple cannery with public funds, is also at work in this situation. Private enterprise will not build the slaughter house because not enough meat is available locally to keep it going; dairy farmers and the few people who produce beef cattle will not improve their lands and increase their herds unless and until they see a sure market for their beef in the form of a modern processing plant. Again and again Puerto Rico has discovered that the first venture capital must in a situation of that kind come from the government—even though the plant may later be sold to private interests.

A few decades ago the island's principal crops, after sugar, were coffee, citrus fruits, tobacco, and the foodstuffs that were grown largely on a subsistence basis. The commercial growing of citrus fruits was strangled by competition from Texas and received its death blow during World War II, when ships were not available for transporting the crops to the mainland. Coffee, produced in the western mountain regions, has always been a typically Puerto Rican crop, produced by Puerto Ricans on lands owned by Puerto Ricans, left alone by absentee capital. Until about 1917 Puerto Rican coffee was cherished in Europe, where it commanded high prices. As indicated in Chapter 3, however, that did not mean that living conditions in the coffee hills were correspondingly good. They were terrible, and the coffee regions are today Puerto Rico's most stricken areas and the island's most fertile producers of migrants to New York.

A disastrous hurricane and the disruptions caused by World War I ruined Puerto Rican coffee as an export crop. Today it is produced primarily for consumption on the island, where it is protected by a special tariff on imported coffees. Nevertheless, it is still decidedly a sick crop. Hundreds of acres of once flourishing coffee lands have been abandoned and are reverting to "virgin" forest because it no longer pays to cultivate and harvest them; their abandonment increases unemployment and accelerates the exodus of migrants. The remaining coffee plantations, producing the beans under shade trees, are having a difficult time between uncertain markets and rising labor costs.

The diagnosticians, as usual, differ widely. Some claim that coffee, like the anil that was once planted by the early Spanish settlers, has simply outlived its value as a Puerto Rican crop and should be replaced by such things as good, marketable oranges, avocado pears, and cacao. Others say that a good living can still be made in coffee, on "family-size" farms where children can be used as cheap labor; what the large planters think of that idea is not known. Still others point out that Puerto Rico's methods of producing coffee remain among the world's least efficient. The island's average annual yield is about 150 pounds per acre; Hawaii's growers produce a ton per acre as a result of modern methods of cultivation coupled with the selection of high-yielding stock. Puerto Rican technicians have found and tested what seems to be an excellent high-yield strain of the bean, which matures in the sun and does not require expensive shade trees. Its universal adoption could materially increase the profit per acre, cut labor costs, and release for other uses at least half, and perhaps three quarters, of the more than 150,000 acres of land that now comprise the world's most poorly managed coffee plantations. However, it is difficult to overcome old habits sustained by natural conservatism; the availability of better beans and better methods, plus an active government campaign to encourage new plantings, have to date brought barren results. In the face of financial uncertainty, the mere fact that it takes a tree of the old type five years to mature and start bearing, though the new bean

matures somewhat earlier, militates against an energetic re-
planting program.

Puerto Rico imports more than $125,000,000 worth of
foodstuffs annually, while thousands of acres of its lands,
well suited for food production, fail to produce for the local
commercial markets. The problem there is less a lack of
skill and enterprise on the part of the farmers than an ar-
chaic marketing system under which Puerto Rican farmers
cannot hope to compete with their well-organized competi-
tors on the mainland. A farmer may be able to produce the
finest cabbages found anywhere, but if the local produce
market squeezes him down to a ruinously low price, or if
he has to engage in the precarious practice of peddling them
from house to house, he will not go far economically. The
large hotels, the army camps, and the wholesalers find it
better business to order their cabbages, their asparagus, and
their oranges from the well-organized United States market.
The solution to that problem again lies in industrialization
—the erection of canning and other processing plants; in
education in such matters as grading for quality; in the creation and regulation of markets; in the organization of co-
operatives, and in the improvement of agricultural methods.
But meanwhile our cabbage grower, having no dependable
market for his crops, can get no credit for improving his
land and his methods, and may simply have to stand by
while his topsoil is washed away.

The tobacco industry has been helped greatly through the
promotion of cigar factories, one of them the world's largest.
Socially, however, it leaves much to be desired. For instance,
the women who work in the warehouses stripping and grading the leaves have long received the island's lowest wages
—less than thirty cents per hour. The industry maintained
that it could not afford higher wages and has now begun to
mechanize its stripping operations, thereby putting the production of cigars on a sounder financial basis while also
accelerating technological unemployment.

One can go on indefinitely listing the things that are wrong with Puerto Rico's agriculture. The important thing to consider, however, is that the Puerto Ricans realize those wrongs and are doing everything they can to right them.

The island has long been alert to the possibilities of crops new to Puerto Rico which may, in one way or another, prove more profitable and less precarious than those now being raised. At present the *acerola* cherry, native to Puerto Rico, inspires much hope and more publicity. Previously regarded as a weed, it has recently been found to be richer in vitamin C than is any other known agricultural product. However, the introduction of new, specialized crops is itself accompanied by many economic risks. During the depression the Federal Relief Administration did excellent work in introducing vanilla, and helped a number of Puerto Rican farmers to produce that well-paying crop. Vanilla did well for a time, but is today no longer being produced commercially on the island, owing to diseases and to fluctuations in the world market. Some years ago my friend Catesby Jones introduced Indian pepper to Puerto Rico, where it grows very well, producing large quantities of superior quality. But he had no sooner made a technical success of growing the very stuff that Columbus had been looking for in Puerto Rico in 1493, than the world price of Indian pepper dropped so sharply that the prospects of Puerto Rico's new crop now look dim.

The Economic Development Administration, well aware of the crucial tie-up between manufacturing and agriculture, is making every effort to bring new industries to Puerto Rico to process agricultural products and so to give farmers improved markets for their crops.

Out of these various problems, which seem so confused as to be almost chaotic, there is now developing an agricultural master plan to guide future action, drafted by the economist Dr. Scott Keyes. The most dramatic part of that plan, growing out of a study of soils and topography, was the division of all the island's agricultural lands into three general categories, namely: those that are fitted for mechanized cultivation; those that are fitted for clean cultivation by manual methods; and those that, being steep or otherwise unsuited for the conventional kinds of agriculture, should be under permanent protective cover. Keyes studied local problems of agriculture as well as local and export markets, and drew an idealized, schematic map showing the locations and areas of lands that should theoretically be devoted to various crops. Sugar cane, for instance, which today grows on 360,000 acres, can meet all quota requirements if entirely mechanized and concentrated on approximately 300,-000 acres of flat coastal lands. Pineapples, sweet potatoes, and truck-garden crops are classified as mechanizable and are given their proper places and areas on Keyes's map of hypothetical good practices. Some of his dairy cattle, using a projected total of 125,000 acres, are scattered on the flat coastal plains where mechanization is possible for the production of fodders; some are in the areas of manual production on proposed family-sized farms; some are on the steep hilltops that demand permanent protective cover. The same is true of swine and poultry. Coffee and fruits are produced in part in the zones of manual farming, but to a much larger extent in the "protective-cover" belts. Tobacco, bananas, and starchy vegetables are shown on the master map as belonging entirely in the zones earmarked for manual cultivation.

The most startling aspect of Keyes's plan is his recommendation that approximately half a million specified acres be taken out of cultivation and planted to forests. These will eventually provide the raw materials for a lumbering industry and related wood-processing plants; in 1956 more than five million dollars' worth of lumber and wood products were imported, and the figure climbs steadily. Technical advances, too, promise to stimulate the island's forestry business and thereby lead toward a sound forest policy within which Keyes's half a million acres—today's forest cover comprises a scant 100,000 acres, or about five per cent of the total land surface—can be profitably forested and managed. For instance, the *yagrume* tree grows rapidly and well in Puerto Rico, but has hitherto been regarded as a useless weed, a pest. Then a few years ago a company established a million-dollar sawmill near the city of Ponce, exclusively for processing *yagrume* wood, which is light, suited for many uses for which balsa is used, and well adapted to being chopped and ground for the various chemical treatments that now create other products, such as "synthetic lumber," out of natural woods.

The agricultural plan is a symptom of Puerto Rico's growing sophistication in planning. While it may or may not produce an eventual scheme for rural zoning, its most immediate value is found in its guidance of governmental efforts. For instance, the government's Forest Service now has a studied plan for its future acquisitions; by the same token, the Social Programs Administration has warning to be careful not to create new family-sized farms or rural communities on lands that have been earmarked either for forests or for intensive mechanized farming.

The Keyes plan will probably not lead to a policy of agricultural zoning by which farmers are told what they may or may not plant; but it does lay the foundations for concerted government action along many lines which will eventually steer Puerto Rico toward a technically, economically, and socially sound agriculture.

In the *American Forests* article previously quoted, Monroe Bush praises the Puerto Rican government for its general progressive attitudes and for the dramatic progress that it has brought to the island, but criticizes it for still thinking of its land problem more in terms of tenure and ownership than in terms of improved production and financial returns. He outlines a land policy roughly comparable to Keyes's, but adds that "it leaves unanswered many pressing questions, such as what to do with the agriculturally unemployed once the island's land is producing income at a rate approaching its inherent capacity." But he also adds that "a labor surplus is a problem for the entire economy, which must not and cannot be resolved by simple recourse to unsound, short-sighted land-management." He ends his article by saying: "Staggering as the political problems are in the application of such a policy, Muñoz Marín and his colleagues possess incredible skill in leading the people toward decisions that advance the well-being of the whole society. Despite the narrow limits of the land on this fantastically overpopulated island, it is to be hoped that the government will find a proper way to move toward land use compatible with the un-limited promise which lies before these remarkable people."

12

The Battle for Production

WHEN a few of us laid the foundations for systematic planning in Puerto Rico—in the stormy days of the Reconstruction Administration—we put a number of dreams on paper while more than half suspecting that they were doomed to remain dreams. Puerto Rico was an agricultural land and seemed fated to remain one. It might be improved as such by the curtailment of undue exploitation by the sugar corporations, but it could never aspire to create a healthy economy based in large measure on manufacturing. To be sure, we managed to get such manufacturing off to a fair start by building a cement mill, but that was built with federal money and was therefore a sport, an abnormality of the depression years.

Why could not Puerto Rico help itself out of its dreadful dilemma? Why did every local effort to remedy local ills seem foredoomed to failure? Why, with a certain amount of local capital available, did Puerto Rico not build factories to make at home some of the things that were being imported from the continent, thus improving the balance of payments and giving local employment? Before the PRRA's creation, the Federal Relief Administration had studied such matters and arrived at a number of dramatic answers besides the obvious one that the sugar interests, wanting to continue their operations in a reservoir of cheap labor, could be counted upon to do everything in their power to prevent rival industries.

One of the island's difficulties was that poor as it was, it was still the second largest market in the Hemisphere for American manufactured goods and farm products, the largest being Canada. It was also a place where U.S. manufacturers could dump their seconds, their misfits, their out-of-style clothing—everything they could not sell on the continent. In those days manufacturers would not stand by idly while new local industries threatened their profitable Puerto Rican market.

The various American soap companies, for instance, sold so much of their product in Puerto Rico that they maintained twenty-two representatives there. When a Puerto Rican began to make soap locally, the price of the imported product dropped to such low levels that the local enterprise was forced out of business. A Puerto Rican plant for making candy for local consumption was similarly forced into bankruptcy by the dumping of mainland candies.

It took nothing more than a plan to refine gasoline on the island to start a price war that reduced the cost of imported mainland gasoline to fantastically low levels. When the plan was abandoned, the price of gasoline went up again.

A local plant was erected to manufacture lime near the town of Fajardo. Immediately the steamship companies reduced the freight on imported lime from ten dollars per ton to three dollars, thus forcing the new plant out of business.

Under such conditions capital had good reason to stay out of local manufacturing. Puerto Rico seemed doomed to remain stagnant—its people less an agricultural people than cheap labor in a rural sweatshop of industrialized agriculture—unable and not permitted to marshal the many skills that are required for a program of industrialization and diversified agriculture.

The conditions described existed not merely in the cutthroat depression days. As many a colony has discovered, they were inherent in the exploitative institution of colonialism. One reason why Puerto Rico has been so outstandingly successful in its industrialization program is that today's industrial world has entered an era of unprecedented expansion. Investors and manufacturers are today actually searching for new fields of enterprise, as well as new customers with purchasing power. The erstwhile competitive morality has undergone drastic changes, and Puerto Rico has been transformed into "a new American industrial frontier."

The results, as expressed by statistics, are sensational. In 1940 the island's gross product was $287,000,000. In 1958 it was $1,286,000,000. In 1940 Puerto Rico's net income from agriculture was $70,000,000, that from manufacturing—largely devoted to the processing of sugar, to the distillation of rum, and to needlework—was $27,000,000. In 1958 agriculture produced a net income of $155,000,000, and manufacturing one of $233,000,000. Puerto Rico is no longer primarily an agricultural country; manufacturing began to outstrip farming in 1956 and is today moving ahead, aided and promoted energetically by the government. In 1940 Puerto Rico's imports, almost entirely from the United States, totaled $107,000,000; in 1958 the figure was $728,000,000. During the same period the exports rose from $92,000,000 to $467,000,000. (The apparently "unfavorable" balance of trade, with imports exceeding exports by far, is in this case not unhealthy. Compensating factors are federal expenditures in Puerto Rico, as for the armed forces, the post office, and the like. Federal grants in aid, monies sent to relatives on the island by Puerto Ricans in the States, and the fact that Puerto Rico does not contribute to the federal treasury also serve to balance the economy.)

Power

In one sense, as industrialization is intimately and inescapably interlocked with the provision of abundant low-cost electric power, the great effort began—almost by accident—as far back as 1908. In that year the insular legislature created the Puerto Rico Irrigation Service for the purpose of increasing agricultural production in the island's southeast. The organization's first project was completed in 1915, bringing water down from the Carite Reservoir in the mountains and incidentally generating the electricity needed for running irrigation pumps. The surplus power was wired into the district's towns and rural areas, which had previously received nothing at all from private companies; it created so clamorous a demand and was so effective in the improvement of the living standard that the generation and distribution of low-cost electric power, in the beginning a by-product of irrigation, eventually became a major activity of the government.

Before 1936 a number of Puerto Rican cities were served with electric power—inadequately, poorly, and at high rates —by a few private companies that lacked the means or the financial incentives for expanding with those cities and had not the vaguest intentions of expanding into the rural areas, where the majority of the people hadn't even the money to buy kerosene for one miserable lamp each. But even then hydrogenerated government power had begun to prove itself and its social benefits. Step by legal step, the private companies began to be absorbed by the government, which was working feverishly to generate ever more power and distribute it to all parts of the island in an integrated system, today known as Puerto Rico's "Little T. V. A."

The generation and distribution of electric power—at first exclusively from hydroelectric plants, but now, as virtually all the available hydro sites have been developed to capacity, from a growing number of steam plants burning imported fuel oil—has become an island-wide government service, administered by the autonomous Water Resources Authority. There are still those who decry that fact as "creeping social-ism," inimical to private enterprise. However, the owners and operators of factories on the island, whose lucrative pri-vate enterprises are in part made possible and sustained by government power, do *not* so decry it, nor do the private en-terprise manufacturers, wholesalers, and retailers of about $46,000,000 worth of electric machinery and apparatus—of motors, bulbs, neon signs, electric irons, and washing ma-chines, which were imported in 1958.

When Senator Robert A. Taft visited Puerto Rico in 1943 he was annoyed by the several 150 per cent Americans who tried to tell him that the government's entry into the power field was unconstitutional. He didn't believe it. It was a fool-ish thing to say to an eminent lawyer, to the son of a former Chief Justice of the U. S. Supreme Court who had previously as President in 1912 signed the first federal power act ever passed by Congress. Moreover, while Senator Taft did not like to see government go into the power business, he agreed that in Puerto Rico the government hardly had an alterna-tive.

In 1925 the government generated and sold a little more than 10,000,000 kilowatt hours. In 1958 the figure was 1,299,000,000, produced in an interlocked island-wide sys-tem of hydro and steam plants and sold for a gross revenue of $34,000,000. The 500 new factories that had been estab-lished with government help by the middle of 1958, giving employment to 35,000 workers, were attracted by the power network, and today all of Puerto Rico's cities and towns are served by it at individual rates that are about half as high as they were in the days when the government first started the legal fights to oust the private generating companies.

An important feature of the power program is its constant

expansion to reach more of the rural poor—those who still live in small shacks in the hills and who need light to study by, power for refrigerators, power for electric irons, etc. During the fiscal year 1957-8 alone, lines were built, and the system extended, to reach more than 10,000 new rural customers, whose low rates are in part compensated for by the slightly higher rates paid by those who can afford them. The total number of customers in the rural electrification program now comes to 140,000. If a man cannot afford to have his house wired for electricity, which happens often, the Water Resources Authority pays a contractor to wire it for him in case he wishes it, and later adds the cost to the customer's bills in easy payments stretched over five years.

In addition, the Authority, primarily because it developed out of the days when public power was a by-product of irrigation, helps the island to maintain a relatively high rate of agricultural production, by operating three government irrigation districts with a total area of nearly 57,000 acres, while the water from some of its dams, after turning turbines, is also used to supply a number of towns with good drinking water.

Meanwhile, the growth of the power services and the creation of new steam-generating plants continue dramatically. Year by year the plans for further growth keep mounting, the new jobs for Puerto Rican technicians multiply, special training programs prepare more technicians for better jobs. Now, too, the Water Resources Authority is dealing with the federal government for the acquisition of a nuclear power reactor for fostering the use of atomic energy to aid the peaceful war on hunger and poverty. At the time of the present writing, economic conditions are not yet right for such use; the Authority, being an autonomous government agency with the power to float bond issues and engage in other "private" business, must always conduct its operations in a thoroughly businesslike manner. But the plans exist, personnel has been trained, the technical research is being done, and the agency is looking ahead!

Manufacturing

Intellectual leaders who are concerned with today's revolutionary emergence of vast parts of Africa are expressing much worry over the fact that they can see no way of developing their countries except through socialism, which has an evil reputation in the western half of the "Iron Curtain" world. If they study Puerto Rico's experiences, they will realize that they needn't be too worried—always provided that they don't remain too dogmatic in their thinking. True, Puerto Rico is one of several proofs that the modern day's "emerging" societies cannot do their jobs without substantial *borrowings* from socialism; but if they borrow too much and too enthusiastically, within the framework of the capitalistic world in which they must survive and prosper whether they like it or not, inevitable circumstances will either suggest or force workable adjustments with capitalism.

In Puerto Rico, of the five factories that came to be run by the government on a Socialist basis during the Tugwell regime, only one—that for making cement—was a success from the start. The others—for making glassware, paper and pulp products, clay products, and shoes—gave employment and in turn helped to support other industries, but they cost the government money. After Luis Ferré bought all but the shoe factory and operated them at considerable profit, he crowed that he had been able to make them go where the government of the Popular Democratic party had been unable to, and that people should therefore vote him into the governor's job and let him lead Puerto Rico into statehood.

But things weren't that simple. The shoe factory, manufacturing footwear for local consumption, was doomed before it was built. To be sure, the people of Puerto Rico bought many shoes, but they bought so many shapes, styles, and sizes that one factory couldn't supply them all, and so few of any one shape and style that they couldn't keep a factory going. The government withdrew from the business and rented its plant to a continental manufacturer, making shoes for the vast United States market; he got along quite well. All the government plants, too, suffered from the facts that their wages were determined politically, rather than economically, and that precisely because they *were* government plants they were peculiarly vulnerable to labor troubles. Relatively high wages were insisted on by the legislature as an example to other industries, regardless of whether or not business operations could sustain them. Moreover, as there was a widespread impression that the government had gone into manufacturing as a kind of work relief to take up the unemployment slack, organized labor insisted on much feather-bedding, went on strikes to support it, and could count on only feeble opposition from a government that described itself as being "of the poor, for the poor," had much sympathy for organized labor, and included a legislature with many members who were labor leaders on the side.

Moreover, while it is not too difficult for a government to manufacture a number of things, the commercial operations of distribution and selling are much simpler for private operators than for government. Even during the Tugwell regime the new government realized this and wanted to switch to tax exemption as a means of attracting private capital. But Tugwell was against tax exemption and vetoed the bills providing for it. Not until Tugwell was out and Piñero sat in the Fortaleza as interim governor could the necessary legal steps be taken.

Under today's policies exemption of taxes on corporate profits—which in the States mount to fifty-two per cent, and in Puerto Rico to thirty-seven—are offered for ten years to new industries or to new branches of industries established in the States. No help of any kind is given to runaway industries that may close their doors on the continent in order to open in Puerto Rico. If workers are needed with special skills, the government will train them at no cost to the investor, and do much free research and industrial engineering for which private firms are used on the continent.

Finally, the government provides factory buildings at low ✕ rental, which may eventually be purchased by the tenants. As experience has shown that most of these factory buildings fall into definite categories of size and proportions, many factories have been, and are being, built in advance of demand in order to be ready when a prospective tenant comes along. Their designs and locations are controlled by the Planning Board, which, by means of its program of urban planning and zoning, strives to prevent the growth of industrial slums around the new industries.

While investors are warned that low wages should not be regarded as an incentive for establishing industries in Puerto Rico, as it is the government's aim constantly to raise wages, there can be no question that the wage differential between the mainland and the island has been, and still is, such an incentive, which compensates in part for the freight that has to be paid for shipping raw materials in and finished products out.

The soundness of such policies is attested by the fact that Puerto Rico today experiences one of the highest investment rates found in the capitalist world. Investment in new construction, machinery, and equipment has increased from an annual rate of $29,000,000 in 1940 to $274,000,000 in 1958, and the autonomous, government-owned Development Bank, now headed by Dr. Rafael Picó, has played a strong role in bringing about those conditions. The bank was established in 1942, and its powers and responsibilities have since then been expanded on several occasions. One of its most important functions is that of making loans to private investors. Such loans, as for the construction, expansion, and improvement of industrial and commercial buildings, for the acquisition of machinery and equipment, for the financing of inventories, and for hotels and other essential tourist facilities, are made entirely on the bank's evaluation of the risks involved, whether to large organizations or small, new or long-established, locally or externally owned, tax exempt or subject to taxation. In addition, the bank is the repository of government funds, as well as the government's fiscal agent in the matter of floating bond issues.

That the government today strives to attract and aid private enterprise does not mean that it has abjured its own entry, on one basis or another, into the industrial field. In all developing economies, the vicious circle referred to in Chapter 10 can be broken only by government action. A case in point is the famous Caribe Hilton Hotel. In 1947 the government not only wanted a first-class hotel in which to house as well as impress prospective investors, but also planned seriously to foster the tourist industry that is today pouring millions into the economy. The trouble was that tourists weren't coming because there was no good hotel, and private enterprise didn't build such a hotel because the tourists weren't there to fill it. Therefore, the government spent $7,-200,000—exactly the same amount the United States once gave Russia for what is now the forty-ninth state—to build the Caribe Hotel, and later made a contract under which the Hilton chain would run it in return for one third of the profits. The venture worked astonishingly well and got the present tourist industry off to a flying start.

The cannery for pineapples and the slaughter house referred to in Chapter 10 are other examples of government action to break that vicious circle.

It might be said that the Puerto Rican government stands ready at any time to use temporary socialism for the purpose of strengthening and abetting capitalist development. Meanwhile, the capitalist investors and potential investors who now flock to the island are almost unanimous in praising the

Puerto Rican officials for honesty, hard work, dedication, and the eagerness to serve. Those who have done business in other Latin American societies, or even in the United States, and who come with money for greasing palms and opening doors, have an immediate and pleasant surprise: no favors can be bought. Except for occasional petty pilfering on a municipal level, there is no bribery or other financial corruption in the government. Having been in close contact with Puerto Rico since 1935, I venture to say that the island has by far the most consistently honest government in the Western Hemisphere.

The 500 new factories that were established under that program by the end of the fiscal year 1957-8, giving employment to 35,000 workers, attest to the program's success. The goal, however, is to establish 2,000 new factories by 1975—the target year for attaining a standard of living comparable to that found in the United States in 1955.

The industries that were attracted in the beginning were often fly-by-night affairs that took their tax exemption for a number of years and then either went bankrupt or took their profits elsewhere. The government's general policy in those days, as expressed by Teodoro Moscoso, Head of the Economic Development Administration, was: "The best industry for Puerto Rico is any industry. Anyone willing to take a risk on us will be cordially welcome. A good entrepreneur should know enough about his own industrial activity to be able to determine with a reasonable degree of certainty his chances of success on the island. So far, the mortality rate of our new industries is considerably lower than that in mainland United States." By and large, the statement still holds good; potential new industries are not turned down because the government wants other kinds, or wants them to locate in some place other than that of their own choice. However, the experience of years has indicated that certain industries have better chances for success than do others. Much of the old home-needlework industry has in recent years left the island because of rising wages, and has sought greener sweatshop pastures in Japan and the Philippines. (It is interesting to note that some of the operators who made the move have come to regret it. Philippine workers, they complain, accept lower wages, but the Puerto Ricans know much more about skilled, honest, and conscientious work.)

Heavy industries such as rolling mills for steel are, of course, out of the question for a country with no resources to speak of. Nevertheless, in addition to twenty-nine sugar mills, Puerto Rico's list of *relatively* heavy industries is impressive. It includes two cement mills, two petroleum refineries, a paper mill, an ammonium plant, a general iron works, a flour and feed mill, a glass factory, and two clay refractories. Certain other industries have proved so successful that they have begun to give definite character to the program. The brassière, the baby pants and clothing industries—as apart from sweatshop work—are well established, as are shoes and plastics.

"The growth of industries processing metal articles, machinery and instruments," says the Economic Development Administration's report for 1957-8, "is significant and encouraging, as is the high employment potential of such factories. These are light industries which require more workers and higher capitalization per worker than does the clothing industry. . . . They can pay higher wages than can clothing, and are in a far better position vis-à-vis competition from the southern states." Accordingly, the Administration has undertaken special studies toward the furtherance of such industries. The processing of agricultural crops —as, for instance, through canning and the manufacture of cigars—is coming up in importance. Current agricultural planning, which calls for the return of twenty-five per cent or more of the total land to forest cover, presages the growth of a new forest-products industry, using woods in all the variegated means developed by modern technical advances.

Puerto Rico has lately begun to gain importance for the

canning of tuna fish, caught originally off the Galapagos Islands and now also in the South Atlantic. As most of the finished products are sold in the eastern United States, it is cheaper for the companies concerned to can them in Puerto Rico than in California, whence transportation by rail or ship to the eastern seaboard is expensive. The residual fish meal, moreover, helps to support Puerto Rico's growing cattle industry. Although Puerto Rico's deep surrounding waters had always seemed to rule against the establishment of commercial fisheries on the island, the almost sensational growth in recent years of sport fishing as a lure for tourists and sportsmen has begun to throw so much new light on the relative abundance of deep water food fish that a local fishing industry, supporting canneries and perhaps freezing plants, has now begun to loom as a decided future possibility.

In recent years some of the largest United States corporations have established branch factories on the island and have thereby reduced the program's "temporary" aspects, which it seemed to have earlier by virtue of the ten-year period of tax exemption. Such organizations as the General Electric Company, the International Latex Corporation, and Remington Rand realize that tax exemption is meaningless unless there is a profit before taxes. After the ten-year exemption period such things as wages and productivity become critical profit factors. What becomes important at this point is that the Puerto Rican workers, besides drawing somewhat lower pay than do those on the mainland, are quick, conscientious, self-respecting, dependable, and loyal. A large number of those workers are women, whose wages now give them an economic and moral power they had never dreamed of in the old Spanish society. Because of this definite culture change in Puerto Rico's life, it is unlikely that the men will long continue to play the dominating role they had previously enjoyed since Ponce de Leon first colonized the island in 1508.

The Economic Development Administration is now especially interested in industries that can in turn support other industries. The newly established refining of oil, for instance, though slowed down by oil regulations on the mainland, has attracted the United States Carbon and Carbide Company to make anti-freeze and other products out of the refineries' "waste"; the capital investment in such ventures is so large that the cessation of tax exemption after ten years can hardly cause them to pull up stakes. A flour mill, recently completed, while having to depend entirely on imported grains, will not only cut down shipping cost—as the grains can be shipped in bulk, whereas the milled flour was previously shipped in packages—but will, through its by-products, contribute materially to Puerto Rico's cattle culture, to say nothing of hogs, chickens, and other animal products. It will also contribute to the success of the new slaughter house.

Puerto Rico has long been a heavy importer of rice—in bags and packages. New plants for processing and packaging rice in San Juan harbor will soon be able to receive the grain in bulk, thus reducing shipping costs, and will also help to support other industrial and agricultural ventures.

So the planning goes—more and more toward integrated, interrelated new industries that can be promoted in clusters. Not only has Puerto Rican manufacturing outstripped agriculture as a source of income, but it is now itself beginning to take on the aspects of technical integration and maturity. All that, of course, puts a heavy burden on the educational effort. Industrialization and good standards of living are impossible in a society with a high rate of illiteracy; the transformation of an agrarian society into a semi-industrial one demands the acquisition of many skills at all levels.

The other side of the picture is this: while integration in the technical and economic sense, within the industrialization program itself, is progressing rapidly, "regional" integration is lagging far behind. A number of towns in certain well-defined regions have benefited immeasurably from the industrialization program, have indeed been transformed beyond the wildest dreams of a few years ago. Others have not only not benefited, but are actually going downhill economically and are contributing their major shares to the constant, restless movement toward the larger centers on the island and toward that largest of all Puerto Rican cities— New York. There is an effort to use rent differentials for spreading industrialization more evenly throughout the island; a manufacturer moving to one of the more backward towns can even get his factory building rent free. It doesn't work very well. The problem must obviously be attacked in a new and integrated fashion. The reasons why manufacturers don't want to establish themselves in certain regions are themselves indicative of potential solutions to the problem. Manufacturers don't like to establish plants in towns that have execrable telephone service, inadequate labor forces, and whose connections with the nearest shipping ports are by narrow, winding roads unsuitable for quick transportation and the heavy trucking of raw materials. In several instances no amount of tax exemption, no amount of rent exemption, no amount of cajolery and salesmanship on the part of the Economic Development Administration could overcome such formidable industrial handicaps. And *because* such difficulties keep industries out of certain parts of Puerto Rico—notably the western mountains, where the coffee industry is located—the labor force there grows smaller yearly as people stream into the more prosperous areas or out of Puerto Rico.

As an island, Puerto Rico needs low-cost shipping for economic health. But today the cost of shipping, and especially that of loading and unloading ships, rises constantly. That calls for drastic and sometimes costly technical improvements at the ports, as for instance through the bulk-loading of sugar, cement, and other products, and for the shipping of various mixed products in large containers or trailers. Such measures reduce the amount of labor utilized and thus

lead to dock strikes, which have themselves been known to
scare away potential industries. The government steps in
with relief measures to tide the workers over the first impact
of technological unemployment. New plants keep coming in,
but they seek locations near the good ports that have been,
and are being, modernized. Also, they want good roads between factories and ports. That means primarily the harbor
of San Juan, which is expanding by leaps and bounds, not
without its full share of growing pains. On the south coast
Ponce harbor is also showing a healthy growth, which in
turn makes it the center of a lively industrial boom. But today Puerto Rico, which had twenty active seaports a quarter
of a century ago, has only three that are used for general
shipping; of these the one at Mayagüez, at the island's western end, has begun to show alarming symptoms of decline,
though it may recover as a result of industrial promotions.

One compensating solution is found in the "industrial
ports" that are created especially to serve special industries.
For instance, the new oil refineries on the south coast and
near San Juan maintain such "ports"—special piers built exclusively for unloading crude oil. But that spells the corresponding decline of other ports, which used to receive large
gasoline shipments for their districts. The various competing
oil companies now obtain all their gasoline from the two refineries and truck it to their several distribution centers.

The west-coast port of Mayagüez has recently declined because of natural economic shifts to other parts of the island
and also because the roads serving the city of Mayagüez have
long been inadequate (though they are now being improved).
A scheme is therefore afoot to make Mayagüez the scene of
a "foreign trade zone," a kind of manufacturing and processing compound into which foreign raw materials and
parts can be shipped duty free for processing and eventual
reshipment.

⅄ The communications problem is still serious. To date the
island's telephone service has failed dismally to keep pace

with the demands made on it. At one time there was talk of expropriation, following the example once set in relation to the private power companies. But expropriation has been a dirty word in the American language since Mexico applied it to the oil fields, and a society that is striving hard to attract United States capital doesn't want to hear it bandied about too freely. The increase in telephone rates, granted by the government in 1958 at some political risk, may now give the company the means and incentives to expand and improve its services.

The matter of roads is now assuming paramount importance. Twenty years ago the island's roads were adequate and even relatively excellent for the conditions and needs of those remote times. Today, even though many dramatic road improvements are visible in some parts of the island, the improvement program lags far behind the need, and in some sections the system is still so antiquated that it acts as a brake on economic progress. But good roads are not brought by Santa Claus. They must be paid for, and even though a certain amount of federal money is available for their construction, that money must still be matched. Where is the money to come from? Through another boost in taxes? Through bond issues, which will put the burden of payment on future generations while also demanding current tax monies for amortization and interest? Through a combination of the two? A relatively small increase in the tax on gasoline, the price of which is kept down through government control, might permit such a combination, but it would raise the island's transportation costs and might create a number of new political enemies for the Popular Democratic party—among the drivers of taxis and other public vehicles.

Then, too, there is the problem of water. Like many another country, Puerto Rico has hitherto been smug in the belief that it had plenty of surface water; suddenly it has awakened to the fact that it hasn't at all—at least not where needed. Many potential new industries require large quantities of water, not only for industrial uses, but also to serve the population clusters of their workers; on the relatively arid south coast there is also a growing need for irrigation water. Now a program has been started jointly with the United States Geological Survey to explore, gauge, and map the ground water resources, the deposits beneath the surface that might be safely pumped up at certain rates without being "mined out." In certain parts of the island, many conditions combine to create settings favorable for decentralized industrial development, but such development is still impossible until adequate supplies of water can be provided—either piped in from one of the dwindling surface sources, or pumped from subsurface sources that have not yet been found.

Such, and many others, are the pressing problems of a society that has set out to modernize and industrialize itself. They must and will be solved, but the solutions take time and cost effort and money. As already stated, Puerto Rico has set itself the goal of achieving by 1975 a general and well-distributed standard of living comparable to that of the United States in 1955. To do that, it will have to reshape and modernize its entire pattern of life, not only its seaports, roads, telephone services, and water facilities, but its town life as well, its educational and health facilities and their distribution, its recreational facilities, and finally the distribution of its population.

Every governmental agency wrestles with those problems today, if only because the voters in the more backward regions may someday express their annoyance at the polls. The Planning Board has organized a "Bureau of Integrated Regional Planning" to rechannel general progress and chart it by regions, rather than by academic subject matter, and—as now—by the glowing statistics that seem to present Puerto Rico as one homogeneous island, uniformly blessed by progress.

The Tourist Industry

Poor, tired Governor Winship—who probably deserved better than to occupy the Fortaleza during the turbulent days of the PRRA—had one idea, and one only, for improving Puerto Rico's economy. He wanted to create a tourist industry to exploit the island's natural beauty and fine climate, as well as its "picturesque," poverty-stricken natives. To accomplish that he put a tax on salt, staged elaborate pageants in San Juan, and offered prizes for beautifying roadsides by planting hibiscus. He even coined a slogan: "You may not find a pot of gold at the end of the rainbow, but you can always find a garden of flowers." The country people called him "the Beautician in the Fortaleza"; his numerous political enemies accused him of wanting the hibiscus shrubs as screens to hide the countryside's universal misery from the eyes of sensitive visitors. Certainly he thundered hard and loud against San Juan's evil slums because they would offend the eyes and noses of tourists, but his somewhat unique urban renewal program seemed unpractical because the slum dwellers didn't want to obey his stentorian orders that they "go back to the hills where they came from."

Also, he seemed completely to overlook the fact that there were no hotels in Puerto Rico to house the tourists for whom he ardently longed, but who never came.

As stated previously, in 1947 the new government—finally rid of its autocratic Winships—decided to do something about the matter and primed the pump with what is today known as the Caribe Hilton Hotel, famous as a show hostelry in the Caribbean and as one of the world's most profitable hotel properties. That started a chain reaction, ably speeded by systematic promotion.

As a result of various vicissitudes and changes, the initial public-relations program to lure tourists has by now changed into the "Commonwealth" advertising program, which, through the combination of texts and gorgeous colored photographs, blown up to full-page size, sells to readers a kind of "package" that includes Puerto Rican scenery, pleasant living, rum, economic opportunity—and Pablo Casals.

Like any other industrial plant, a hotel is no better than are the people who work in it; one couldn't take the machetes away from cane cutters and field hands, stuff those people into uniforms, and expect them to function well as bellboys, waiters, cashiers, and clerks. Swiss instructors were therefore imported, and a hotel school was established jointly by the Economic Development Administration and the Department of Education. Courses in that school last ten months and include many aspects of hotel work plus a working knowledge of English. Students are paid twenty dollars per month, plus free uniforms and at least one good meal per day. Not all of them stay in Puerto Rico after completing their courses. Some go to Brazil or some other Latin American country that is building up its tourist industry and can use trained bilingual employees; some go to the United States Southwest where hotels have many Spanish-speaking guests; a number are undoubtedly now working in the Waldorf and other New York establishments. Such migrants give Puerto Ricans a good name wherever they go and help to make things easier for other migrating Puerto Ricans.

Hotel guests must find something pleasant to do, within their own refined and sophisticated tastes, besides lolling on their establishment's grounds, swimming in kidney-shaped pools, basking on beaches under the tropical sun, continuing the game of bridge that was started in some other country, and patronizing the bar. In 1947 the government hit on legalized gambling—besides the regular weekly lottery—as a lure. A number of casinos in as many hotels are now sources of relatively high income, besides helping to draw visitors to the island. Their croupiers and other employees are trained under the same government supervision, which is extended so rigidly to the operation of the casinos themselves that the latter are known as by far the most honest in the Caribbean area, and perhaps in the world.

As "everybody" had known for centuries that the fishing was poor in Puerto Rican waters, the government imported a sport-fishing captain from Florida to test whether that knowledge was in accordance with the facts. The result was a chain reaction: a surge of interest in sport fishing; the investment of much money for equipment in that expensive sport; the establishment of thirty world records for fish of various sizes caught on lines of various strengths; exuberant photographs of victorious fishermen with their catches; annual fishing tournaments that drew increasing numbers of *aficionados* from many states in the union; the description of Puerto Rican waters by Estéban Bird—a prominent local banker who by now can't stay away from the water with rod and reel—as the world's best grounds for blue marlin; and a decided boost for Puerto Rico's public relations and the tourist industry.

Some of the new hotels have excellent tennis courts. International tennis matches are now staged on them, and the several world champions they attract in turn attract visitors to watch them perform.

The new El Comandante race track near San Juan has a great advantage over many continental tracks in that its season lasts almost the year around. It is another fine new tourist attraction.

The Laurence Rockefeller interests have created the "Dorado Beach Resort," an hour's drive from San Juan, where visitors can play golf on one of the world's finest eighteen-hole courses, under the aegis of President Eisenhower's former pro, Ed Dudley, and enjoy tennis, swimming, bar entertainment, and pig roasts, with local talent singing and dancing. Special airplane service transports guests between the resort and San Juan's International Airport.

Because discriminating visitors like to eat well, the Economic Development Administration gives all possible help, encouragement, financial aid, and promotion to the task of establishing first-class restaurants that serve both Puerto Rican and world cuisine, in surroundings acceptable to sophisticated world travelers.

When Pablo Casals moved to Puerto Rico from France in 1956, the entire island was overjoyed. The fact that the world's greatest musician, a fine person of integrity, a staunch and unrelenting defender of human freedoms, now makes his home there is a source of deep pride to all Puerto Ricans. The great impact of his presence and activities on Puerto Rico's musical life and culture began to be felt immediately. Quite aside from their cultural value and importance to the entire Western Hemisphere, his annual music festivals, at which the world's greatest musicians perform the world's greatest music, are an important attraction for visitors, as is the presence of the genial "Don Pau" himself. The new Puerto Rican symphony orchestra, organized by Casals, and the projected conservatory of music will do much for the island's cultural life.

To be sure, such things are symptomatic of Puerto Rico's general growth and increased prosperity as well as sophistication, quite aside from the tourist business. But they are watched and accelerated with much satisfaction by the Commonwealth's Department of Tourism, which is accomplishing wonders in the advancement of its own particular branch of the economy. New hotels spring up constantly, and private capital is pouring into Puerto Rico for the purpose of building and operating them—usually aided in some way by government capital. A recent survey lists four hotels, with 335 rooms, as worthy, before 1949, to be regarded as offering "tourist accommodations"; by the end of 1958 the number of such hotels had grown to thirty-nine and the rooms to 2,790. For 1946-7 the number of nonresident hotel visitors in Puerto Rico is listed in the same report at 20,925, who

spent $1,199,000 on the island; in 1957-8, 99,279 such vis-
itors are listed, spending $10,948,000.

That stream of visitors adds immeasurably to the activities of Señora Felisa Rincon de Gautier, who has won world
fame as San Juan's beloved and superbly efficient mayoress
and city manager (she is something of both), and who is
herself no mean tourist attraction. One of Muñoz's first and
most ardent co-workers, who now directs the affairs of
Puerto Rico's capital, she takes time out—from keeping the
city immaculately clean and in repair, expanding it, tending
to the poor and distressed, holding wayward political workers in line, running the Popular Democratic party at her
local level, making many trips abroad to spread good will
and receive well-deserved honors—to greet a constant and
swelling stream of visitors in a ceaseless round of entertainment. Distinguished guests receive the keys to the city from
her; a bewildering and variegated number of groups—cham-
bers of commerce, American mayors, policemen, teachers,
journalists, actors, dentists, doctors, scientists meeting in
conventions, military men's and women's clubs—sample her
hospitality constantly.

As "Doña Fela" presides over Puerto Rico's principal port
of entry, her warm personal hospitality is symbolic of the
Commonwealth's.

The season of 1958-9 broke all records. The brand-new
luxury hotel La Concha had to take in guests even before it
was finished—a week before its formal opening—and was
filled to capacity almost immediately. Virtually every hotel
room, every boarding-house room on the island, rich or poor,
shabby or elaborate, low cost or high, was filled for a time,
as were all the planes that carried some of the frantic over-
flow to such places as the Virgin Islands. Not all of that
boom, however, can be credited to the laudable efforts of the
government's Department of Tourism. Fidel Castro had
something to do with it by scaring tourists away from Cuba
with the turmoil of a revolution well won. In the Dominican

Republic Generalissimo Trujillo contributed to Puerto Rico's success by inviting—as through the famous Galindez case—attention to his country as "a well-ordered graveyard." Possibly the prevailing troubles in Egypt, the Far East, and the Middle East helped to channel a share of the "Hilton Chain Globe Trotters" away from the Cairo and Ankara Hilton hotels into the one in San Juan.

Many problems, of course, remain to be solved, and their solution creates others. Today's main problems stem from that old and ubiquitous poser, "distribution," which here needs to be straightened out both regionally and seasonally. So many visitors come to San Juan, where most of the island's new hotels were built, that a number of Puerto Rican residents worry lest their beloved capital be turned into a second Miami.

A long coastal strip in and beyond San Juan has been zoned as a belt for hotels, and now other valiant efforts are being made to further decentralize the industry. The small new hotel, El Barranquitas, in the central mountains is beginning to be known. In the southwest the little fishing village of La Parguera, near the famous "Phosphorescent Bay," is attracting an increasing number of visitors to its resort hotel. The charming "old-style" city of Ponce on the south coast is beginning to be invaded, and a new tourist hotel was completed there in December 1959. The entire southwest part of the island may well before long become known as Puerto Rico's Riviera. In the east, near Fajardo, now only about half an hour from San Juan by a magnificent new highway, and in the vicinity of el Yunque—the mountain of the famous rain forest—large potentialities for a thriving tourist business are being studied, explored, and developed. In the western interior the so-called coffee region is dramatically beautiful; all planning for that region's restoration to prosperity includes a heavy emphasis on recreational projects.

Meanwhile, the "drive-yourself" car business and the running of conducted tours are thriving. More and more of the tourists who a few years ago were content to stay in San Juan now go out and discover Puerto Rico for themselves, exploring the island, finding its "native" restaurants, exclaiming over the sections that are still "unspoiled" by tourists, being charmed by the simple and friendly country people.

The uneven seasonal distribution of visitors presents difficulties that are perhaps even greater than the regional. But there is today a definite policy to sponsor relatively inexpensive boarding houses in various parts of the island—modest inns, *pensions* in the style of the French—and thereby to attract a growing number of teachers who take their vacations in summer, as well as secretaries, college students, writers, artists, and professional people with modest means but with a deep personal interest in the things they see around them. The new policy is still in its earliest stages, in part because its implications are not yet fully understood by the men who shape Puerto Rico's public-relations policies. To date—and very successfully—those men have labored to attract tourists by stressing "sophistication" rather than Puerto Rico itself, and at times by consciously avoiding all mention of certain picturesque Puerto Rican realities. They have shaped their policies by the idea, stubbornly adhered to, that any mention or photograph of dramatic curves in mountain roads, any official admission that oxen are still widely used for plowing and hauling carts, may cause people to think that Puerto Rico is "backward." At one time they even arrived at the decision that the long-established word *jíbaro* must never be used to denote the island's friendly country people. In Ecuador, they argued, *jíbaros* are bad Indians who cut off people's heads and shrink them down to baseball size; using the word in public-relations efforts to attract tourists to Puerto Rico might scare away a number of potential visitors who harbor aversions to having their own head chopped off and transformed into portable souvenirs.

Nevertheless, the new policy of "rural *turismo*" is bound to be a success before long. Inevitably, a large number of people who are more interested in the island than in sophistication continue to discover Puerto Rico's charming rural realities and have begun to create a swelling demand for simple, low-cost accommodations.

The total number of visitors arriving in Puerto Rico for all purposes, by ship and plane, from everywhere, was 78,377 in 1951 and 207,000 in 1958. Truly the island has become America's crossroad in the Caribbean.

13

Labor

Puerto Rico's revolution has brilliantly fulfilled its original promise: to provide land for the landless and jobs for the unemployed. But there is no end to the fulfilling, no terminal point for the task. When a reporter recently asked Muñoz Marín: "Where do you go from here?" the Governor laughed and said: "Good heavens. We aren't here yet."

The past twenty years have seen a tremendous effort. Half a thousand new factories now employ tens of thousands of workers; the land-distribution program has established thousands of new independent farmers; migration to the mainland has eased the pressure of population by removing hundreds of thousands from the island. *And yet* thirteen per cent of the island's total labor force is still officially listed as "unemployed," to say nothing of the thousands who are only partially employed, or poorly employed at bottom wages. In 1940 the official figure was lower, listing only eleven per cent of the labor force as being unemployed. The comparison, however, is more dramatic than valid. The standards by which "unemployment" is judged have meanwhile become far more exacting; by today's standards the 1940 figure would be immeasurably higher. The starving sugar workers, the animal-like coffee laborer described in Chapter 3, were certainly listed as being employed.

Now, as indicated in Chapters 10 and 11, a reshaped, modernized Puerto Rico must deal increasingly with the problem of technological unemployment. At one end more people obtain jobs; at the other, as it is vital that efficiency be maintained in competition with other societies, they lose them to machines; in between, labor grows sophisticated and struggles more effectively for higher wages and better living conditions. That endless cycle is not unique to Puerto Rico, though it is there made more serious by the fact that the island has no empty geographical frontier.

The years 1958 and 1959 saw an unusual amount of labor trouble. Stevedores, seeing their livelihoods threatened by the introduction of new mechanized methods of handling cargoes, walked out on several occasions. The telephone workers struck, disrupting communications for weeks by cutting trunk lines and private lines. Taxi drivers tied up their cabs for a time; the bus drivers threatened to walk out and thus to stop most of Puerto Rico's transportation of passengers.

Continental labor leaders have discovered a fertile field for organization in Puerto Rico. During the season of 1958-9 the AFL-CIO held its annual convention in San Juan. Dubinsky, of the International Ladies Garment Workers Union, has been active in Puerto Rico in a sane and decent manner; his union has even gone into partnership with Rockefeller's IBEC Corporation to provide good housing for workers, and Dubinsky as well as Postosky, of the Amalgamated Clothing Workers, have declared themselves in favor of wage differentials between Puerto Rico and the mainland United States, as the lack of such differentials would close too many shops and throw many people out of work. While such leaders are welcome on the island, the racketeers are by no means welcome, and men like Hoffa have so far been unable to gain a foothold.

Though the wage differentials are needed, and though they play a role in attracting mainland capital and industries, all government officials are emphatic in stating that they are in no way to be regarded as an incentive to starting factories in Puerto Rico. It is the government's stated policy to raise wages as rapidly as circumstances permit. The differentials are maintained for the purpose of compensating for the need for importing raw materials and exporting finished products at shipping rates that are the world's highest; the differentials also compensate for the fact that Puerto Rican labor, for all its devotion and all its mounting skills, still does not measure up in efficiency to that on the mainland.

The situation, naturally, has deep political implications. Advocates of statehood can use the wage differential as a tempting bait for labor; a general federal minimum of one dollar per hour, which at the time of the present writing seems destined to be raised to one dollar and twenty-five cents, has a strong appeal. The fact is, however, that such increases and other drawbacks of statehood—in a society whose economy is still far from being on a par with that of the mainland—would almost inevitably mean the wholesale closing of factories.

In the troublesome dichotomy between more jobs and greater efficiency, between more employment and higher wages for fewer workers, between wider distribution of the land and its more efficient use, lies *the* great problem of modern Puerto Rico. The problem demands great flexibility in matters of government policy and in the functioning of such agencies as the Department of Labor; it may yet, in the end, result in the formation of a new political party. The time may come when a rising political leader wants to give a stevedore the chance to cast a vote against the Popular

Democratic party, in protest over the modernization of the seaports, without also apparently voting for either statehood or independence, neither of which he may want.

Despite the current restlessness, however, despite strikes and dissention, there can be no doubt that the Popular Democratic party is a warm friend not only of labor, but also of labor organizations. One test of that statement is not only the wording, but also the effectiveness of its labor legislation. Many a Latin-American country has fairly good labor laws. In most of them they remain inactive; they stay on the books largely as decorations. Students of Puerto Rico are constantly surprised at the manner in which the Puerto Ricans not only take pains to pass good laws, but even take them seriously and enforce them to the best of their abilities.

Puerto Ricans are justly proud of their labor legislation and regard it as the most advanced in the United States. What other country has written such legislation into the Bill of Rights, the fundamental, basic document of its constitution? The Commonwealth's Bill of Rights, besides prohibiting child labor and stating that "persons may join with each other and organize freely for any lawful purpose, except in military or quasi-military organizations," goes on to say that "the right of every employee to choose his occupation freely and to resign therefrom is recognized, as is his right to equal pay for equal work, to a reasonable minimum salary, to protection against risks to his health or person in his work or employment, and to an ordinary workday which shall not exceed eight hours. An employee may work in excess of this daily limit only if he is paid extra compensations as provided by law, at a rate never less than one and one-half times the regular rate at which he is employed."

Having thus established some basic principles, the constitution goes on to recognize the workers' right "to organize and to bargain collectively with their employers through representatives of their own free choosing in order to promote their welfare." The next section establishes labor's "right to strike, to picket and to engage in other legal concerted activities, "though it also recognizes "the authority of the Legislative Assembly to enact laws to deal with grave emergencies that clearly imperil the public health or safety or essential public services."

The telephone strike referred to previously led to much understandable public grumbling to the effect that such emergency legislation "to safeguard the public health or safety or essential public services" seemed definitely in order; there was even clamor for the company's expropriation in the manner in which all the private electric-power companies had once been expropriated. However, the legislature did nothing and prudently left the matter in the hands of Mr. Fernando Sierra Berdecía, the genial, intelligent, respected but overworked Secretary of Labor.

On the other hand, the restlessness stirred up by the bulk loading of sugar, which threw thousands out of work while saving the sugar producers and shippers more thousands of dollars, did give rise to special legislation. The law levied a special tax on the production of sugar, both in the field and in the mill, and provided for its distribution, as unemployment compensation, to the approximately 3,000 dock workers and 1,200 workers in sugar mills adversely affected by the new system of shipping. There is, however, a time limit on the tax and the compensation, stipulated on the theory that other jobs for the unemployed stevedores will be created before long.

In addition to the constitution's provisions, legislation has been passed to take care of nearly all aspects of labor's life and of its relations with management. The most important fields of such legislation have been those of minimum wages, industrial peace, employment, and workmen's compensation.

The question of minimum wages is especially difficult in an old society with many long-established norms and patterns, both in the field and in the factory. Often these cannot be disturbed drastically without causing shutdowns; legislative efforts to raise wages to a prescribed minimum result in little social benefit if they actually bring about the payment of no wages whatever. It is, of course, impossible to avoid such consequences entirely. For example, the home needlework industry, which in 1935 paid wages as low as three cents per dozen for hemming and embroidering hand-kerchiefs, has now departed to Japan and the Philippines.

Two laws govern minimum wages in Puerto Rico: one is the Puerto Rican law, which applies to all industries, including agriculture; the other is the Federal Fair Labor Standards Act, which applies only to industries manufacturing for interstate commerce and has since 1940 made special provisions for Puerto Rico. They operate in similar ways. The island's industries are divided into several groups and subgroups, and hearings are held every two years to determine the minimum wages those groups are able to pay. Those wages—in the determination of which management, labor, and government experts all have a voice—then become law for the ensuing two years.

For the purpose of enforcing the Federal law, commissions appointed by and in Washington visit the island every two years, make investigations, hold hearings, and decide on specific minimum wages for specific industries. If the two wage-determining bodies, the local and the federal, differ from each other in their recommendations, then the higher of the two minimum wages is the one that is chosen and adopted as law.

The situation has raised a political question that has never been quite settled. Should the Congress of the United States have the power to pass laws pertaining to the Commonwealth of Puerto Rico without the specific consent of the Puerto Ricans, expressed either through direct vote or through the island's legislature? The entire matter of Puerto Rico's freedom to manage its internal affairs is often debated around that one issue alone. The advocates of independence make much of the fact that Congress still possesses such legal right, and claim that Puerto Rico is therefore still a colony of the United States. However, the government's official position is that as Puerto Rico has free commerce with the United States, it is reasonable that Congress, in order to protect mainland labor against unfair competition, should exercise control over wages in the industries that ship their products to the mainland.

The fact that in a number of industries, principally those dealing with metal work, affecting some 25,000 workers, the minimum wages have by such means already been brought up to the one dollar per hour prescribed by Federal law for the states, testifies to Puerto Rico's growing industrial maturity. But that does not scare away continental manufacturers interested in establishing factories on the island. In the states the figure is usually a true "minimum," a floor, rather than a ceiling; in Puerto Rico it also tends to be a maximum. However, says the government, that is the point at which government action in regulating wages has reached its limit; from then on, unless the federal minimum is raised above the present one dollar, organized labor must assume the task of raising wages through the orderly processes of collective bargaining.

In general, minimum wages run the gamut from twenty-six cents per hour for hand sewing on gloves to a dollar in the top industries, with some forward-looking U.S. companies deliberately paying more than the legal minimum in order to improve their labor relations. The industries in the low wage brackets are those that have shown to the government's satisfaction that they cannot afford to raise their pay. Hence, as they operate in what must remain a rising labor market, some of them either pull out, as did a number of the needle-work industries, or mechanize, as has been done in recent years in cutting tobacco. Such mechanization then creates technological unemployment, and the Department of Labor maintains that it is precisely the victims of such unemployment who are the hardest to place in new jobs. The women who lost their jobs in tobacco cutting were at the lowest end in the wage scale; they were also the least skilled and now find it increasingly difficult to find jobs in a society that is daily placing greater value on individual aptitudes.

Until the educational system, with its strong emphasis on vocational training, has succeeded in raising the general level of skills, and the Economic Development Administration has provided enough new jobs for everybody, the Commonwealth must rely increasingly on social assistance and unemployment compensation.

Puerto Rico's labor movement had its earliest beginnings just before the Spanish-American War—though in those days of Spain's rule anybody who talked about the rights of workers was regarded and persecuted as a dangerous radical. The movement received impetus under the aegis of the United States at a time when labor slowly began to feel its strength. But the movement's growth was a long and painful uphill struggle. The feudal type of management that was inherited from the Spanish regime, the management introduced by the sugar corporations during the early decades under the American flag—which was no less feudal for being more efficient and slightly more generous—retained a strong contempt for labor. Conciliation and arbitration were not regarded as proper functions of the government. Labor relations hovered constantly between the uneasy industrial peace under which the workers perforce accepted starvation wages, and the sporadic conflict of strikes, which only too often amounted to desperate, savage warfare. Fields were burned, properties destroyed, lives lost. Being weaker than management by the usual norm of "lasting power," labor was inclined to intensify its violence.

All that is changed today, partly because of the government's progressive attitudes, partly because the new industries being established on the island bring with them ideas on labor relations which may be old in the United States, but are new in Puerto Rico. The former methods are now being replaced by work contracts, collectively bargained, while the government's Department of Labor offers its free services for conciliation and arbitration. While labor is encouraged to organize and to use its collective strength to strive for higher wages and better working conditions, both it and management are also encouraged—through a continuing process of education and experience—to adjust to a new day's new ways. In the states those new ways emerged gradually from a long period of strife that resulted in sporadic legislative actions. In Puerto Rico, entering the industrial scene later and having to run very fast to catch up, they were legislated into the picture during the transformation's earliest stages.

Conciliation services are offered by the Department of Labor at all times—during strikes or during the negotiations of work contracts—for all types of discussion. At times the conciliation services are requested by one party to the dispute, at times by both, and sometimes—when public interests are involved—by the legislator from the district or the mayor of the town concerned. At the conciliation table the workers have the same weight management has; the government leans neither way, but gives its advice according to the merits of the case and on the basis of the public good. However, the rulings of the conciliator are not binding; they merely represent efforts to bring the two parties together.

Arbitration services, on the other hand, must be requested by both parties to the struggle, and are devoted largely to settling disputes over the interpretation of existing contracts. Such arbitration may draw out for weeks or months, but both parties requesting them must agree beforehand to accept the arbitrator's decisions. Obviously the law's effectiveness depends entirely on the faith the people of Puerto Rico —and of management—have in the government's good faith and fairness.

According to a revealing statement in the 1957-8 report of the Department of Labor, "The original concept of the union as an organization devoted to the attainment of higher wages and better living conditions is gradually changing. Today the union is beginning to be regarded as an agency for the achievement of social services for the worker and his family, including medical plans, retirement systems, protection against unemployment and other aspects of social security. . . . These changes have greatly complicated the functions of the conciliator as well as of the arbitrator. Today the unions' objectives, and their concepts of negotiation, have become far more complicated, requiring much more study, making both conciliation and arbitration more difficult, and demanding of the conciliators and arbitrators much more skill than formerly, as well as a better understanding of all the questions involved."

Although strikes are played up heavily in the newspapers, one hears much less about the department's effectiveness in preventing them, in maintaining industrial peace. During the fiscal year 1958, 217 controversies, all of them potential strikes, were conciliated; special services were rendered in 196 more cases; arbitration was requested and given in another 192 instances; thirty-nine strikes and seventeen threats of strikes were settled through collective bargaining with the help of conciliation. More than ninety per cent of the cases were settled peacefully, a record which few, if any, states can match.

The basic principle in Employment Security is that a worker who suffers from technological unemployment or a temporary lay-off is entitled to help from the government until he can again be placed. The government admits its responsibility in the matter of creating jobs; when a worker, through no fault of his own, becomes unemployed, the society has a responsibility toward him. Again, that responsibility was freely acknowledged in the constitution as origi-

nally written, which stated that "the Commonwealth also
recognizes the existence of the following human rights:

"The right of every person to receive a free elementary
and secondary education.

"The right of every person to obtain work.

"The right of every person to a standard of living adequate
for the health and well-being of himself and his family, and
especially to food, clothing, housing and medical care and
necessary social services.

"The right of every person to social protection in the event
of unemployment, sickness, old age or disability.

"The right of motherhood and childhood to special care
and assistance."

Having boldly proclaimed such "welfare-state" rights, the
original Bill of Rights goes on to admit: "The rights set forth
in this section are closely connected with the progressive development of the Commonwealth's economy and require, for
their full effectiveness, sufficient resources and an agricultural and industrial development not yet attained by the
Puerto Rican community."

The next paragraph, however, pledges the government to
do everything in its power to bring about conditions under
which the various stipulated rights may be fully achieved by
the island's people. Meanwhile, until such conditions have
been achieved, the Department of Labor, bolstered by special
legislation, must do everything it can to find employment
and cushion the evil effects of unemployment.

Those provisions of the constitution were adapted from
the United Nations "Universal Declaration of Human
Rights." However, when the constitution was submitted to
Congress for ratification, that body objected to the provisions
on the grounds that they were "un-American," despite the
fact that the United Nations declaration had previously been
ratified by the United States. As a result of the Congressional
objections, that section of the constitution was eliminated

by Puerto Rico's Constitutional Convention. Morally, however, as a statement of intent, and in the government's policy
and actions, its provisions remain in force.

As stated in Chapter 2, the Department's Migration Division, while neither encouraging nor discouraging migration
to the states, labors constantly to help those who do migrate.
That division is part of the Bureau of Employment Security,
which also runs an employment agency and administers unemployment compensation. Recently, it may be added, the
latter activity has become connected with the federal em-
ployment-insurance program.

The increase of the number of people applying for jobs
through the employment service is indicative of Puerto Rico's
current trends. Between the years 1957 and 1958 the island's gross product increased from $1,204,000,000 to $1,-
286,000,000; the net income rose from $1,014,000,000 to
$1,079,000,000; the per capita income rose from $446 to
$469; the number of new factories promoted or helped by
Fomento rose from 499 to 577. *Nevertheless, the number of
clients asking the Department of Labor to find jobs for them
also rose from 103,753 to 121,188 or 16.8 per cent.* That increase, however, is not entirely the result of technological
unemployment in Puerto Rico. Net (permanent) migration
to the states *decreased* by more than 20,000 during the same
period, while local job applications increased by about 17,-
000, indicating that it was somewhat due to the recession
on the mainland.

Of the total applicants, 66,267 were placed in jobs, 54,-
087 in Puerto Rico and 12,180 in the States. The employment service's statistics, then, show that there are about 60,-
000 workers in the Puerto Rican labor force for whom
employment cannot now be found and who may well, for
want of opportunity, or lack of skills, or both, be regarded
as forming a permanent body of unemployed.

Like all government agencies, the Department of Labor is

growing by leaps and bounds, though it is still handicapped by lack of funds, still unable to meet all the many demands made on it. For instance, besides the activities mentioned above, it gives courses in labor laws and labor relations to both workers and managers; it maintains a Bureau of Labor Statistics that keeps track of problems and progress in many fields; it maintains special divisions for unemployment compensation in the sugar industry, for the social security of chauffeurs, for accident prevention, for the handling of veterans, and for the determination and maintenance of work standards.

This large and complex government program on behalf of labor and industrial peace grew naturally out of the chaotic conditions the Popular Democratic party encountered in 1940, and has made Puerto Rico a model for labor relations in the Americas. On the other hand, the island's progressive labor laws have impeded the growth and strengthening of the labor movement. Unions became strong in the States through their struggle to achieve the things the Puerto Rican government has given the Commonwealth workers on a legislated silver platter. As a result, the Puerto Rican unions are still relatively weak.

The father of the island's labor movement was Santiago Iglesias, a Spanish carpenter with little education, but a burning messianic fervor. He came to Puerto Rico in 1896, found labor conditions truly terrible, and began immediately to rouse the workers out of their almost hopeless lethargy. He was in prison in San Juan during the Spanish-American War, but when Admiral Sampson bombarded the capital, one of his shells knocked a hole in the wall of Iglesias's cell and conveniently failed to explode. The agitator managed to escape and began immediately to harangue some sugar workers in San Juan's outskirts, telling them not to accept the rotten, maggoty codfish the company store was selling to them at high prices in return for the miserable token payments they received for their work. For that he was arrested and taken to the American land forces, which had by then come close to San Juan.

The American officers were impressed by Iglesias and by the samples of rotten codfish he had given them as indications of labor conditions. They protected him when a Spanish commission arrived to inform them that he was a dangerous character, an agitator and incendiary who belonged in prison. As a result, Iglesias became an ardent admirer of the United States. Later he became a close friend of Samuel Gompers, and still later, from 1933 until his death in 1939, he was Puerto Rico's Resident Commissioner in Washington.

The "Federation" founded by Iglesias was Puerto Rico's first labor organization, composed of a considerable number of loosely knit unions. In 1899 Iglesias organized the Socialist-Labor party, which was some years later transformed into the Socialist party with a platform taken from Eugene Debs's party in the states. That was the party to which Muñoz Marín gave his allegiance in 1920—getting his first experience in political campaigning—to the horror of many people who thought that he should, if only from family loyalty, have worked with his father's Unionist party. The Socialists, however, had small political success until 1932, when they joined with the Republicans to form the Coalition that took over the government as a result of that year's election and held it until 1940, when Muñoz's new Popular Democratic party managed to nose it out. Not until 1952, however, did the Socialist party cease completely to function as a political organization.

The first unions grew out of and within the cigar industry, in which, until recently, every shop had its "reader," a man who kept the workers interested by reading newspapers and other materials to them. Many of these readers were labor agitators on the side, slipping a good deal of exhortation and denunciation of management into their singsong readings.

In the sleepy, out-of-the-world Puerto Rico of those days many cigar makers received their first lessons about the outer world and about labor's rights from their readers. A number of them became labor leaders and organizers, and used these positions to get themselves elected to the legislature.

During the century's first four decades the labor movement grew with the organization of a number of local unions that were independent, not only of the United States labor movement, but also, despite the "Federation," of each other as well.

The movement grew—sporadically, disjointedly—until the modern day arrived with its new conditions and the new powers granted to labor by the government. As stated above, the union is more and more being regarded by its members as an instrument of social welfare, not merely as a means of increasing wages. Moreover, the old system of a number of independent unions is now giving way to the modern system of federations. The movement toward affiliation with the AFL-CIO is gaining headway rapidly and is in no way discouraged by the government. (Typical is the story of the U.S. industrialist, A. N. Spanel, who maintains excellent labor conditions in his plant through paternalistic means, but happens to hate and fear unions with a desperate fervor. His company, the International Latex Corporation, established a factory in Puerto Rico, where it pays wages higher than the legal minimum, grants fringe benefits above those demanded by labor or the government, but will not allow a union organizer anywhere near the premises. Somehow Mr. Spanel formed a high opinion of Muñoz Marín. During his one visit to the island, some years after his branch factory had been established and proved itself to be the most successful of all his various factories in various parts of the world, he requested and virtually demanded an interview with the governor. Eventually the invitation arrived. The industrialist was invited to a cocktail party given at the executive mansion in honor of a visiting group of high officials in the AFL-CIO).

About ten international unions were functioning in Puerto Rico in 1958, and their intensive program included the organization of workers in long-established local plants that have survived from the former unhappy days, whose managers are accustomed to old ways of doing things and are likely to scream much more loudly than do the American managers of new factories. But, on the whole, the international unions go at things sensibly and refrain from making demands that could wreck the entire present effort to raise standards of living.

Meanwhile, the Hoffas and other racketeers still constitute a threat. I asked an official in the Department of Labor what was being done about them. "Officially," came the answer, "very little. The racketeers have so far failed to gain a foothold here largely because our unions, while they may be weak, are certainly honest. There lies our greatest strength."

14

Public Health

ACCORDING to the claims of a once powerful school of thought, tropical diseases impede successful development in the tropics and will always impede it because it is more difficult to control illness in the miscalled "torrid zones" than in the middle latitudes. The uniformly warm and humid climate, runs the argument, is ideal for the propagation of disease germs and of insects and other vectors that spread those germs. Vicious in that it is fatalistic, the claim is today refuted by many public-health experts who work in the tropics.

It is nonsense, say the latter, to blame the natural climate for tropical illnesses, when the man-made social and economic climate is so obviously bad in the tropics that health conditions *must* be correspondingly bad. In the middle latitudes, in the countries that are economically advanced, standards of living are sufficiently high to eliminate widespread malnutrition as a health problem. Residents of the more advanced countries are surrounded by municipal, state, and national health organizations, alerted, equipped, and financed to deal immediately with any threat to the public's health. Much money is spent and great care is taken to see that their water and sewage facilities are not sources of infection. Their meat and other foods, as well as their restaurants, are inspected. They have sufficient doctors, hospitals, clinics, and sufficient private and public income to support them.

The humid tropics, however, have long been the world's colonial regions par excellence, exploited as such. To be sure, capital outflow from the ruling countries to the colonies has been great, but profit returns have been greater. Whatever was left behind was not sufficient to raise wages above the twelve cents per person per day about which Estéban Bird complained, to assure diets and ways of life for the majority which are conducive to general health, to give the tropical society a budget sufficient for creating an adequate sanitary environment, medical services sufficient to meet existing needs, education geared in part to problems of hygiene, and income large enough to support all these out of taxes.

"Public health," say doctors of the U. S. Public Health Service, "is a purchasable commodity. The amount you get is the amount that you can, or are willing to, pay for." It is a good working principle that says, in effect, that public health is a function of an intangible called "standards of living." Modern Puerto Rico is among the several societies (Australia's Queenland is another) which have shown that a tropical society which tackles its health problems by improving the man-made social climate is likely to achieve notable results.

In 1951, at a reception in Washington, I met Dr. Juan Pons, then Puerto Rico's amiable and energetic Secretary of Health, who was succeeded in 1957 by Dr. Guillermo Arbona. I told him about my interest in the tropics and in all their problems, and congratulated him on the remarkable progress Puerto Rico had made in matters of health.

"Look," said Pons. "Let's not talk about tropical medicine, because there is no such thing. There is only a medicine of low standards of living and another of higher. Our experiences in Puerto Rico and the entire world's disease pattern bear that out."

Today we are witnessing a thrilling world-wide drive on communicable diseases, carried forward in the Western Hemisphere by the Pan American Sanitary Bureau in collaboration with the health departments of all the American republics. They are aiming at the elimination of malaria, yellow fever, smallpox, and a number of other devitalizing ailments, and they are training men and women, and sending them out in teams, and buying sprays and spray materials and jeeps, and hiring doctors, nurses, and statisticians, and they are going out to the four corners of every land, and achieving notable results. But they will find—as some learned in Puerto Rico—that those results will be temporary unless and until they are accompanied by settlement and development in such wilderness areas as the vast Amazon basin, and by the improvement of standards of living in such backward areas as Venezuela's hinterlands.

Dr. Bailey Ashford was one of Puerto Rico's heroes. He had won world fame by being the first in the Western Hemisphere to isolate the parasite of hookworm, or ancylostomiasis, and subsequently he had headed, for the U.S. army, the first campaign to eradicate the plague on the island. When I met him in 1931, shortly before his death, he told me why that campaign had been unsuccessful and why similar campaigns—carried on in purely mechanical fashion—were bound also to fail. Talking about the Rockefeller eradication teams, he said:

"Those fellows go all over the world trying to clean up hookworm, but they go at things wrong. They tell people to wear shoes, which they can't afford, and to build outhouses, which they can't afford, either. They dose hookworm patients with carbon tetrachloride, which in their weakened condition is worse than the disease. If they examined people's stools they would see that nature is constantly trying to pass off the parasite. Why don't they give nature a chance? Feed the people: improve their strength. After a while they will find that the hookworm problem is simple."

In 1931, the year Ashford talked to me, Puerto Rico had 397 deaths from hookworm, or 25.1 per 100,000 people. By 1933 (the worst of the depression years), the figures had gone up to 770, or 46.8. Then the relief and reconstruction administrations started their work, and the hookworm figures began to show slow but wavering declines. The war came, and the armed forces helped a great deal with their medical work; in 1944 there were 133 deaths, or 6.6 per 100,000. The next year there was a sudden drop to 48 deaths, or a rate of 2.3, from hookworm. Standards of living began to improve greatly after the war; people ate better and had more money for shoes and latrines; on growing budgets the Department of Health could do more work. The statistics for 1956, far more complete and reliable than had been those of 1931, showed not a single death from ancylostomiasis.

Similar gains are noted in other so-called tropical diseases. Twenty years ago malaria was a scourge in Puerto Rico, as it also was in India, Africa, the Amazon basin, many other tropical countries, Washington, D. C., as far north as Ohio, and in Saratoga, New York. Between 1931 and 1934 malaria caused about 3000 deaths annually on the island, with rates of close to 200 per 100,000. In those years that rate was about six times as high as it was in the malaria belt in Alabama, Florida, Mississippi, and South Carolina. Mortality, incidence, and rates began to go down with the advent of the PRERA and the PRRA, but the figures for 1941 still show 2,382 deaths at a rate of 124.6. From that point on, however, the figures show a sharp decline, reaching zero in 1955. The fact that no cases of malaria have been reported since the latter date does not necessarily mean that the disease has been eradicated; it may still be dormant in a few people's spleens, or it may be reimported by a sick sailor or two. However, being no longer needed, the Health Department's

Bureau of Malaria Eradication was abolished in 1955. The spraying of DDT in the interiors of houses was primarily responsible for the disappearance of malaria; however, the raised standard of living, which provided funds for the drive and improved people's living habits, as well as their health and resistance to disease, was another essential factor in getting rid of the disease.

Before 1940 Puerto Rico's three greatest killers were, in the order given: diarrhea and enteritis (a kind of grab-bag name for several gastro-intestinal diseases), tuberculosis, and malaria. In 1937 diarrhea and enteritis caused 8,590 deaths at a rate of 483.5 per 100,000, or more than ten times the rate in Hawaii, and more than fifty that in Connecticut; in 1956 the figures were 1,796 and 79.3 respectively, and the chart for the ailment, in the office of the Secretary of Health, keeps dropping steadily. Tuberculosis killed 5,182 Puerto Ricans in 1936 at a rate of 297.3 per 100,000; the island's several tuberculosis hospitals were constantly overcrowded, and thousands of patients could not be accommodated. 1956 saw 831 deaths from the disease at a rate of 36.7.

Such figures, which are studied with enormous interest by medical visitors from Asia, Africa, and Latin America, are in themselves dramatic indices of Puerto Rico's new vitality. In partial explanation of the distressing earlier health statistics, an unpublished PRRA report prepared in 1936 said: "The Puerto Rican laborers are subject to a process of slow starvation which for hosts of unemployed becomes habitual, pressing hunger. Meat and milk, for example, are such luxuries that the daily per capita consumption is measured in ounces and spoonfuls." On the other hand, in line with Dr. Pons's dictum that there is only a medicine of low standards of living and another of higher, several other diseases now plague the island to an increasing extent. Not only do rising standards of living bring their own ailments, but the fact that the Puerto Ricans' life expectancy has risen from 46 years in 1940 to 68 in 1958 has also increased the menace from the several diseases of age. So, for instance, we find that cancer killed 676 in 1931 and 1,682 in 1956; diabetes caused the death of 44 in 1932 and 165 in 1956; deaths from heart ailments went up from 1,466 in 1931 to 2,525 in 1956, when heart trouble was a far more serious disease, statistically considered, than were tuberculosis and diarrhea and enteritis.

In 1906 Governor Beekman Winthrop wrote: "Although it may be possible, through the introduction of more advanced sanitary mediums, to reduce Puerto Rico's death rate, this rate is not excessive for a tropical island." In that year it was twenty-three per 1000. In 1940 about 35,000 Puerto Ricans died on their island, or 18.4 per 1000. When the mortality rate dropped to twelve per 1000 in 1947, Dr. Pons thought that things had gone about as far as a public-health program could bring them. In his report for that year he wrote that the tuberculosis rate might be reduced slightly by direct action, that minor improvements in the total health situation could be expected here and there, but that the death rate was leveling off. "I expect," he wrote, "that at this point in our accomplishment any marked reduction in our mortality rates in the years to come must be in proportion to the improvement in economic level at which our population struggles, rather than to any increase in our direct health-promoting efforts; and that the smallest unfavorable change in our economy will have an immediate effect on those rates."

There was no unfavorable change; the economy kept improving, though not rapidly enough to suit the impatient Secretary of Health. Budgets for public health increased; efforts to reduce illness and death increased to correspond. In 1957 the death rate was 6.9 per 1,000, which is lower than that of the United States. The following year, however, it climbed to 7.2, possibly because the population is growing older while many of the younger and healthier people are migrating to the States. The "crude" death rate here referred to is one that has not been adjusted to the population's age and age groups. Puerto Rico's death rate is at present one of the world's lowest, but it will quite possibly continue to climb as the island's population grows older and becomes increasingly afflicted with the ailments of age. Such a climb will in no way indicate a decline of general health conditions. "As an index of general health," said a world authority to me recently, "give me a good solid heartline. A country's general health is indicated by the number of deaths it has from cardiac diseases." (It should be noted that the Soviet Union now crows that its death rate of 7.5 is "the world's lowest.")

Such figures, I know, distress a number of demographers who seem today to be terrified by the word "overpopulation." However, the birth rate is also dropping, though not as rapidly as is the mortality.

Just as Puerto Rico is beginning to achieve social and economic health, it is also moving toward a proper balance between population numbers and the developed resources sustaining the population. Year by year the Puerto Ricans produce more to eat; at the same time, they have begun to produce fewer Puerto Ricans to share the food. That is as it should be, in line with demographic trends often observed in many parts of the world, and also in line with the theory advanced by Dr. Josué de Castro in his book *The Geography of Hunger*. According to his theory, for which the author reaped vituperative abuse from many scholars, human fertility tends to rise with malnutrition and to go down as nutritional standards rise. While he cannot prove his theory experimentally, his many enemies cannot disprove it, either. However, they know that nutrition improves immediately with the same rise in living standards which is usually accompanied by declining birth rates.

Dr. Jacques May, who is in charge of the American Geographical Society's studies in Medical Geography, became aware of those matters some years ago and formulated an

ambitious, systematic program of research in Puerto Rico,
aimed at arriving at possible conclusions regarding the complex interrelations between public health on the one hand,
and on the other such matters as economic indexes, employment, manners of individual living, cultural *mores*, ways of
living together, attitudes and habits of government, sanitary
environment, psychological environment, and possibly natural climate as well. Unfortunately he failed to find the
needed financial backing. His study would have helped to
clarify man's understanding of the relations between himself and his environment—of which man himself is the most
important component.

Adequate and energetic medical treatment is, of course,
only one phase of any public-health effort; the provision of
an adequate sanitary environment is another. The quality
of drinking water available to the people is one of several
indexes of such an environment.

To judge by his book *The Stricken Land,* Governor Tugwell seems to have been greatly preoccupied with San Juan's
untrustworthy water supply. He seems to have considered
it symptomatic of all of Puerto Rico's ills; at times his book
reads as though having to put up with it, having to boil and
filter his drinking water, was among the worst of the hardships he had to endure in a backward and improvident society.

He wrote about conditions during 1942-6, which were
infinitely better than they had been when the United States
first stepped into the Puerto Rican scene. In contrast to his
complaints, however, it is significant that since 1950 the
San Juan water supply has been approved for interstate
commerce. That means that steamers and airplanes putting
in at the capital may now fill their tanks from the city water
system with no thought of further purification, with no danger of their crews and passengers catching diseases from
polluted water. It also means that the life of some future
Tugwell will be far easier and less worrisome in the capital.

If you should move there tomorrow, you may throw away most or all of the common advice, oral and printed, about how to stay healthy in the tropics. Precisely as you may forget about the daily quinine pills for prophylaxis against malaria, so you may now drink from the common water supply, from anybody's tap, in any hotel or restaurant, without having to go through the common tropical ritual of boiling, filtering, and adding so many chlorazene pills that it smells worse than Chicago water. In fact, if you come from some place other than Chicago or Milwaukee, you may even be bothered by the fact that the San Juan water already smells and tastes of chlorine. You will not be bothered long; Chicagoans have long since become accustomed to it, and so will you. A little chlorine is better than a lot of typhoid and dysentery.

In matters like the provision of safe drinking water, the Department of Health must of course work closely with other branches of the government, such as the Aqueduct and Sewer Authority. Every year more of Puerto Rico's communities and municipalities receive filtering and other plants for purifying their water, as well as improved distribution systems. In his latest published report the Secretary of Health stated that in 1956 alone his department's Bureau of Environmental Sanitation "encouraged the Puerto Rico Aqueduct and Sewer Authority to supply drinking water to 203,695 subscribers (approximately 1,018,471 people). The Section approved 96 construction plans for new water supplies and alterations or extensions to existing ones."

Puerto Rico's "rural aqueducts" are important in the general health program. A decade ago most of the island's rural women had to carry their water in old gasoline tins, converted into pails, often for long distances and even more often from polluted sources. Today every effort is made to purify the springs, rivers, and other sources of water, and long pipelines, with hydrants conveniently spaced, run along road after road, bringing good water from safe sources to the countryside's populations. Their construction proceeds steadily in a continuing program as funds become available; it will not be long before every family, rural and urban, has access to an ample and safe source of water. Such programs, of course, capture the imaginations of the people themselves. A number of rural communities are now anticipating routine governmental efforts and are installing their own water supplies—with government help, but with their own labor and limited funds.

For building latrines, too, considerable direct participation of the people has been enlisted. Twenty years ago Puerto Rico was a pesthole for hookworm, one reason being that the people had no shoes; barefoot peasants became infected by walking on soil that was polluted because virtually nobody in the rural areas had a latrine. The Department of Health is today building latrines as rapidly as funds and staff permit, at a cost of about ninety dollars each. Now, however, a number of communities have decided not to wait for the government's program to reach them; they organize themselves for group action, ask the government for technical help and advice—and perhaps for some financing as well—take up collections among themselves, donate their labor, and build latrines at a cost, to the government, of less than twenty dollars each. As an added health measure, the government gives shoes to the rural poor, while the Health Department's Section of Soil Sanitation inspects dwellings and privies and carries on research projects aimed at evaluating "the importance of the use of sanitary privies in regard to the incidence of Bilharzia, hookworm and other intestinal parasitic infestations in the rural zones of the island."

"How have we lengthened our lives so much in so short a time?" asked Muñoz in a nation-wide radio broadcast on Columbus Day 1953. "Largely by involving the people themselves in the determination of their own destiny."

As a result of these programs, the periodic inspection of restaurants, stores, ice plants, bottling works, and factories

—to say nothing of private homes—and a campaign to teach the rudiments of sanitation to the individual poor, the sanitary environment has been so drastically improved since 1941 that Puerto Rico is today, in its sanitary as well as its social and economic aspects, virtually a new country.

Puerto Rico's present low death rate seems all the more remarkable when one remembers that over eighty per cent of the island's people are still, despite rising standards of living, medically indigent, and that of that eighty per cent an appreciable number are still medically all but inaccessible, in part because they live in remote sections of the hills, and in part because they superstitiously follow the hocus-pocus of *curanderos* or *curanderas*—male or female folk healers who flourish in all the world's isolated and poverty-stricken communities.

Despite the fact that there were about 500 doctors on the island in 1940 as compared to 1,745 today, and the number of persons per physician was reduced correspondingly from 3,672 to 1,325, over eighty per cent of the medicine practiced in Puerto Rico must be public medicine and therefore a drain on a budget already low and overstrained when compared with those of the various states.

In addition to managing six tuberculosis hospitals and five general hospitals, the department maintains seventy-six public-health units in the various districts. Each of these is a clinic (though some have small hospitals attached to them) for the treatment of such diseases as tuberculosis, syphilis, and heart trouble. Each unit, however, is also an important educational center in which doctors and nurses constantly talk to patients about various health problems, as well as a field outpost of various suborganizations, such as the bureaus of Tuberculosis, Venereal Disease, Maternal and Infant Hygiene, Crippled Children, Malaria and Insect Control, Public-Health Nursing, and Sanitation. It is largely through these centers and through its Division of Social Welfare that the department manages to reach a large number of the rural poor, who also, because of their poverty, constitute the greatest single reservoir of disease.

The ultimate aim is—through the public-health units, the department's Division of Public Welfare, the Division of Hospitals, and through close co-operation with the educational system for health instruction, school lunches, and public milk stations—to reach into all walks of Puerto Rican life and into all of the interlocking phases of any one walk of life. Always the work comes back to education in its manifold forms—and to pioneering in education. One unique but gratifyingly succesful practice is to talk about general-health problems to patients in hospitals, where they and their visitors are more receptive to such talks than at any other time.

Mrs. Glenola Rose was one of my students in the area-studies course I had the honor to conduct in Puerto Rico in 1952. A mature woman and an interested one, with a vast variety of experiences in matters of public health in many parts of the world, in the term paper she wrote for the course she had this to say about the Rio Piedras public-health unit:

"Among the seventy-six public-health units one is unique, that at Rio Piedras. It is the training center for all personnel for all public-health units in Puerto Rico."

After describing the plant, the staff, and the varied activities of this unit—which includes the offering of services in prenatal, well-baby, preschool, and school clinics, control programs for tuberculosis, venereal disease, malaria, and communicable diseases, programs designed to combat cancer and heart disease, education in nutrition and all other matters of health—she calls attention to what is undoubtedly one of the greatest factors in Puerto Rico's success. "One is impressed with the enthusiasm and response from every person involved, both patient and staff, from the janitor up. This atmosphere appears to result from the insistence that every person is valuable in his own right—true democracy. One of the ways of giving satisfaction is the custom of giving a diploma at graduation to anyone finishing a course of training. The Puerto Ricans are eager to be educated, take pride in securing an education. Janitors as well as other employees get diplomas. But, so do mothers, who are taught how to care for themselves and their families. There are constant graduation ceremonies. The people are being taught to want what they should have and to be proud of wanting it!"

In describing his program to the second regional meeting of the American College of Physicians in November 1950 Dr. Pons said: "It is imperative that we put into the attitude of people, into their everyday conscious thinking, that illness and infirmity are to a very large measure preventable, that they are cancelable liabilities, and that it is unnecessary to suffer them. . . . We must teach people to seek the services that prevent them, rather than those that remedy them. We must see that the communities co-operate in a constructive manner with the agencies dedicated to the promotion of health. When we accomplish this, then we shall have the greatest of any progress in medicine to report."

While Pons's report on the problems and achievements of Puerto Rico's Department of Health was noteworthy, I doubt if the American College of Physicians liked hearing it, especially at a time when many of the doctors in the United States were frightened by the bogey of socialized medicine.

"It is interesting indeed," Pons went on to tell the American College of Physicians, "that a small epidemic outbreak in Puerto Rico brings forth all our might to prevent a few deaths in as many days and that public opinion becomes manifestly impatient if that might is not immediately forthcoming; yet, there is no great worry over the fact that some 60,000 women give birth each year (164 daily) in dingy, substandard homes in the rural areas without any of the benefits of present-day medicine. Certainly a small epidemic outbreak offers no greater urgency than the fact that hundreds of children do not have a wholesome home and

appropriate food; the death of a few during an epidemic outbreak is not a more serious matter than the fact that hundreds of families are each month left to suffer hunger and
misery upon the death or infirmity of the breadwinners."

Continuing in that vein and dealing with the obstacles
that result from limited budgets, he said: "We now have on
the waiting list of the Crippled Children's Bureau, 1,009
children waiting for orthopedic treatment of one kind or
another, 556 children waiting for plastic surgery, and 1,358
waiting for treatment of remediable ocular conditions; most
of them have been waiting for much too long, and we do
not know just when they can be taken care of. We know of
824 cerebral palsied children who are receiving little if any
expert care.

"Screening surveys have shown that our schools, with an
approximate enrollment of 400,000 children, contain some
38,000 with visual difficulties readily correctable, and some
25,000 children who are hard of hearing; little is being done
about them. One study has indicated that there are no fewer
than 400 children under eighteen years of age who are blind,
most of them from causes that could have been prevented."

Pons complained about conditions of 1950, which have
improved immeasurably since that date. He is quoted here
to illustrate a widespread attitude of mind; in his own field
the then Secretary of Health personified a society impatient
to get things done. But even while such men and the entire
society complain, Puerto Rico keeps progressing in its public-
health affairs, with amazing statistical results.

The Department of Health is today a vast, sprawling organization with many branches, each busy with its own
share of the complex total task. While ambulatory X-ray
plants photograph hundreds of thousands of chests in the
drive against tuberculosis, other trucks distribute to public-
assistance beneficiaries food donated by the Federal Department of Agriculture. Plans are now well under way to con-
struct a modern medical center in San Juan's Rio Piedras

section. There is a psychiatric hospital, a psychiatric training center, and a project for mentally retarded children.
The Bureau of Health Education goes deeply into all phases
of Puerto Rican life. The Mental Health Bureau is "mainly
concerned with the basic function of promoting and maintaining the mental health of the people of Puerto Rico as
part of the objectives of a public-health program." The Bureau of Medical Social Service strives to improve and tie
together the social services of all the other bureaus. There
is a Bureau of Nutrition and Dietetics that works hard to
improve the island's nutritional levels, making studies and
surveys and offering consulting services, as well as in-
service training. The Hospital Service and Construction Bureau strives to enlarge and improve the island's hospital
facilities. The Bureau of Cancer Control attempts to curb
the inroads of cancer. The Office of Pathology and Medical
Education does laboratory work besides training workers in
special fields. Specific bureaus deal with communicable diseases, while others are concerned with venereal diseases,
heart diseases, and tuberculosis. Among the many bureaus
are those of Health Laboratories, of Nursing, of Maternal
and Infant Hygiene, of Crippled Children, and of Oral
Health. Some of the activities of the Bureau of Environmental Sanitation have been recounted earlier. The Division
of Hospitals runs hospitals, while the Division of Public
Welfare, with a complex system of programs in many fields,
is as yet the closest thing on the island to a general Department of Public Welfare.

Such divisions and subdivisions are, of course, common
in large governmental departments. The results of organiza-
tional efforts, they do effective work, though it is a fact—
increasingly recognized today throughout the world—that
the compartmentalization of effort they represent brings its
own serious drawbacks. The battle between compartmentalization and integration is a universal phenomenon in Puerto
Rico, and in that connection the new "Bayamón Health and

Welfare Regional Program" is of special interest. Believing that the lives and affairs of people and societies are not compartmentalized and are truly integrated, the Department of Health is now carrying out activities in the region served by the Bayamón District Hospital, aimed not only at integrating all its own activities and services for improved health, but also at co-ordinating its activities with those of other government agencies and of the various municipalities.

A pamphlet published by the Department of Health in 1957 begins as follows: "When all the agencies for curative medicine, preventive medicine, public health, and social service within a given geographic area are coordinated under a single system, the term *regionalization* is used to denote the organization." It is an important venture, the first of its kind under the American flag, which is attracting attention from medical circles in all parts of the world. In Puerto Rico it may yet lead to further administrative pioneering. In 1957, in his annual message to the legislature, Governor Muñoz Marín asked for something similar, at least in a localized experiment, for all the various governmental efforts. What he asked for, in effect, though he has not yet received it, is something similar to Egypt's imaginative "Demonstration and Training Area of Naguib," which has a population of some 300,000. In that instance governmental appropriations are made for the region in question, and not for the various government departments active in it. The Naguib area is administered by a committee composed of representatives of all those departments, who must spend the monies appropriated in accordance with integrated master plans.

Perhaps the most important single explanation of Puerto Rico's remarkable success in matters of public health is found in the fact that the island's Department of Health not only subscribes to, but also abides by, Craig's dictum that "the days of monastery medicine and the ivory tower are gone." Medicine, according to Howard Reid Craig in his book *Introduction to Social Medicine,* is "an integral, interrelated, and interdependent part of a functioning social and economic system which to be viable must exist in a continuing state of flux."

The vision of a future Puerto Rico with the world's lowest death rate and one of the world's best climates of sanitation and health is not necessarily one of the distant future. As yet, the figures, curves, and charts dealing with mortality and incidence of various diseases, with infant mortality and maternal deaths in childbirth, have shown no indication of discontinuing their dramatic drops. The vision of a Puerto Rico with the world's lowest death rate is realizable in the near or immediate future of another decade or two—barring a local catastrophe of a world calamity.

15

Education

WHEN the United States took over Puerto Rico in 1898, the island's educational system was extremely limited and church-controlled. With characteristic energy and good will we started to do something about the matter immediately. Commissioners from Washington were appointed to expand and reorganize the system according to the latest and best continental patterns. They built schools, hired teachers, worked with vigor and devotion to improve something that was obviously bad, and wrote enthusiastic reports, which were characteristic of our national exhuberance of those days. As early as 1900 Dr. M. G. Brumbaugh, the first Commissioner of Education under the American flag, proudly informed the U.S. government that the average Puerto Rican child already knew more about Washington, Lincoln, Betsy Ross, and the American flag than did the average child in the United States.

Educational policy, which is a knotty matter everywhere, was in those days not at all knotty in Puerto Rico. Politically determined, by and in Washington, it had one obvious major aim, and one only, namely: to make "good Americans" as rapidly as possible out of as many Puerto Rican children as possible. Hence the children learned about Betsy Ross and the American flag; the question of whether or not they learned as much as they should about the responsibilities involved in taking their places as Puerto Ricans in the Puerto Rican society was hardly considered.

For the children it proved confusing, especially as it seemed obvious to the American commissioners of education that one couldn't be a good American—learn about Betsy Ross, with perhaps a little arithmetic and writing thrown in—except in the English langauge. It was therefore decreed very early that all the teaching in all of Puerto Rico's public schools must be done in English, thus forcing the teachers immediately to learn a new language if they wanted to hold their jobs. The results were chaotic. Children who had never heard anything but Spanish at home and in the streets now had to learn the three R's and various other subject matters—including the history of a culture alien to theirs—as expounded to them in English by teachers who hardly knew English themselves. Many a time during these early decades, especially in the higher grades, many a teacher closed the classroom door against the enemy in order to bootleg a little comprehensible Spanish into her conversation with her students; a supervisor who caught her at it might well have been sympathetic, but had to discharge her just the same, thus accentuating the teacher shortage, as well as resentment against the United States.

Immediately after taking over the government, the American rulers began to send promising Puerto Rican students to the States for an education. The first group presented difficulties. Where should they go? They were not citizens of the United States, and as colonial subjects they didn't have the full rights of American boys and girls. But the fact that they were undeniably West Indians offered a solution: they were sent to that training institution for other colonial subjects—Carlisle Indian School. But then some of our better private schools opened their doors to Puerto Ricans, and those of the second group had better luck.

One of them was José Padín, who had the good fortune to be taken in by Haverford College. However, the fact that Haverford was a Quaker institution distressed his Catholic relatives. When he returned to Puerto Rico four years later, they asked him with much apprehension whether those godless people had diverted him from the true faith and had made a Quaker out of him. His classic and revealing answer was: "I couldn't make the grade."

In 1930, while Theodore Roosevelt, Jr. was Puerto Rico's governor, Herbert Hoover appointed Padín Commissioner of Education. Things began to change immediately, though uneasy stirrings also began to be felt in Washington. The daring new commissioner set out to reshape the educational system to fit the island's needs. He even managed to abolish the rule under which all the teaching had to be done in English, and to substitute for it a system whereby the teaching was done in Spanish, but English became a required subject of study. Also, he encouraged the teachers to express their opinions. Many of them held such opinions before, but they had kept them prudently hidden from the Americanizing commissioners of education.

The so-called Second Unit Rural Schools, established by Padín during the thirties, represented the first truly Puerto Rican educational effort designed to fit Puerto Rican realities, integrated with the island's indigenous life. These took the pupils from the seventh grade through the tenth, and their organization and basic ideas have been studied and adapted by many Latin-American countries.

Previous to the establishment of those schools, most of the educational effort had been confined to the towns and cities; the rural areas had a few poor equivalents of the Little Red Schoolhouse, in which the three R's and other subjects were taught by rote. That was bad, of course, in a society that was still predominantly rural, and one whose human strength consisted primarily of the impoverished peasantry. The new program of the Second Unit Rural Schools began with detailed studies of all the various rural areas in which they were established, of their type or types of agriculture, their health conditions, their relative isolation from the rest of Puerto Rico, their social conditions and characteristics. As a result of such studies, the operations and educational programs of each of the Second Unit Rural Schools were then shaped in such a manner that the school came directly to grips with the problems of the community which it served.

Each school had (and has) a farm on which the boys are taught agriculture in addition to their regular academic subjects. Facilities exist for teaching the girls cooking, canning, and other branches of domestic science. In the early days the teaching of social studies was aimed primarily at the understanding of the particular communities in which the schools were located; much emphasis was placed on vocational training; instruction in health and hygiene was made an essential part of the curriculum. Boys and girls, as today, were encouraged to join such organizations as the Future Farmers of America, so becoming, through devotion to their own particular problems, also identified with the vast agricultural world beyond Puerto Rico.

The work of the schools soon became intimately tied with that of the Office of Public Welfare. Social workers attached to them strove to help the children and their parents and to bring about a close relationship between the school and the community's various individuals. Mothers' clubs and parent-teacher associations strengthened that relationship. Thus the school became also a community center; its influence on adult life came to be felt widely, as for instance through night classes for adults, the organization of co-operatives, and the joint tackling of many other community problems.

Such innovations were revolutionary in Puerto Rico a quarter of a century ago. The Second Unit Rural Schools have by now been drastically modified. Today they are largely rural junior-high schools with some vocational aspects added, but this means only that Puerto Rico has changed. The psychological and cultural division between city and country is now not nearly as drastic as it was three decades ago; people by the thousands have flocked to the towns to take industrial jobs; new roads have united city and country more than ever before; the growth of literacy, the radio, and other means of communication have brought about accelerated exchanges of information.

The stress Padín placed on health and hygiene in the Second Unit Rural Schools has since his day been greatly intensified throughout the educational system. The phenomenal success of the Department of Health in reducing the death rate is due in no small measure to the increased emphasis on health and hygiene in the school system, and to the island-wide program for training teachers for health instruction. Health is further improved by the more than $9,000,-000 spent per year, including a sizable amount from the federal government, on school lunches and milk stations, while the Department of Education also distributes free shoes to the poor.

Vocational training, even of the most rudimentary type, was a welcome innovation when the Second Unit Rural Schools were established. Today all of Puerto Rico is vocation-minded to such an extent that individual public schools can no longer cope with the entire problem of vocational training in an industrializing society and have been supplemented by vocational schools.

Padín was and is modern Puerto Rico's great culture hero in education. He set the pace and the norms for adjusting education to the changing culture's changing needs, and he achieved success largely because he insisted that the teaching, the talking, the discussions, the planning, be in the language that teachers, students, parents, administrators, knew best. But in 1936, in view of the dangerous tensions arising from Colonel Rigg's assassination, a number of eminent members of the U. S. Congress visited the island to see for themselves what the trouble was. Among them was Senator King of Utah, Chairman of the Senate's Committee on Insular Affairs, and his rather novel manner of correlating one problem with another in order to reach a solution came to have far-reaching effects on Puerto Rico's educational system. It was obvious that there was trouble in Puerto Rico; it became equally obvious to King that few Puerto Rican children knew English. There, to the powerful senator, lay the key to the Puerto Rican "problem."

Padín's resignation was accepted, and his successor's appointment was confirmed by the Senate only after he had pledged himself again to put major stress on the teaching of English. Again English became a political football, rather than a desirable subject of study. In Puerto Rico the Commissioner of Education found himself in much trouble and resigned in 1945. From then until 1948 there was no commissioner at all, no responsible head of the school system, as qualified Puerto Ricans refused to accept the job unless they could work out the problem of English instruction according to their best judgment and by the best pedagogic means, instead of obeying the U. S. Senate, whose members included few, if any, skilled educators. The federal law providing for the election of 1948, when the people elected their own governor for the first time, also stated that the governor would appoint his own Commissioner (now Secretary) of Education, responsible to the people of Puerto Rico rather than to the Senate of the United States.

One result has been a dramatic expansion of education in all its forms and institutions. Puerto Rico's sudden upsurge of interest in education, of popular hunger for learning, is not unique to the island; it is symptomatic of a similar surge in all the world's new emerging societies—in Ghana and Nigeria, Thailand, India, Indonesia. Many of the thousands of visitors from such countries are particularly interested in the methods used in Puerto Rico, not only for expansion, but also for effective instruction. There is still much groping, much study, much dissention. But Puerto Rico is not unique in that respect, either. Even in the United States modern educators are obviously and bitterly at each other's throats— in magazines and in books, on lecture platforms and in board meetings, in faculty meetings and in personal gossip —over the vital issue of whether or not today's education prepares American pupils and students for the demands of the future.

There are many in Puerto Rico today who are proud of the obvious progress that has been made, of the goals toward which the educators are working, of the means used to achieve those goals. There are others—and some jingoistic U.S. journalists echo them—who again make a political foot- ball out of the subject of English. They claim correctly that today's children are not yet learning English fast enough and well enough, and insist that this proves the present govern- ment to be extremely nationalistic and to be actually aiming at the island's eventual independence. Still others are dis- tressed because education in the States is as yet much bet- ter than that in Puerto Rico.

Whatever the situation's realities, the statistics that in- dicate progress are impressive.

In 1940 the total enrollment in schools, public and pri- vate, elementary, intermediate, and high, was 296,679. By 1958 the figure had more than doubled, to 614,000. In 1933, 61,655 children were born in Puerto Rico; 28,121 of them, or 42.3 per cent, found their way into the schools in 1940. In 1958, 67.2 per cent of the 85,455 children born seven years earlier were in the first grade.

One of the prime aims of the Department of Education is to make schooling universal, to create conditions under which every child of school age is actually in class, and illit- eracy is finally eliminated as a social scourge. Another aim is to keep the children in school as long as possible, with a maximum number continuing through high school. The increase in enrollment in high schools, public and private, has been phenomenal. In 1940 it was 12,440; in 1958 it was 59,312.

The regular school program is accompanied by a special adult educational program aimed primarily at the elimination of illiteracy. Its standards are high, defining literacy as the equivalent of a third-grade education, rather than as the mere ability to read and write. The program was inaugurated in 1954 with the organization of 548 groups in both rural and urban zones, and an enrollment of 17,892. In 1958 there were 1,782 groups, with 32,895 students. A total of 118,258 adults had by then taken advantage of the courses offered. Results in a nutshell are: in 1898, 85 per cent of the population was illiterate; the 1950 census, which judged the matter solely by answers to the question "Can you read and write?" listed nearly 25 per cent of the population as being illiterate; the 1960 census will show the figure to have been reduced to 10 per cent; by 1970 or earlier the entire population may well be literate, even according to the "third-grade" definition.

The University of Puerto Rico shows a similar growth. Its enrollment of 4,987 in 1940 had grown to 16,753 in 1958. A School of Medicine and a School of Dentistry have been added, and today the university is becoming an inter-American center for the study of atomic energy and its peacetime applications.

Vocational schools, public and private, show a corresponding growth in a society that is hungry for education and training.

The number of teachers has risen from 6,294 in 1940 to 12,302 in 1958.

According to a United Nations report of 1957, 29.9 per cent of Puerto Rico's total population was in that year enrolled in the elementary, secondary, and vocational schools. The figure was the world's highest; that for the United States, 22.2 per cent, came next. If you lump all the Puerto

Ricans who are today taking courses of one kind or another, in the regular public and private schools, in night classes, in vocational schools, in the university and in other institutions of higher learning, you find that well over one third of all the island's people are receiving some kind of formal education. Again the figure is the world's highest; in the United States it is less than one fourth.

Such statistics are all the more remarkable in view of Puerto Rico's relative poverty. Every government department makes clamorous demands on the limited budget, but education has top priority. Approximately one third of the budget now goes for educational efforts. The Department of Education spends about sixty-seven dollars annually for every pupil enrolled in its schools and its various special didactic activities. Admittedly that is low when compared with the $200-odd spent by New York and New Jersey, but it is remarkably high when compared with the twenty-four dollars Puerto Rico spent per pupil in 1940.

The teachers, as dedicated a group as one can find anywhere, are necessarily overworked and underpaid. Despite heroic efforts and dramatic gains, there are not yet enough teachers and classrooms to meet the urgent needs. Nearly seventy per cent of the pupils in the urban and rural public elementary schools suffer from the "double enrollment" system, under which a teacher has one class in the morning and another in the afternoon, while the pupils receive only half a day's schooling. Admittedly that system, which is regarded as a temporary makeshift to get as many children into the schools as rapidly as possible, has its limitations as pedagogy.

The question of language is intimately tied up with that of culture, and both are extremely difficult in the present era of rapid culture change—much more difficult than they were during the revolutionary period of 1940-8. In those days it was relatively easy to recognize the vital importance of Puerto Rico's getting its own education into its own hands.

The basic principle that education had to be shaped to fit Puerto Rico's cultural life was easy to grasp; the matter of defining that life in an era of rapid change was more difficult, took longer, and led to much conflict.

The truth of the matter is that modern Puerto Rico is not exclusively a society with an old Spanish culture. It is a society that prides itself on bridging the gap between the Latin and Anglo-American cultures. Its "dual citizenship" in the political sphere exists also in the cultural. In fact, Puerto Rico is today a bi-cultural society in which the educators are hard-put to incorporate both sides in their curricula and methodologies.

In an excellent pamphlet published in 1956 by the Department of Education, Leonard S. Kenworthy went so far as to say: "With close economic and political ties with the United States, with rapid industrialization and urbanization, and a growing feeling of kinship to the States, the question of how much of their Spanish background can be retained in the next generation continues to cause controversy. Certainly older and even middle-aged people are proud of their Spanish cultural heritage, but whether this pride can be developed in the oncoming generation is still open to question. Already most of the African and Indian heritage has disappeared; whether the same will eventually happen to the Spanish heritage remains to be seen."

In the matter of art and music, in which, according to Kenworthy, the Puerto Rican schools are still deficient, the culture question must necessarily play an important role. However, the question of English instruction is still by far the most difficult in the educational struggle. It is widely recognized that the Puerto Ricans must make every effort to become relatively bilingual as rapidly as possible, though the governor has added the cogent admonition that they must be careful not merely to become "semi-literate in two languages." As stated above: when the process seems too slow, the political opposition that advocates statehood charges the government with nationalism and with secret aims for independence; on the other hand, when a consultant some years ago urged intensification of English instruction largely because migrants to New York are handicapped by not knowing the language, he was widely attacked for wanting to use the school system to train Puerto Ricans primarily for export.

Some years ago the Department hired Dr. Charles C. Fries, former Director of the English Language Institute of the University of Michigan, to make studies and recommend solutions. The present program is based on his recommendations. Under his supervision the Department wrote the "Fries American English Series" of texts, as well as teachers' guides for the various grades. They were printed by the Department of Education press.

Today English is taught daily as a required subject in all the grades from one to twelve. In the first three grades it is taught as an oral subject; reading and writing are not begun until the third grade. The general aim is to so shape courses and methods that high-school graduates can take full advantage of the university, where a number of non-Puerto Rican faculty members lecture in English, and where a number of texts are perforce also in that language. In the English classes in high school special stress is placed on United States history, culture, and literature.

The program for English instruction, aided by special texts that were designed to meet Puerto Rico's specific needs, has been planned with great care and skill. But it cannot become effective immediately, if only because too many of the teachers are themselves still deficient in their knowledge of the language. As a result, the island's sixty-three Catholic schools and the new Catholic university in Ponce are today more effective in their teaching of English than the public-school system can be. The public-school system must take its teachers as they come and laboriously train them to be better. If they don't know much English, they must be taught. The Catholic schools have no difficulty in sending to the States for excellently trained English-speaking nuns. The difference, like everything else in Puerto Rico, has political repercussions. For years, and especially since the Commonwealth constitution provided for the complete separation of Church and State, Puerto Rico's two bishops have railed against Muñoz Marín over what the bishops called the "godlessness" and "materialism" of the government's present policies. At the same time, the bishops have tried in all conceivable ways, though without success, to regain a foothold in the school system, which had been virtually controlled by the Church during the Spanish days. In that situation it is easy for the opposition parties to fish for the Catholic vote by announcing that *they*, at least, are good Catholics, and to line up with the bishops in the never-ending war on the governor and his dramatic programs. They gain relatively few votes by such tactics, but that merely shows that in a society in which some eighty per cent of the people are Catholics, the political maneuverings of the Church and the political pronouncements of its local officials are not taken as seriously as they might be in the States, where the Catholics are a minority.

The public-school system cannot hire skilled continental English teachers, if only because they would cause friction by having to be paid more than Puerto Rico's teachers receive. Under the present system the regular class teachers handle English in the first three grades, though some of them necessarily do it by rote, knowing little English themselves. After that, however, the language is taught by a special corps of teachers who do nothing else. Improving their skill and preparation has been described in a recent official report as one of the department's most pressing problems. Between 1955 and 1959 more than 300 were sent to the States on special scholarships for a year each. Summer institute scholarships are planned for more. Special English classes for teachers have been and are being organized. A good supervisory program to keep track of results and to devise new methods is in the process of being created.

The department also offers special adult courses in English free to all Puerto Ricans who plan to migrate to the States.

All of which costs much money that is also badly needed for many other things, from nursery-schools to highways, from seaports to hospitals.

In a society that is rapidly drawing closer to the United States by means of its accelerated industrialization, vocational training ranks high in importance after English. In that field Puerto Rico has also developed an impressive program, which fascinates visitors from Latin America, Asia, and Africa, whose countries, too, face the drastic changes and new ways of life that result from industrialization. Although systematic vocational training in agriculture, in home economics, and in trade and industry was begun in 1931 under the United States Smith-Hughes Law, it had its greatest impetus after 1948.

After World War II the government bought a wealth of war-surplus machinery and equipment and used it for founding what was then the world's largest single vocational school, in which some 3,000 students soon began to learn fifty different trades, ranging from welding to cooking, from carpentry to electronics, from blacksmithing to airplane mechanics. After 1950, however, the school was decentralized for the purpose of better serving all of Puerto Rico's people. Today vocational training is offered in the general categories of agriculture, industrial arts, home economics and native handicrafts, business, trades, practical nursing. It is offered in distinct vocational schools, in the regular public schools, and in night classes, to young people, adults, and veterans, by regular teachers and specially trained itinerant teachers. In special cases it is offered to prospective workers in new factories which could previously not have found their required skills in Puerto Rico. In 1940 some 450 students received vocational training. By 1958 the figure had risen to 118,749.

Ever since Padín organized his Second Unit Rural Schools, the island's educators have been in close touch with the people, the voters, the parents. In March and April, 1958, the Department, under the leadership of Dr. Efraín Sánchez Hidalgo, Secretary of Education, organized public hearings in all parts of the island, at which more than 102,000 adults expressed themselves on what they wanted from the school system. Carefully studied and tabulated, the results were revealing. While a few diehards lamented the new directions and wanted to see a return to the "good old days," by far the majority wanted the new programs speeded up and made more effective. They wanted to do away with the system of double enrollment. They asked for much more stress on English, more history, more geography, more information on the wide world of which Puerto Rico is now becoming a functioning part. They asked for stricter standards, under which their children would be promoted from class to class *only* on merit. They requested more homework, drastic cuts in absenteeism, and greater retention in the schools, aimed at having the pupils go as far as possible, preferably through high school. They seemed to be thoroughly aware that the present serious problem of technological unemployment is at least partly rooted in inadequate education. A large number talked about the dignity of the teaching profession; they wanted both the pay and the prestige of the teachers to be increased. Many were interested in the school health programs and asked for annual physical examinations for pupils as well as teachers. Some wanted the school lunch program extended through the serving of light lunches at ten in the morning. Finally, the testifying parents demanded an even closer relationship than has existed heretofore between the school and the community.

I have been a teacher in the States. I have attended P.T.A. meetings, have talked at P.T.A. meetings. The kind of vital interest that was shown in Puerto Rico by 100,000 adults attending special hearings may well be envied by thousands of U.S. educators.

In response to the demands that both the skills and the prestige of teachers be improved, the department has worked out a series of norms and procedures for teacher promotion. Today teachers may be promoted *only* on merit; seniority, nepotism, and political influence no longer count in the process.

The department's publication activities are extremely important. A number of the texts, for instance, have to be specially written to fit the island's needs. Sometimes they are books that are available in the States in English and need merely to be translated into Spanish; more often, like the "Fries American English Series," they must be created from scratch. Then, too, the department publishes three periodicals, *Educación* is a monthly with a circulation of 16,000, distributed to teachers, dealing with a great variety of educational problems. *Escuela* is a weekly paper distributed free to pupils in the elementary and high schools; it deals with literature, art, science, general information, the English language, biographies, and school notes. More than 300,000 copies go every other week to pupils in the elementary schools; on alternate weeks 100,000 copies go to the high schools. Finally there is *Semana,* a weekly with a circulation of nearly 300,000 copies, published for free distribution to adults. A magazine with cultural orientations, dealing with a miscellany of things from all over the world, it is designed to improve the level and widen the scope of the people's cultural interests.

It should be added that all traces of political partisanship are excluded from those publications, as they are from the Education Department's radio and television stations.

Station WIPR—TV, in San Juan, was opened in 1958, and is the only television station in the Spanish-speaking world that deals exclusively with educational programs. Previously there had been educational radio, as there still is. Commercial advertising is as rigidly excluded as is politics from both the radio and television programs. Music (for instance the Casals festivals), literature, drama, the problems of labor, of health, of education, news of the day and the world, play important roles in the programs. Now the medium of television is being studied toward the end of organizing courses in subjects for which the teacher-shortage is most acute. Courses in mathematics and physics were successfully transmitted in 1958, and at the time of the present writing a course in conversational English is being offered to a total enrollment of more than 3,000. Among the new courses offered in 1959 and given by various members of the university faculty are: Universal Literature; The Spanish Language; The Structure of the Universe; and Principles of Economics. New television courses are being developed constantly; Puerto Rico's educational pioneering in that field is impressive. All students enrolling in such courses receive free specially prepared printed materials to accompany the broadcasts. Final examinations are required for credit.

All such steps, and many more, are completely new to the Puerto Rican scene, and some are new to the general scene of education. But they represent a ferment that will inevitably bring good results within a relatively short time. The most important aspect of that ferment is perhaps the encouragement of self-criticism and the invitation of criticism from without. In 1959 the Commonwealth brought three eminent European educators to Puerto Rico, to study the educational system and make pertinent recommendations. One was Danish, the second German, and the third Italian. Their report, which they had agreed to make unanimous in all its specific parts, was not yet available for public perusal at the time of the present writing, but that they were asked to prepare it is important.

An educational system taken in its entirety is always a mirror of the total society in which it functions. When the society is in rapid change, socially, economically, politically, the educational system must struggle against the inevitable lag also to change. But Puerto Rico is today not only examining its own problems, but is also reaching elsewhere throughout the world for solutions to those problems; precisely as many parts of that world are reaching toward Puerto Rico for solutions to *their* problems. Let the present trends continue another decade, and Puerto Rico may well develop educational innovations as important and effective in their way as Denmark's world-famous folk high schools are in theirs.

16

Civic Employment

In a message to the legislature, March 20, 1952, Governor Muñoz Marín discussed health activities and education as being vitally necessary for improving the standard of living and for the purpose of giving impetus to economic expansion. For such ends, he said, the government would need money—and ever more money. Where was that money to come from? It would come "from six sources, most of which are not at present being adequately used: (1) taxes which are collected; (2) taxes which are [now] not collected; (3) federal aid; (4) the issuing of Commonwealth and municipal bonds; (5) economies effected by running the government more efficiently; (6) civic action in the community to solve its own problems. There has been only very slight action on the part of the community, except through the government, in creating on its own initiative a school, or a cooperative, or in helping to purify the waters of a river, or to provide a library, or to provide food and shelter in cases of extreme necessity."

The governor talked about community participation in terms of cash returns to the Commonwealth. However, the poet and humanist who constantly distinguishes for his people between creation and mere acquisition, who coined the subtle and deeply human term "Operation Serenity," does not think merely in terms of cash returns. When, under Agriculture's Social Programs Administration, men, women, and children give of their own time and strength to build their own new modest homes and those of their neighbors, when the Co-operative Development Administration persuades groups of neighbors to organize themselves into associations for joint action toward improved economic strength, Muñoz is even more aware of the spiritual than the financial returns. Puerto Rico's new drives toward organized self-help at community levels are the island's most eloquent expressions by far of a new, modern phase of its ancient sense of creative, democratic civilization.

With the aim of fostering the growth of the creative human spirit, of encouraging people to help themselves through their own efforts, the Division of Community Education was created by legislative action May 14, 1949. Operating within the Department of Education, it started from scratch with inadequate funds, no staff, no materials. All it had was a vital idea blessed by the governor and his legislature. The Statement of Motives of the bill creating the organization, written by Muñoz Marín himself, says in part that it is to give "to the communities and to the Puerto Rican Community in general the wish, the tendency, and the way of making use of their own aptitudes for the solution of their own problems. . . ." The statement goes on to say: "The community should not be civically unemployed. The community can be constantly and usefully employed in its own services, in terms of pride and satisfaction for the members thereof."

Fred G. Wale, formerly with the Julius Rosenwald Fund, was appointed head of the division. Throughout the succeeding decade he has strived both creatively and defensively to adhere to the organization's prime aim of education and training in the basic democratic processes. His basic philosophy is admired by many, attacked by some. His sole aim is education in the spirit and processes of community self-help. Having acquired that spirit, he insists, communities will decide for themselves on the creative programs to which they wish to dedicate it, and will seek means for learning the required skills.

Puerto Rico's Division of Community Education is known outside of the island for the excellence of the documentary films it makes and uses for the purpose of arousing civic consciousness. The New York and Chicago offices of the Commonwealth's Department of Labor lend such films to schools and other institutions. UNESCO and the Technical Co-operation Administration of the U. S. Department of State purchase many copies for distribution throughout the world.

One of these films is the famous *El Puente, The Bridge*. Simply, but with a high degree of technical and artistic excellence, it portrays the story of how and why a rural community built a foot bridge over the apparently peaceful Río Cañabón.

A small stream, easily forded in good weather, the Cañabón flows near the city of Barranquitas. About a hundred children who live near its bank have to cross it twice daily on their way to and from school, as do their parents bound to or from the city. In rainy weather, however, the crossing used to be dangerous, if not impossible, because the river becomes torrential. Flash floods roaring down from the mountains have in the past threatened the lives of several people who were caught on the stepping stones of the fords; a few years ago a schoolboy was swept downstream by such a flood and narrowly escaped either drowning or being battered on the rocks. If it rained while the children were in school on the other side, they couldn't get back—sometimes for days at a stretch. The result was that if it even looked like rain, mothers would not permit their children to go to school, while many of the men in the sixty families affected also had to stay at home and lose working days and wages.

It is estimated that before the bridge was built, a hundred children lost about half of their school time. For decades the people affected had clamored to various government officials for a bridge. Once the neighbors had built a makeshift wooden bridge, but it was washed down the river in the first flood.

Then in 1949 the Division of Community Education selected one of the most respected men in the district, brought him to San Juan for a training period, and sent him back with the title of Group Organizer.

He began to discuss community problems with the people, and to distribute thousands of booklets on life in Puerto Rico, on health, on new ways of doing things, on many subjects that were interesting but had nothing to do with a bridge. He visited everybody for miles around, driving a jeep on the often all-but-impassable roads, and after a while he began to paper his district with colorful posters announcing free movies on certain nights. On those occasions he set up a portable screen on a hilltop, turned on a portable generator he had in the back of his jeep, and showed a film of Puerto Rican life to the assembled people, many of whom had never seen motion pictures before. The films were fascinating, but they were still in no way related to the bridge that was on everybody's mind.

In December 1950 a group of twenty-four neighbors called on him to discuss the question of why a government would spend so much money on movies, but not a cent for providing safe passage across a river that constantly cut into their earning power and the education of their children. He listened sympathetically and hinted that the community's people might build the bridge themselves. That was not exactly a new idea, but it was staggering in its implications and almost an impossibility to isolated countryfolk who had no money and few, if any, of the required technical skills. But the organizer kept encouraging them, and from the time of the first discussion the bridge became the central theme of his conversations in the community. Twice a month, between January and July 1951, he organized meetings to discuss the bridge from all angles. Gradually, those meetings began to result in action.

Members of the community raised $125 among themselves in pennies, nickels, and dimes. One man had had some construction experience; encouraged by the organizer, he designed a concrete bridge, specifying for reinforcement two old truck chassis he had seen in a junk yard in Barranquitas which they might hope to obtain as a gift. The design was submitted to the local district engineer of the island's Department of Interior; he checked the plans, improved on them, and gave advice for construction. A school was being repaired nearby, and there was some lumber left over; the people asked for this lumber and obtained it as a donation. People waited on the mayor of Barranquitas and persuaded him to contribute eighty bags of cement and 600 pounds of iron rods from the city's stock. Other donations—of cement, of nails, of tools, and of the two truck chassis—began to come in. By July 1951 the community had gathered all the materials needed for their bridge.

The people now elected one of their neighbors as project foreman. He began his work on July 12, sending out daily calls for the number of helpers he would need for the job— after regular working hours in the fields, on Saturdays and Sundays, whenever people had a few hours or a day to spare. He had no labor problems. When he called for ten helpers, fifty were likely to come—men, women, and children—eager and interested.

The bridge was completed after twenty-two days, during which about sixty people had contributed their work, and even the dedication, attended by the entire community, was something new in Puerto Rican affairs. The local politicos were present only as welcome guests, not to make speeches.

The little boy who had been swept down the river the year before made the principal speech, and a mother cut not only one ribbon, but a dramatic series of them.

After the bridge's completion the Division's staff in San Juan undertook the preparation of a new documentary film, depicting the entire story, from the troubled school situation that had existed before the bridge had been built, the misadventure of the boy who had nearly drowned in a flash flood, the anguish of the parents when the weather looked threatening, through the first talks of the group organizer, the talks in the community, the gradual growth of community determination, the efforts to obtain materials, to the actual construction and dedication. The script was written carefully, and the picture was made on the scene with no professional actors; the community's people played the same parts they had played while planning and building. Incidental music was composed for the picture; posters were painted and reproduced by the silk-screen method.

That *El Puente* is today being shown in many parts of the United States and in many foreign countries is an incidental result. It was designed to be shown throughout Puerto Rico to hundreds of rural audiences, not for the purpose of persuading them to build bridges, but to stimulate them into saying: "Those people are poor country people, just like ourselves. If they could solve one of their community problems in that fashion, why can't we get together, discuss our own problems, and perhaps swing into some kind of similar action?"

In the *barrio* Mariana, the sugar zone, where most workers earn their poor livings by cutting cane, individual farming is almost unknown. The people, however, wanted to augment their food supply. The group organizer encouraged them—with talks that went on for months and covered every phase of the problem—to create a community garden. They obtained land from the local school in return for the promise of vegetables for the school lunches. They sent soil samples to the Agricultural Extension Agency, had them analyzed, and requested advice on proper practices from that agency and the Soil Conservation Service. They obtained good seeds from the university's experiment station, on their promise to set aside a portion of the garden for growing seeds for future years. They took up a collection of pennies and dimes for the purchase of fertilizers and the materials for the fence that was needed to keep cattle out of the garden. The entire community turned out to prepare the soil and cultivate the garden under the direction of an elected foreman. Among the results were: (1) crops so large that they astonished members of the community; (2) an education in proper agricultural practices, which, as the result of direct experience voluntarily sought and intimately related to the community's problems, was far more effective than any mere lecture courses could have been; (3) close liaison between the community and the various agricultural agencies which promises large returns in the years to come; (4) marked improvement in individual gardens of the neighbors and some decrease in cash expenditure for food; and (5) increases of the school lunches given to children.

The *barrio* Santa Olaya in Bayamón had only two one-room schools serving the first four grades. For fifth grade and up, children had to walk a long distance to another school and cross rivers that were sometimes in flood. This meant that few children in the *barrio* ever went beyond the fourth grade. The hard-pressed government had no money available for the construction of another school. Finally, stimulated by the group organizer, the community decided to build a school for the fifth and sixth grades. Committees were appointed to consult with various agencies on the proper plans for such a project. One group went to San Juan to visit the Planning Board, not only obtaining much valuable technical help and advice, but also returning to spread the message among their rural neighbors of what the Planning Board, always an august body in the eyes of simple farmers, meant to the people of Puerto Rico. The Department of Education promised to provide a teacher as soon as the school was finished. Collections were taken up. As the *barrio* was poor and was able to raise only eighty dollars in two months' time, it was decided to build a wooden school instead of the concrete building that had been envisaged in the beginning. Wood, nails, tools, and paint were gathered wherever they could be found, and the *barrio*'s entire population turned out to do the work, the women preparing hot meals while the men labored.

The planning of this venture had begun in March 1951. The school was inaugurated in September. As usual, the community itself conducted the inauguration, but one of its members was a Puerto Rican soldier from Santa Olaya, recently returned from the Korean War. He made the main speech, expressing his pride in being able to participate in that one example of the things he had fought for on the other side of the world.

Now the community of Santa Olaya has begun to study other problems. Its people have talked of their need for a water tank for the school and have considered building a community center.

The directives of the Division for Community Education called for the use of "motion pictures, radio, books, pamphlets and posters, phonograph records, lectures and group discussions," and one of the first steps was the rental of an old market hall in San Juan, which was converted into a studio, office building, and general workshop. While one group in the Division began the important work of selecting and training an adequate staff for work in the field, another group in the studios and in the shops turned out materials for use by those representatives. A similar organization in the mainland United States would be able to obtain a wealth of such materials at little cost in the form of rented films and educational pamphlets and posters, turned out by the thousands in Washington and in various other cities. But in

Puerto Rico the need was for materials in Spanish, dealing in the simplest possible terms with various aspects of the Puerto Rican problem. It was therefore necessary to start from scratch to create these materials. This was done with the help of a group of young Puerto Rican writers, artists, composers, photographers, printers, and other craftsmen, who were thereby granted new outlets for their own creative impulses.

The old market is today a beehive of activity. The booklets that are there produced include an annual almanac stressing the Puerto Rican scene and dealing with such special subjects as good land use, health, etc. The almanac form assures that thousands of country people refer to it again and again throughout the year. There are special booklets on health; there is one on life in various parts of Puerto Rico, produced for the benefit of those many rural people who have never been far beyond their own valleys; there is another on how people live in various other parts of the world, how they work and how they shape their environments toward the improvement of life.

By March 1959 the division had produced forty films and had eight more in production, varying, one from the other, over a wide range. Like *El Puente, Una Voz en la Montana* (*A Voice in the Mountain*) re-enacts the entire story of a community effort; it deals with the finally successful struggles of an illiterate laborer to organize a night class for illiterate adults. *Los Peloteros* (*The Ballplayers*) runs one and a half hours and is the longest film made by the organization. Although its script is fiction, it is eminently and recognizably true to Puerto Rican life. Both as an example to adults and as a warning to beware of pitfalls it tells, charmingly, the story of the trials and tribulations endured by a group of poor boys in their efforts to raise money for uniforms for their baseball team. *Modesta* is a film that tells the apocryphal story of how a group of country women won improved treatment for themselves by staging a revolt against their hus-

bands. It won signal honors in both the Venice and Edin-
burgh film festivals during the summer of 1957. However,
despite its recognition abroad, and despite its present role in
fostering a concept of their own worth and dignity among
Puerto Rico's rural women, it was *not* borrowed by the group
of nine eminent Moslem educators who went to Puerto Rico
for ideas a few years ago.

Several films reproduce musical expressions of the island's
folk life and lore. There are films that deal with problems of
soil erosion, agricultural improvement, consumer education,
health, and the like. They derive their beauty in part from
their simplicity; each of them is clearly understandable by
every *jíbaro*, educated or illiterate. Together they comprise
a new expression in Puerto Rico's folk art.

A number of the posters used for advertising the films are
now collectors' items, and several of them are nearly always
reproduced in the various annual books, published in several
countries, dealing with the world's best poster art.

The report of March 1959 also lists twenty-eight books
and booklets written, designed, illustrated, and printed in the
Division's central shops for free distribution throughout the
countryside. These, like the almanacs, cover a wide range of
subjects: nutrition; housing; the world of children; problems
of migrants to the mainland; family life; the rights of
women; Christmas songs; hurricane damage. Most of them
were prepared to complement specific films.

The Division has forty-three field workers, each supplied
with a jeep, a projector, a generator, and other needed equipment. Mrs. Wale, Doña Carmen Isales, is in charge of the
important work of selecting and training field representatives. Hundreds of applicants for these field positions have
been interviewed. The hard lesson the successful candidates
have had to learn is that it is not at all their job to persuade
people to build bridges, schools, roads, to create gardens, or to
build latrines. It is to encourage people to develop the initiative, the ability to plan, and the needed discipline which will

eventually result in community-created bridges and the like. At first it is always difficult for prospective group organizers to realize that they are not leaders or teachers, that they are merely catalytic agents whose job it is to encourage people to develop and act upon their own ideas. A group organizer may be firmly convinced that the thing his people need most is a new and pure water supply. But he says nothing about it, and if they develop a desire for a kitchen in which school lunches may be cooked for their children, or an improved road, or a community center, he encourages them to translate that idea, and not his own, into action. The basic concept there is that community spirit and enterprise have a much better chance of growing around an idea that springs from the community itself than around something a government employee preaches as being for the people's good.

I asked Doña Carmen about her standards for selecting organizers. She said: "They must be respected at home, believe in our basic philosophy, dedicate themselves to it, and prove their ability to work democratically. We don't discriminate against people who hold a Ph.D. or a Master degree. A number of our men have graduated from the university, but one has finished only eighth grade. He has the confidence of his people, his work is outstandingly effective, and he has by now, through sheer interest in his work, learned to write analytical reports that any highly trained social worker could be proud of. UNESCO published one of them recently."

Although the Division's general philosophy and approach seem eminently sound and bring dramatic results, they are not universally accepted or understood by professional people. Many Puerto Ricans may grant that the Division of Community Education is doing good work, even though they may know next to nothing about its fundamental purposes.

I have heard at least one eminent Puerto Rican educator rail against the program because he thought that it embodied a serious basic error: one cannot trust uneducated and often illiterate people to choose their own paths for salvation; they

simply don't know what is good for them. Before being permitted to embark on community projects, said the critic, they
must be educated in such things as the co-operative movement, the value of good housing, the benefits from drinking
milk and brushing teeth, the dangers lurking in impure
water; they cannot merely get together, discuss community
problems, conclude that too many children are sick or that
they need a road, and then go out on their own initiative and
get the information they need for effective remedial action.
People don't do that kind of thing, he said; they don't know
enough; they need guidance. But more and more people *are*
now doing them, and the critic himself is coming around to
the point of supporting the program.

The critic had voiced a point of view common in many
parts of the world. Many countries have community programs today, and their great value is being recognized to an
increasing extent. Such programs play important roles in the
current transformations of India, Israel, and the Philippines.
The United Nations and the U. S. International Co-operation
Administration foster them in many countries. Often they do
much to spread and strengthen the spirit of democracy,
though they are also used by the nondemocratic countries.
Even Generalissimo Trujillo likes to see people doing things
for themselves, as long as they do the things he tells them
to do; it saves him money. The construction of the Moscow
subway, with private citizens turning out by the hundreds
of thousands to donate their labor, was a community project on a vast scale. China is today rebuilding itself in large
measure with the voluntary labor of millions of Chinese who
may well like to improve their lives through such work, even
though it was planned and directed by their Communist
overlords.

But when we study the approaches of other community
programs, we find that virtually all of them differ from
Puerto Rico's in one vital respect. They are, in effect, extension programs whose field workers have been trained as

technicians. The latter learn something about agriculture, construction, child care, sanitation, or co-operatives, and then go forth to spread their various gospels and to organize communities along specific, dictated lines. A field worker in Puerto Rico's Division of Community Education who becomes a technician in anything but the subtle business of helping to foster people's faith in themselves has outlived his usefulness as a group organizer. He may eventually become valuable as the director or foreman of a project decided upon by the community, but he is through as an educator.

That lesson must be understood by the field workers, as well as by all those who for one reason or another are in a position to collaborate with the Division. It is being learned, step by step as specific cases arise, and is now also beginning to influence American education. On two occasions, in 1958 and 1959, I have seen groups of thirty students from Sarah Lawrence College come to Puerto Rico for some ten days. On both occasions they spent at least half their time with the Division of Community Education, living in the modest homes of group organizers, attending community meetings, watching projects grow through discussion, seeing the films that helped them to grow. Both times the girls went back to Bronxville, New York, enormously stimulated. Vast new vistas had been opened for them. They had seen a way of teaching that was new to them, and had learned many exciting things that illuminated and invigorated their more formal classroom work.

The Division's methods often seem slow and cumbersome if success is to be measured by the number of community projects undertaken. Now, however, ten years after the Division's creation, the insistence on hurrying nobody, on merely aiding communities in clarifying their own problems and setting their own pace, has begun to pay dramatic dividends. A number or projects are now in various stages of progress, and many of them tie in directly with established government programs. As pointed out in other chapters, various governmental agencies are dedicated in part to the task of bringing to the island's people, as rapidly and as cheaply as possible, the benefits of electric power, of abundant pure water, of schools and free lunchrooms for children. All communities want such things immediately, but it is not always possible to bring them to any one community at a specified time. Suddenly, however, an authorized delegation from one part of the interior arrives in San Juan for a talk with the proper government official, and says: "We have studied our situation for a long time. We have too much illness and we know that the construction of a pure water system will help us to combat it. Give us technical help and advice, and perhaps some money for materials, and we will do all the construction and digging, without charging for the labor." Sometimes such delegations ask for money; sometimes they don't. Everything, including financing, has been thought out and talked out before the delegation goes elsewhere for help, and all rural communities take a deep pride in doing as much as possible by and for themselves. Now the particular delegation referred to is offering actively to help the government in one of its important programs, and so, also, to save the government and the taxpayers money.

So many offers of such "partnership" have been made in recent years that the government has created a special committee to deal with them, and has established a fund of $300,000 per year for meeting the requests. The committee is composed of the Director of the Division of Community Education and three top officials in the Department of Public Works. In that agency there is now an entire section that does nothing but render technical assistance, as requested, to the communities in which the Division's field men are working.

In April 1959 there were no fewer than 192 applications for such help, of which fifty-one, involving a total estimated cost of over half a million dollars, had been approved and were actually being carried out. The approved projects included four small schools, six community centers, fourteen roads averaging 1.5 miles each, nineteen aqueducts to bring good water to communities, one well plus pipes for the distribution of its water, and a school lunchroom. There is no estimate of how many meetings were held in the fifty-one communities involved before the requests were made—before decisions had been reached on priorities among the many things that any community might undertake at any time. The important thing is that no community sends a delegation beyond its borders with a request for help without first having gone over the entire problem so thoroughly that it knows exactly what it is doing.

Once such a request is received, the government committee's technical staff drafts detailed plans—as for a road or a water line—accompanied by a complete estimate of what it would cost to build the project by government efforts. These budgets are then mimeographed, and a copy is given to every family in the community concerned. Then begins the work of analyzing the estimates to determine what part of the total cost can be met by the community, in the form of skilled or unskilled labor, trucks, tools, various kinds of materials, rights of way over the land. That requires more meetings— nobody can know how many. Finally the community talks as follows to the San Juan committee: "The cost of the project is estimated at so and so much. But we are prepared to carry this or that percentage of it ourselves, according to our own calculations and division of labor. Can you help us with the rest? Give us technical supervision and let us go to work."

As stated, the fifty-one projects under way in April 1959 had a total estimated cost of over half a million dollars— $582,965.13, to be exact. But after studying the estimates, the various communities decided that they could themselves take care of $308,397.22, or more than half. All they finally asked for and all that those roads, pipelines, schools, etc., are costing the government is $274,567.91.

After Puerto Rico had turned the corner with the election

of 1940, one heard poor people everywhere on the island say of Muñoz Marín: "He is our leader who has given us faith in ourselves." The Division of Community Education was created for the purposes of helping that faith to grow and of channeling it into constructive action. A number of Puerto Ricans, who are today justifiably concerned over the problem of Muñoz Marín's successor, have begun to agree with Doña Inés, the governor's wife, who said to me in 1951: "That is the program which will produce the island's future leaders."

17

Culture Changes

THE Puerto Ricans have remained "Latin Americans" to a far greater extent than have the Mexicans in our Southwest. Their language, religion, literature, folklore, and abiding belief in the individual's worth had come to them from Spain at the height of her power, and remain integral parts of their culture. That culture, however, was modified after the conquest's first wave. Almost from the beginning there was a strong infusion of Indian blood and Indian adjustments to the environment. In many parts of the interior most of the rural Puerto Ricans still look like Indians. The aboriginal inhabitants were not exterminated as ruthlessly as some historians have claimed; many fled to the interior mountains, maintained themselves as long as they could, but gradually through the centuries took on the white man's ways, learned Spanish, and intermarried with the whites. Only their language and culture were exterminated, so that now little is left of them—a word here and there, some root crops, the hammock, and a few palm-thatch houses, which are rapidly being replaced by concrete constructions. African slaves, too, came to add their blood to the common stream, and their rhythms to the music. French, Italian, Corsican, and South American Creole settlers were taken in their stride, absorbed as Spanish-speaking Puerto Ricans.

As colonial subjects the Puerto Ricans were in no way full-fledged Spaniards. "Disdainful of metropolitan commands," they began, slowly, to alter their first heritage into something truly "Puerto Rican." They developed their own folklore, music, arts and crafts—however rudimentary and primitive —their own ways of living together, which in many ways set them apart from the Spanish officials, clerics, businessmen, and soldiers who infested the capital and often despised the rural people. What is typically Puerto Rican in the island's culture was developed in large measure as a social mechanism for defense against alien overlords and ubiquitous poverty. The foundation of the social structure came to be the family, each close-knit and huge, including all relatives of all ages and varying degrees of legitimacy, each a vast and smoothly functioning mutual-aid society, held together by the fact that there was no other social aid and no political power for attaining it.

But despite such modifying influences, Puerto Rico has through the centuries kept alive something vital of Spain's ancient culture, as is attested by the several great Spaniards who have settled on the island in recent decades and obviously feel at home there. Among those notable migrants— who are themselves sources of deep pride to the island's people—have been Juan Ramón Jiménez, winner of the Nobel Prize for Literature, who died in San Juan in 1958, and Pablo Casals. One doubts, however, if Don Juan and Don Pau, both embattled democrats and fighters for human dignity, would have liked living in Puerto Rico before 1940, when we Americans were still running things with a rather high hand.

The coming of the North Americans—regarded by many Latins as materialistic, godless, Protestant enemies—precipitated a profound culture crisis. Members of the lower classes, to be sure, may not have been seriously disturbed about their new masters from the United States. They were already accustomed to being exploited by their Spanish overlords, and we Americans proved somewhat more humane than the Spaniards had been. But the intellectuals and the upper classes often found it difficult to adjust themselves to the new regime. At one end were the fanatics who wanted by any and all means to retain Puerto Rico's culture—all of it, regardless of whether or not it had outlived its usefulness. It was from that element that the Nationalists drew their adherents, and it was the members of that group who regarded the assassination of Colonel Riggs as a patriotic act. At the other end, and especially in business and professional circles, were the new super-Americans who set out enthusiastically to change their cultures with the same ease with which they changed their coats. They embraced "Americanism" passionately with a terrible, uncritical fervor, and became a ridiculous element in Puerto Rico's life.

There was the famous story, for instance, of the salesman from Illinois who was introduced to one of these superpatriots. Asked what part of Illinois he came from, he answered "Springfield."

"Ah," came the impassioned answer. "You must indeed be proud. Springfield, Illinois, the home of Abraham Lincoln, 'the Emancipator,' the greatest man who ever lived. Doesn't it fill you with pride to have sprung from the soil made sacred by Lincoln?"

Whereupon the salesman turned to another man and said: "What's the matter with him? Is he nuts?"

The cultural nationalists and the superpatriots still exist in Puerto Rico, though in modified form; today they don't feel that they need to parade either their Puerto Rican culture or their Americanism quite as fervently as they once did. Side by side with them in today's cultural scene are the remnants of the former unassimilated Spaniards who stayed on the island after the advent of the Americans. These are the "Spanish merchants" who are still identifiable as a class and continue to feel superior to the Puerto Ricans. They have their own social life and their elaborate, exclusive club, where they maintain "white supremacy" and have worshipped at the shrine of Francisco Franco since the outbreak of the Spanish Civil War. Under the American flag, too, came a number of Americans, and their influx has accelerated dramatically since the end of World War II. Now there are about 25,000 of them. In many ways they, too, have their own life, their own social affairs, their own schools, their own church services, their own Jewish center. A few of them still talk in terms of an "American colony" and like to tell everybody who will listen that the Puerto Ricans "hate us." But, the former gulf between continental Americans and Puerto Rican citizens of the United States is now narrowing rapidly.

The year 1940 was every bit as great a turning point in the cultural sense as in the economic. The Spanish-oriented indigenous Puerto Ricans had never before been able to achieve great and constructive things for themselves—except the near-miracle of survival *as a people*. Now suddenly, and without experience in such matters, they released their latent energies by "borrowing" a number of culture traits from Anglo-America. From a broader viewpoint: after 1940 the Anglo-American culture of the United States effectively joined forces with Puerto Rico's Latin American culture in the effort to reach a common goal. The far-reaching importance of that union, especially in the realm of inter-American relations, is only now beginning to be realized. But Puerto Rico's leaders and people are aware that their Commonwealth could not play an important role in those relations, could not capture the imaginations of the twenty Latin-American republics, were it not for the fact that Puerto Rico, while changing fast, remains essentially and proudly "Latin American."

When I talked to Muñoz Marín in San Juan in 1931, im-

mediately before he entered politics, he was deeply and re-
sentfully concerned with the effect the United States was
having on his people. The old, leisurely habit of sitting in
coffee houses for hours, discussing politics and praising or
damning poets, was giving way to a frenetic chase after the
dollar; the coffee houses themselves were disappearing in
favor of soda fountains. Up in the hills many *jíbaros* were
giving up their ancient faith and turning for salvation to the
Holy Rollers and other hysterical sects. The former solid
structure of family life showed signs of cracking. The people
were losing their cultural identity under the terrifying impact of the United States. Where would it end? Such thinking had much to do with the fact that Muñoz was in those
days an ardent advocate of Puerto Rico's independence. He
was afraid that under the American flag the Puerto Ricans
would turn into second-class citizens, similar to the Mexicans in Texas and in New Mexico. It was not until he had
found the formula for political action by which the Puerto
Ricans could save themselves by their own indigenous efforts
and thus retain a pride, *as Puerto Ricans*, in their own culture and life, that he also turned his back on independence
as a means of salvation.

Muñoz is profoundly, poetically aware that societies draw
the strength and unity that nourish their creative genius
from their own past, their historical roots, their culture, the
living thoughts of their forebears, and that nothing is
socially more devitalizing than their rejection—perhaps
through shame deriving from a colonial feeling of inferiority
—of their own cultural roots and evolutions. In all his actions and in all his speeches he strives to keep alive, in the
people of Puerto Rico, a proud sense of *being* Puerto Ricans
and thus also of being Latin Americans. Although while he
is one of the island's most ardent baseball fans, he is nevertheless apprehensive about the rapid influx of American innovations in the cultural scene and about English words in
the language, and does his personal best to keep them at a

minimum. At times he reminds one of Henry Ford, Sr., who, having done more than any other single individual to change the old American "way of life," grew sentimental and tried his best to preserve—or at least to immortalize—it through such monuments as Dearborn Village.

Muñoz's efforts, as translated into government programs, are immensely valuable. The officials of the government in power now respect Puerto Rico's cultural heritage, and work to keep it alive and viable; under Spain and the United States that heritage was largely ignored by the government to the point of being despised.

The Institute of Puerto Rican Culture, established by the legislature during the 1950's, plays an important role of balance and guidance in today's turbulent culture changes. Headed by Ricardo Alegría, an able anthropologist, it engages in a wide variety of activities. The excavation, study, and preservation of pre-Columbian archeological sites and artifacts are entrusted to this Institute, as are the study and recording of folk music, folklore, and old festival rites. Workshops and instructional help are provided for artists and aspiring artists. The Institute's exhibitions include permanent collections of folk art as represented by home-made guitars and similar instruments and the carvings of saints and the Three Kings, for which Puerto Rico is now becoming famous among collectors. There are also both permanent and temporary collections by modern Puerto Rican painters, engravers, and sculptors, while an increasing amount of attention is paid to the world art the Puerto Ricans had no chance of seeing a few decades ago unless they traveled to New York, London, Rome, or Paris. During 1958 the Institute's fine exhibition hall was for seven weeks used for the display of some of the world's greatest paintings borrowed from museums in the States and in Europe; at another time it housed a display of native African art—carved masks, objects of cast metal, textiles, artifacts of ivory, and the like.

That growing interest in the world's great art also appears

in the field of music. A few decades ago sophisticated Puerto Ricans, many of whom tended to reject Puerto Rico's indigenous music as being poor and naïve, had little opportunity to hear the world's best music unless they left the island for cultural refresher courses in New York. After World War II, however, when money became available for hiring artists, more and more famous musicians came to the island for concerts and concert tours. When Pablo Casals decided in 1956 to make Puerto Rico his permanent home, he stirred up a fervent interest in music, while also, by his own attitudes, strenghtening respect for Puerto Rican songs and other musical expressions. The annual Casals Festivals are today much more than tourist attractions; they are a source of deep pride to thousands of Puerto Ricans. The new Puerto Rican Symphony Orchestra, founded, directed, and at times conducted by "Don Pau," was considered impossible until the immediate time of its founding; today it is an integral part of the island's cultural life, and the government sees to it that it plays a number of open-air concerts where thousands of *jíbaros* can hear the world's greatest music free. Such activities have led toward the eventual creation of a Puerto Rican Conservatory of Music to train native musicians of the first rank.

The Institute of Puerto Rican Culture is also active in the preservation and restoration of buildings remaining from Spanish colonial days. In the interior town of San Germán the Porta Coeli Church, said to be one of the oldest in the Hemisphere, but long in a state of half-ruination, is now being restored. Those of San Juan's old fortifications which have been relinquished by the federal government are similarly being restored as historic monuments.

Following detailed studies by a number of experts, the Institute now heads a movement toward the eventual restoration of "Old San Juan," the Spanish walled city, to something of its earlier aspects. Public buildings in that part of the capital, for instance, cannot be changed except in manners prescribed by the Institute's experts. The government cannot, of course, exercise such control over privately owned houses; however, if you buy a house in old San Juan, and then repair and renovate it according to plans and designs furnished by the Institute of Culture, your reward is tax exemption for a number of years.

Most of the streets in Old San Juan are still paved with the glazed bricks that were once brought from Spain as ships' ballast; the city government is today not permitted to replace that paving with concrete; if necessary, it must be replaced with new glazed bricks. New neon signs may no longer be erected in that part of the city; a business establishment that has an old one must take it down within a period of years calculated to give the owner his money's worth in usage. Slowly, the old city—which had since the turn of the century degenerated into a vast, fetid, overcrowded slum—is being restored to its pleasant aspects of a century and more ago, while a number of good new shops, curio stores, and restaurants are moving into it. Like the French Quarter of New Orleans, which was once fashionable, then a slum, and is now fashionable again, Old San Juan is at the same time becoming a major tourist attraction.

Shortly after the American occupation, following the Spanish-American War, a number of overzealous citizens claimed that the massive old walls and gates, erected during the sixteenth, seventeenth, and eighteenth centuries, were outmoded and stood in the way of progress. As good Americans and progressive men of the world, those people were ashamed of such reminders of an age that was at the same time sleepier and more turbulent. On one festive occasion a large number of San Juan's inhabitants tore down one of the city's gates and a section of its walls. Those who remember that day of rejoicing now regret it bitterly. There is growing sentiment to the effect that the U.S. army and Washington's Department of the Interior should relinquish the old Morro and San Cristóbal forts and give them back to the people of

Puerto Rico, in whose history they once played so powerful a role. The American Commander in Chief of the armed forces in Puerto Rico lives in the beautiful "Casablanca," the "White House," which was built by Juan Ponce de Léon and belonged to the latter's descendants until the United States took it over. His occupancy of that lordly mansion was in the beginning undoubtedly arranged as a symbol of the United States's overlordship on the island. As such, it is today as out of date as is the former imperial Caribbean commission, and a number of Puerto Ricans now urge that the high military officer relinquish the island's most important single historic monument and give it to the Puerto Rican people.

As one of several conscious efforts to preserve and respect old culture values, the Institute of Puerto Rican Culture was founded precisely because the island's culture is changing with a dizzying speed. A new middle class, with new values, is rapidly growing in what a few decades ago was essentially a two-class society. Old social orientations are disappearing, and new relationships, new values—as yet but imperfectly defined and accepted—are beginning to take their places. Virtually everything described in this book—every bit of progress and change in agriculture, manufacturing, education, health, labor relations—both symbolizes and demands a cultural reorientation so drastic as to be almost terrifying. Many Puerto Ricans cannot keep up with such changes. "Where," wailed an old friend to me in 1958, echoing many others, "have the fine old days gone? What has happened to our old family unity, to the human respect that we had for each other, to the leisure with which we once contemplated and discussed our problems, to our intellectual honesty? They have been eliminated, replaced by a mad scramble for money, possessions, mediocrity."

The fact that he was only partly right didn't mean that he was not wholly distressed. Where *did* the good old days go? They went the way of the wolf packs of homeless waifs which once infested the cities. They went the way of ubiquitous starvation, illness, despair. Many another society in today's world is discovering that the good old ways of life can be preserved only at the cost of also preserving the bad old ways of misery.

My friend's distress over the modern scramble for material things is reflected on a higher level by Governor Muñoz Marín, whose thesis of "Operation Serenity" is an exortation to his people not to be carried away by the shabby instinct for mere acquisition for its own sake. It was reflected in part by the government itself when in 1957 it imposed new excise and license taxes on automobiles. The more expensive the car, the higher both taxes are today; the newer the car, the more costly the annual license plates. The taxes were imposed in an effort to cure people of the senseless habit of buying new cars every year—thereby often remaining inextricably in debt to the finance companies and exporting millions of dollars annually that could be put to much better uses at home—for no better purpose than that of keeping up with a neurotic American trend.

The revolution of 1940 could take place, *had* to take place, for no other reason than that the good old ways of life had begun to break down long before, and the survival of Puerto Rico's people demanded that new ways be devised. The outstanding Puerto Rican composer, Rafael Hernández, wrote his haunting song *"Lamento Borincano,"* "Puerto Rican Lament," a decade before that climactic year. For a long time it was, and to some extent still is, Muñoz Marín's theme song, and when his people want to honor him, they serenade him with it. In two verses, the song describes the joy with which a *jíbaro,* singing happily, makes his way to the city with the mare that carries his crop to market. He plans to buy his old woman a new dress with the sale's proceeds. But the city is dead, the market is deserted, there is no sale. Sadly the little countryman makes his way home again in the evening, weeping and crying: "What will become of my Borinquen and my sons?" The song's melody became an immediate international success. It became a dance tune, was pirated in the United States, and was published with sentimental English words and the astonishing title: "Cuban Moonlight." In Puerto Rico today a number of upper-class people dislike hearing it, and dislike especially having visitors hear it; they are deeply ashamed of the former days of misery which gave rise to the present day of creation and hope.

The widespread desertion of rural areas and the phenomenal growth of the cities were symptomatic of Puerto Rico's modern culture changes long before the 1940 revolution. The movement is, of course, accelerated by today's industrialization, but what is truly new is the responsible attitude the present government takes toward it. Before the rise of the Popular Democratic party, there had been sporadic attempts at slum clearance and the creation of decent low-cost living quarters; after the great turning point these efforts came to form major parts of the government's many social programs.

When people first began to stream into the cities, they had no place to go. One after another, they took over fetid, infested areas, swamps, wastelands that nobody else seemed to want, and created new slum settlements. The city authorities could not cope with that frenetic trend. The newcomers built their houses at night and acquired uncanny skills at putting them together between sundown and sunup; when the sanitary inspectors arrived in the morning, they found the *faits accomplis* of new slum sections, housing thousands of people and often tapping nearby power lines for stolen electricity. The growth of city slums was accelerated immeasurably by every hurricane, which scattered parts of houses, doors, windows, to be picked up by all who wanted them.

The clearance of such slums and the substitution of decent houses immediately became one of the new government's major concerns. It will remain one for years to come.

Thousands of people still stream into the cities and still have no place to go on arrival. As fast as one slum is cleaned out, a new one springs up—especially in San Juan. Meanwhile, however, Puerto Rico's urban-renewal program is attracting world attention.

On a per-capita basis and almost on an absolute basis no part of the American Union, no state, uses federal aid for low-cost housing as enthusiastically and as well as does Puerto Rico. That, however, is only partially the result of the present government's deep concern for the welfare of its poor. It is also related to the fact that in Puerto Rico one finds fewer powerful financial interests vested in slums than on the mainland, where many real-estate operators find it more profitable to own and operate crowded tenements than to manage better types of housing. The sorry spectacle of powerful churches owning city blocks of rat-infested, crumbling tenements, of universities drawing their monies from such dwellings, of southern investors going in for "nigger housing" because its occupants must be content with very little and are not permitted to demand improvements, has never been a part of Puerto Rico's cultural scene. In Puerto Rico, in other words, it is less difficult than it is in the continental United States to oust the owners of slum dwellings, which are no less disgraceful and socially dangerous for being exceedingly profitable.

Originally Puerto Rico's municipal housing projects consisted of the rows of apartment buildings, attractively designed, laid out with playground space and other aids to good urban living, which one now sees in most of the cities. The apartments vary in size to accommodate variously sized families; each, moreover, has electricity, water, a kitchen, and a bathroom—utilities unknown to the tenants in their early slum existence. Rent is charged according to ability to pay. A man with a large family but a small income may live in a three-bedroom apartment for as little as $3.50 per month. His neighbor, with a smaller family but a large income, may have to pay up to $30 for a much smaller apartment. Keeping track of incomes is a task for social workers —and not always a pleasant one. If the first man's income goes up, or his sons take jobs or join the army, his rent is raised to correspond; if the second tenant's income rises above the legal limit governing occupancy of municipal housing, he has to move. Both may become so annoyed with the Popular Democratic party that they vote against it at the next election. As the only opposition parties advocate independence and statehood respectively, their actions give rise to many claims that the Puerto Ricans are growing tired of their Commonwealth status.

While slum clearance goes forward at an astonishingly rapid pace, it must not be assumed that all slum dwellers are overjoyed at being forced to move into better houses as their former quarters are condemned. Slums are themselves a way of life, with much to commend it in a climate as gentle as Puerto Rico's, and the Puerto Rican slum shacks, bad as they are, have never been as evil as the New York slums into which migrants are herded after they leave their beloved island. Life in those shacks, as opposed to the overcrowded San Juan tenements, involved a certain amount of individual freedom and a resulting minimum of governmental regimentation. But even the recalcitrant ones are eventually nudged, cajoled, lured into one of the new housing projects. After that, and often to their surprise, they are subjected to a patient process of education, designed to "take the slums out of the people." They must be taught not to throw their garbage out of the windows as they had in their former homes in "el Fanguito," the notorious "Mudhole." They are taught new ways of living together in civilized surroundings; it requires much patience, but the labor brings results. Many of the more enthusiastic are taught— but never coerced—not to become so elated over their fine new homes that they mortgage their souls, buying new furniture on the installment plan.

San Juan's San José housing project is a model for the island and an active experimental ground for new ways of handling old problems. Its present population is about 30,000, which means that it is a separate city within the capital. And it *is* a separate city, energetically evolving ways of life that differ radically from the old ones, though the spirit behind them is typical of Puerto Rico's "good old days." An attractive city, it is as immaculately clean as San Juan itself—under the stewardship of that dedicated "housekeeper," Mayoress Felisa Rincón de Gautier. Section by section, block by block, its apartment buildings show the progress in architecture and attractive color schemes which themselves help to instill pride.

Visitors to San José are shown the shopping center and the large community hall in which tenants discuss their problems and inaugurate courses of remedial action. They see a free library, a free dental clinic, a baby clinic, and a pleasant nursery in which working mothers can leave their children during the day. They are shown the well-equipped classroom in which women who enroll in such courses are taught cooking, dietetics, sewing, and even the art of building attractive furniture out of old barrels and boxes. The visitors see a model school, as well as quarters for aged tenants, each of whom has his or her separate small apartment where he can live in dignity and freedom, receive visitors at will, and avoid institutional regimentation.

New things are now stirring in San José. As the system of rentals according to ability to pay creates a certain amount of insecurity, an effort is made to create a class of rooted home owners on the project. If a man has a small house in fair condition in a condemned slum area, he and his family may now be moved to San José, house and all. There they live in the old home, and perhaps they merely paint it and enlarge it. But some of them set to work immediately, building new houses around the old with cement blocks and technical help obtained from the government at less than cost.

Eventually they have two houses, one inside the other, and have to dismantle and remove the small inner one while living on the spot and expanding their quarters into the new outer house.

An adaptation of the aided-self-help process that has proved so effective in the country is now also being used in San José for building new homes, and is giving sections of that vast development the air of clean, decent communities of independent home owners. San José's home owners may sell their houses if they wish, but only to other poor people, approved by the government. Speculating and trading in real estate for mere profit are rigidly excluded.

When Fidel Castros's Minister of Finance came to Puerto Rico early in 1959 with a large mission from Cuba, he shook his head in wonder over San José and said: "We would never dare to try anything like that in Cuba. If we did, the United States would immediately accuse us of being Communists."

Like many other things in Puerto Rico, San José does have Socialist tinges. The proof of the pudding, however, is found in the fact that San José, a city of 30,000 inhabited exclusively by former slum dwellers, has no police station and not a single policeman. While the crime rate rises alarmingly in the rest of San Juan, there seems to be no crime to speak of in the capital's San José section.

The dramatic urban growth has given rise to a boom in the construction industry. Vast new private developments of attractive houses—their design, spacing, and surroundings controlled by the Planning Board under zoning laws—create thousands of new homes for the growing middle class. There is, however, an in-between group of people whose incomes are too high to permit them to live in low-cost municipal housing, and too low for the purchase of homes built by private enterprise, even with F.H.A. help. At the time of the present writing the government is studying the possibility of building homes at a cost of perhaps $3,000, to be sold to members of that class through monthly payments. In addition, the government is considering the possibility of lowering and perhaps even eliminating taxes on homes inhabited by their owners.

The culture changes implied by the growth of the cities are now also indicated by a steady lowering of the birth rate, which a decade or so ago was one of the world's highest and was called "explosive" by demographers. To be sure, 31.8 births per 1,000 per year, compared with 7.2 deaths, is still too high for the comfort of the planners who must think in terms of creating jobs for all those people and who are, to quote Harvey Perloff, "in an Alice in Wonderland situation, where one must run very fast in order merely to stand still." But in 1949 the birth rate was 39 per 1,000, and its steady drop continues year by year. Sampling studies made in Puerto Rico some years ago by Dr. Lydia Roberts showed that families with incomes above $2,000 per year had fewer children than those with less money; women who had completed grade school had fewer children than those who hadn't; people in cities tended to be less fertile than those in the country.

The growing demand for contraception and even for sterilization is a new Puerto Rican culture trait. Though not actively urged or practiced by the government, both are legal under certain conditions. A private agency is doing important work—apparently with considerable success—in testing and demonstrating a new contraceptive pill to be taken orally.

While the Catholic Church is unhappy about that trend, it seems powerless to stop it. Episcopal messages denouncing birth control, and lurid attacks published from time to time in the newspapers tend largely to arouse popular interest; after every such attack, thousands of the rural and urban poor seem merely to say: "this is wonderful—where can we learn more?" Indeed, the Church has become apprehensive over losing its former stronghold on the people. In an apparent effort to combat the trend, it has in recent years established the "Catholic University" in Ponce. It has also induced a number of intellectuals, including several high government officials, to join religious discussion groups, and seems to be covertly in politics on the side of the opposition —especially the Republican Statehood party. Certainly on a number of occasions its high spokesmen have attacked the present government for being materialistic and excluding both God and spiritual values from its programs—an attitude that once caused José Padín to write to me that "it is easy to say that man does not live by bread alone when one's belly is full of bread."

A large proportion of the thousands of Puerto Ricans who migrate to the mainland belong to the most fertile age group, and this also contributes to the present decline in the island's birth rate.

The alarming increase in crime, especially in the San Juan area, is a negative aspect of modern culture changes. When Puerto Rico began to import good things from the United States, bad things came with them. The island's first bank robbery occurred in 1958, followed a few weeks later by the first attempted armed holdup of a bank messenger. The events gave rise to many agonized laments over the passing of the "good old days"; the fact that both crimes seem to have been committed by one or more continental Americans did little to assuage the sorrow. The current rise in juvenile delinquency, the appearance of junior gangs New York style and probably led by Puerto Rican youngsters who have returned from New York, are other disturbing symptoms of the island's growing modernity. Laws remaining on the books from the days when children were both better behaved and considered sacrosanct, and even a stipulation in the constitution of 1952 to the effect that minors may not be imprisoned, make it almost impossible for the police to deal with the rising wave of juvenile delinquency. Burglaries are becoming more common, especially in the San Juan homes of mainland Americans.

The police force is being enlarged to cope with its mounting problems, but its standards are now so high that it has difficulty in finding qualified men. Meanwhile, new civic organizations, patterned after San Juan's "Condado Improvement Association," co-operate with the police to suppress crime, support the Little League baseball movement and other outlets for youth's energies, clean up the beaches, paint their houses, and improve urban life in general.

Puerto Rico's outstanding modern culture trait is the creative restlessness, the eagerness to get things done, which is felt immediately by almost all visitors to the island. To paraphrase Boris Pasternak in *Dr. Zhivago:* everything is growing, fermenting, rising with the magic yeast of life. That does not at all mean, however, that all Puerto Ricans are agreed as to the meaning and desirability of what is going on. A definite "culture war" is still being fought, often unsuspected by resident Americans, but extremely serious and real to thousands of native intellectuals. Like many other things in Puerto Rico, that war finds its ultimate expressions in politics. The two minority parties, one demanding independence and the other statehood, are supported by remnants of the former groups, one of which lamented the passing of the old ways and labored to preserve them, while the other sneered at Puerto Rican culture and tried willy-nilly to take on "American" ways of living and thinking. Both of those groups deny that the island's modern revolution is a true expression of a revitalized Puerto Rican culture. The advocates of independence, the cultural nationalists, accuse Muñoz Marín and his followers of having sold out to a grasping Uncle Sam. The statehood people, among them many 150 per cent Americans, insist that what is happening in Puerto Rico today is nothing but an inexorable outpouring of the United States' creative spirit at a time of unprecedented economic expansion. The Puerto Rican leaders and people, they say, had nothing to do with the matter, and all

claims to the contrary—while effective as political propaganda—are decidedly unpatriotic.

The university, which has experienced a tremendous
growth in two decades, from 2,000 students to more than
16,000, has in some ways become a cultural battleground.
A number of its faculty members are accused of sneering
at Puerto Rican culture, of claiming and telling their students that there has never been such a thing, of insisting that
Puerto Rico has "no history" and that the university is not
interested in the island's past, only in shaping its future.
There is a certain amount of justice in such accusations,
especially when made against some of the non-Puerto Rican
professors from the United States and Europe, a few of them
shallow people, proud of their pseudosophistication, who insist that Puerto Rico has no culture because it has produced
no Shakespeare, Descartes, or Einstein, no history because
it precipitated no Battle of Waterloo. But the faculty itself
and even its non-Puerto Rican members are divided on the
matter. No greater service has been done to Puerto Rico's
pride and integrity than is being done, for instance, by the
American, Dr. Thomas Matthews, whose exhaustive, scholarly history of the "Gruening Era," the days of the PRRA,
is about to be published by the University of Florida Press.

Despite these dissentions the Puerto Ricans as a whole
are—and seem determined to remain—Latin Americans,
closely identified with the Latin-American scene in which
they have begun to exercise important leadership. All their
industrialization, all their borrowings from the United States
in the financial, technical, and managerial realms cannot
change that hard fact. A Latin-American revolution, which
usually means little or nothing to the average North American, is extremely real to the Puerto Ricans; the fall of a dictator is cause for personal rejoicing, as is the strengthening
of democracy in any one of the Latin-American republics.
Most of them even take pride in the venomous hatred such

tyrants as the Dominican Republic's Generalissimo Trujillo display toward Muñoz Marín, and in the fact that Trujillo's government supports a hidden mailing center in San Juan which uses the United States mails to disseminate a steady stream of scurrilous literature to attack Muñoz and his entire program with unbridled and often libelous vituperation.

Now that the Puerto Ricans have taken their own affairs into their own hands, they are prouder than ever of *being* Puerto Ricans, with their own, indigenous culture stream. And it is precisely that growing pride that now brings them closer to the United States. Earlier under U.S. rule, when Washington attempted to ram English down the throats of all the bewildered school children and attempted in a number of other ways to "Americanize" them, there was always a wide rift between the *Americanos* as rulers and the Puerto Ricans as colonial subjects. Today that rift is closing fast precisely because the Puerto Ricans refuse to become "carbon copies of people in the United States," precisely because their strong nationalism in the cultural sense gives them the strength to reject nationalism in the political sense and provides a sturdy foundation for a growing affection for their fellow citizens in the north.

18

Where Now?

IN 1953 the United States officially reported to the United Nations that Puerto Rico was no longer a dependent territory and that Washington would no longer report on it as such. Momentarily the United Nations became a Puerto Rican debating ground. Representatives of the Independence party went to New York to protest against the move on the ground that Puerto Rico was still a colony. They were opposed by representatives of the Puerto Rican government, who claimed that the Commonwealth had entered freely and of its own accord into the compact with Washington defining its present political status, that it had achieved self-government within the framework of the American Union, and that it was, in fact, no longer a dependent territory. A small flurry was stirred by the debate. Fear of Nationalist terrorism caused the bodyguard of Henry Cabot Lodge, America's delegate to the United Nations, to be increased. President Eisenhower made a statement to the effect that if at any time the Legislative Assembly of Puerto Rico adopted a resolution in favor of more complete or even absolute independence, he would immediately thereafter recommend to Congress that such independence be granted. Muñoz Marín officially thanked the President for his generosity, but disavowed, on behalf of his people, a desire for what he called "separate independence."

The official Spanish term for Puerto Rico's present Commonwealth status—"*Estado Libre Asociado*, Associated Free State"—is more accurately descriptive than the English term. In his book *The Art of Politics* Tugwell described the status as "having your cake and eating it too" and as "a first rate political device—one to be ranked with our federal union and with the British Commonwealth." It is conceded to be unique in world affairs, with no precedent in history. Both its importance and its effectiveness grew directly out of Puerto Rico's realities.

Under the present arrangement the United States continues to operate the army, navy, air force, post office, customs service, and various federal agencies, such as the Soil Conservation Service, in Puerto Rico. Excise taxes collected on goods manufactured in Puerto Rico and duties collected in Puerto Rican ports continue to be returned to the Puerto Rican treasury instead of being kept by the federal government, as they would be if Puerto Rico were a state. Incomes earned in Puerto Rico continue to be exempt from federal taxes. However, Puerto Rico is eligible for federal grants in aid—for roads, school lunches, housing, and the like—on a basis of equality with the various states.

Such financial "advantages," plus the fact that Puerto Rico remains within the economic structure of the United States and has free access to America's markets and pool of capital, help to compensate for the island's lack of natural resources. That Puerto Rican purchases from U.S. manufacturers have multiplied almost sevenfold since 1940, and that Puerto Rico is giving the United States a good name throughout the world—worth untold millions in today's propaganda war—indicate that American "generosity" is here paying dividends. Puerto Rico's "advantage" of not contributing to the federal treasury springs from the old American principle of "no taxation without representation." The Commonwealth continues to be represented in Congress by a Resident Commissioner who has a voice, but no vote, can prepare legislation pertaining to Puerto Rico, can argue for or against such legislation, but cannot vote on it.

Although the people of Puerto Rico have been citizens of the United States since 1917, they are citizens in a somewhat limited sense. They can come and go freely within all the areas that are under the American flag. They enjoy all the civil rights and legal protections of U.S. citizens. But, as though to compensate for the financial arrangements that permit their island's dramatic transformation, they lack some of the political rights enjoyed by citizens of the federated states. They vote for their own officials in their own government, but as long as they remain in Puerto Rico they cannot vote for the President or for voting members of the Congress. When I moved to Puerto Rico in 1955 and began to vote as a citizen of the Commonwealth, I voluntarily gave up my political rights as a citizen of the United States. I can get them back, however, and any Puerto Rican can attain them simply by moving to one of the states and establishing such residence there as is required for becoming a voting citizen of that state. In other words, only by being a citizen of one of the fifty federated states can a person be a full citizen of the United States of America.

In matters pertaining to local government Puerto Rico now has a free hand subject to control, not by the U. S. Congress, but only by the Supreme Court, on the grounds of constitutionality. The people of Puerto Rico govern themselves under a constitution of their own drafting which was ratified by Congress (with the minor deletions listed in Chapter 12) and accepted by the Puerto Rican voters in a plebiscite. Neither the Congress nor the executive branch of the United States government (through an appointed governor) can today veto a law passed by the Puerto Rican legislature. In theory Congress can and does still pass laws pertaining to Puerto Rico without submitting them to formal acceptance by the Commonwealth; in practice that ability has been voluntarily curtailed on several occasions. Some years ago, when Congress passed two laws that involved special financial contributions to the federal treasury, it stipulated that those laws should not apply in Puerto Rico unless and until they had been accepted by the Commonwealth legislature. As the laws were good, and promised to benefit the Puerto Rican society, they were ratified in San Juan.

Though that excellent arrangement is new and unique in world affairs, its basic concept—that of local autonomy while retaining economic ties and common citizenship with the former ruling country—is in no way new. Muñoz Marín is often credited with having invented the idea, and Tugwell goes to some length to show that it had cropped up a few years before Muñoz's ascendancy, and that, in fact, even the term *"Estado Libre Asociado"* had been used for a similar proposal in 1922.

Actually, the basic idea began to appear in Puerto Rico as far back as 1808, when the island gained a measure of representation in the Spanish Cortes. It gained strength and appeal after the establishment of the Dominion of Canada, which set a number of Puerto Ricans to thinking along new lines, and was inherent in the thinking on autonomy of Muñoz's father, Luis Muñoz Rivera. Morales Carrión has pointed out that the idea was advocated in the United States by Henry Stimson in 1912, by Horace M. Towner in 1916, and by Theodore Roosevelt, Jr. in 1937, plus several others. It was proposed by Puerto Rico to Congress in 1922. Muñoz Marín's important contributions to the idea were: (1) the specific forms taken by the political arrangement when it was finally put into effect; (2) the fact that after more than a century of talk, it finally *was* put into effect; (3) the imaginative manner in which that was done.

Previous advocates of autonomy expected such home rule to be handed down to Puerto Rico by a benevolent Congress, in a kind of ultraliberal organic act, drafted by Congress with or without consultation with the Puerto Ricans. Muñoz, however, aimed from the start at the *abolition* of congressional organic acts; from the first he labored to utilize the principle of self-determination. The present status was not handed down to Puerto Rico as a bit of enlightened imperialism, as the PRRA had been. The manner of its achievement was in itself a rejection of the imperialistic process. Public Law 600, providing for the new status, was drafted in Puerto Rico, was submitted to the Congress by Puerto Rico's Resident Commissioner, and was passed by Congress on July 3, 1950, with the proviso that it was not to become law unless and until it had been accepted by the island's people. Other congressional acts become law when they are signed by the President; this one was submitted to the Puerto Ricans for signature. The referendum was held in 1951; Public Law 600 was upheld by a vote of 387,016 to 119,169. During the preceding discussions the law had been opposed largely by the advocates of Puerto Rico's independence, who felt that Commonwealth status weakened the chances for eventual independence by voluntarily confirming continued political relations with the United States. Those who were for Puerto Rico's eventual statehood had fewer objections to the law because it in no way precluded, and in some ways even improved, the chances for that status.

Public Law 600 was a simple document, drafted "in the nature of a compact" and in recognition of the principle of "government by consent." It stipulated that the people of Puerto Rico, working through an elected constituent assembly, were to draft their own constitution; the only things Public Law 600 said about that document were that it must contain a bill of rights and provide for a republican form of government. The constitution was then to be either accepted or rejected by the Puerto Rican voters in another plebiscite, and later ratified by Congress. After such ratification, Puerto Rico could start functioning under its new status.

Nothing similar has ever happened in the colonial world. By their own vote and by carrying out the principle of self-determination, the people of a so-called colony could reject legislation passed by the ruling country. But they did not reject it. In the second referendum they accepted the constitution by a vote of 375,594 to 82,877. Congress ratified after a bit of haggling, and Puerto Rico chose July 25 as its own Fourth of July, its Commonwealth Day. It was chosen for its dramatic implications. July 25, 1898, had been the day on which General Miles had landed with his American troops on the island's south coast in the military operation that was to wrest Puerto Rico from Spain.

Puerto Rico's political debate since the establishment of Commonwealth status has centered largely on the question of whether that status is permanent or is merely another way station on the road to something else. Ever since 1808 Puerto Rico's people have passed a succession of such way stations, not one of which was regarded by them as the final goal in their political evolution. During the nineteenth century Spain lightened its former harsh rule by a series of reforms, alternated by occasional setbacks; the autonomy achieved in 1897 was a great step forward, but hardly the final solution. The ceding of the island to the United States after the Spanish-American War was a drastic turning point; the Foraker Act of 1901, Puerto Rico's first American "constitution," drafted by Congress without consulting anybody in Puerto Rico, proved a political setback. The Jones Act of 1917 repaired some of the damage done by its predecessor, but could hardly—especially as it turned out to work poorly—be regarded as the final answer. The right of the Puerto Ricans to elect their own governor, first practiced in 1948, was another great advance, but again not the final answer; too many remnants of the old colonialism still remained.

Governor Muñoz Marín and his Popular Democratic party

insist that as a result of its present arrangements Puerto
Rico has at last attained its final, ultimate status. They do
not claim that it is perfect; they do insist that it is sufficiently
flexible to permit adjustment and improvement. They agree,
for instance, that Congress can still pass laws pertaining to
Puerto Rico without consulting the Puerto Ricans; but they
also maintain that the same good working relations with
Congress that led to establishment of the Commonwealth
status permit its eventual amendment to take care of that
defect. "We have planted a tree," they say. "It is still young,
but it grows older and more sturdy daily. The one thing we
know is that it will not turn into some other kind of tree. A
young oak does not grow into an older elm; it remains an
oak. So the tree of our Commonwealth status will not eventually turn into either independence or statehood; it will
develop into a better and sturdier Commonwealth status."

The two minority parties—one for independence and the
other for statehood—choose to differ. If they didn't, they
would disappear as parties.

The Republican Statehood party, while insisting somewhat vaguely that the status of its choice would improve
Puerto Rico's economy, also waves the flag with an emotional "patriotism." Many of its members claim to be the
only real "Americans" on the island, accuse Muñoz Marín of
working secretly toward independence, and insist that anybody who opposes statehood for Puerto Rico is a traitor to
the United States. At the governors' conference held in San
Juan in August 1959 they were exceedingly busy trying to
persuade the various state governors to support their cause,
while the Independence party staged rallies, waved its own
flag, did its own lobbying, and chanted "Yanqui go home!"
when the various governors drove past their meetings.

Both of the opposition parties, however, have a hard time
reconciling their desires on status with Puerto Rico's economic situation and needs.

Independence seems undesirable and impractical, quite

aside from the fact that in today's *interdependent* world small nations with few natural resources are apt to find the going increasingly rough. To advocate independence is to be willing to throw away the one most important resource that Puerto Rico *does* have—its economic and political relationship with the United States. The sugar business, for instance, is still the island's most important single industry. There is grave doubt about its ability to survive at all if Puerto Rico were a sovereign republic and therefore had to pay duty on the sugar it sells to the States. Cuba, to be sure, does pay such duty, but the Cuban conditions of soil, climate, and topography are so much better than are Puerto Rico's that the larger island can afford the duty. That may be one reason why the cause of Puerto Rico's independence has so many warm adherents in Cuba. At present the production of sugar on both islands for the United States market is regulated by a U.S. quota; if Puerto Rico's industry went bankrupt as a result of independence, Cuba might expect to inherit the entire quota of both.

It has been pointed out, too, that most of the manufacturing done in Puerto Rico today is done for the great United States market, not for the Puerto Rican. There is serious doubt as to whether the General Electric Company could make circuit breakers on the island, or the International Latex Corporation baby pants, if they had to pay duty on shipping their products to the continent. As there is no way in which the United States could give independence to Puerto Rico and then give the new republic anything better than "most-favored-nations" treatment in the matter of tariffs, it is almost certain that General Electric and International Latex and most of the other mainland corporations that now employ tens of thousands of people in their factories would have to close shop once independence was achieved. And then New York would *really* have a Puerto Rican "problem."

Puerto Rico today benefits to the tune of nearly $40,000,-

000 annually from grants in aid which Washington gives the island on a basis of equality with the various states. Matched in varying amounts by the Commonwealth, these grants are virtually indispensable for building roads, creating public housing, providing lunches for school children, and extending the public-health and education programs. Their loss, in the event of independence, would be a disaster to the society.

Leaders of the island's Independence party seem to think that in one way or another they can, if they win an election, persuade the U. S. Congress to give independence to Puerto Rico, while allowing the island to retain all the financial benefits it now enjoys from its relationship with the States. To date, however, they have been vague about how that was to be accomplished, while it is significant that most congressmen who talk publicly about Puerto Rico's potential independence do so in a punitive fashion. It will be remembered that the notorious Tydings Bill of 1936 was drafted to punish "the Puerto Ricans" for shooting their Chief of Police. The independent bill of January 1959 was introduced by Congressman Moulder, of Missouri, because many Puerto Ricans were coming to New York, and many United States industries were opening plants in Puerto Rico; Moulder didn't think that was right. A month later Congressmen Withrow, of Wisconsin, and Jackson, of California, accepted invitations to go to Ciudad Trujillo to address a joint session of the Dominican legislature. Both praised Dictator Trujillo to the skies; both scolded Puerto Rico for being against dictators, and implied that the island was even influencing the United States in that direction. Withrow said that he was certainly going to look into the matter, and Jackson came out flatly for Puerto Rico's independence, presumably as punishment for being against the Dominican "benefactor," and certainly to prevent Muñoz Marín from any longer influencing Washington's policies.

The recent admittance of Alaska as the Union's forty-ninth state and Hawaii as the fiftieth has naturally led to much political discussion in Puerto Rico and has caused redoubling of the Statehood party's propaganda efforts. It is significant, however, that nobody denies that Puerto Rico's tax burden will be increased in the event of attaining statehood, as the present Commonwealth will then have to contribute to the federal treasury as well as maintaining its own. Puerto Ricans will have to pay federal income taxes as well as local; customs receipts and excise taxes on such things as rum and cigars will be kept by Washington instead of continuing to be given to Puerto Rico.

In that realm the debate centers on the amounts potentially involved. Señor Luis Ferré, the Statehood party's perennial candidate for the governorship, points out that Mississippi gives about 8.3 per cent of its gross income to Washington, and that Puerto Rico, if it did the same, would pay less than $90,000,000 per year to the federal government. Dr. Rafael Picó, Puerto Rico's former Secretary of the Treasury and present President of the Government Development Bank, says that the exact amount can be easily determined from Puerto Rico's realities (instead of from vague comparisons with some state chosen at random), and that had the island been a state in 1955, its contribution to the federal treasury in that year would have come to $133,-600,000. In 1959 the U.S. Bureau of the Budget made an independent study of the situation and concluded that in that year statehood would have cost Puerto Rico $188,000,000 in contributions to the federal government which are now not made. Whatever the figure, many people wonder where the extra amount would come from; it is already difficult enough for the Commonwealth to raise its annual budget, which is now close to $230,000,000. It would come from increased taxation, from a drastic reduction of the Commonwealth's present income, and would thus slow down the industrialization program, as well as the programs for building roads and extending the blessings of education and health facilities to the island's people.

Nothing of the kind, says the spokesman for the Statehood party. He points out that the various states today receive larger federal grants in aid per capita than does Puerto Rico, and that the island could expect corresponding increases in such grants if it were a state. His opponents point out that those grants are not outright gifts, but have to be matched by local funds in proportions that vary with the purposes for which they are given. In general, the bigger the grants in aid, the larger the matching funds that must be raised locally in one way or another, at the same time that anywhere from $90,000,000 to $188,000,000 must be sent to Washington as direct contributions to the federal treasury. As one of Ferré's critics has pointed out: "For every forty-two cents that Mississippi receives in federal grants in aid, it not only puts up somewhere near forty-two cents in matching funds, but also pays a dollar in federal taxes."

Ferré insists that the attainment of statehood would somehow result in a marked increase of new industries established in Puerto Rico; his critics insist that exactly the opposite would happen, that it is only the fiscal autonomy now enjoyed by Puerto Rico which makes Operation Bootstrap possible. Not only would tax exemption be impossible, as industries in Puerto Rico would have to pay a federal tax of fifty-two per cent on corporate profits, but the wage differential—which is still an incentive to many new industries— would also be a thing of the past. A State of Puerto Rico would have to abide by the federal government's minimum-wage laws as they apply in the states. Many factories, they insist, that now flourish on wage scales somewhat lower than those on the mainland would have to close their doors in the event of statehood, and it would be more difficult, rather than easier, to attract new industries. It is a matter of record that several U.S. manufacturers who in 1959 were on the verge of establishing branch factories in Puerto Rico were at the last minute scared away by the Statehood party's incessant propaganda activities.

Late in 1958 the Soviet ambassador, Mikhail Menshikov, visited Puerto Rico briefly with his journalist son, Stanislav. Stanislav could not understand how there could be a Statehood party at all, let alone one supported by the island's most powerful industrialists. "What is their aim?" he asked me. "What economic incentive do they have, to subscribe to a program that will probably multiply their taxes by three in the event that they manage to carry it through?"

Although it is difficult to answer such questions to a dialectic materialist, I tried my best to make things plain in my own terms and according to my own thinking. In the first place, there is undoubtedly some hangover from the old days, when struggles between parties were actually struggles for control of the budget, rather than over matters of principle. I had my own serious doubts about whether the industrialists and reactionary large landowners, if ever they won an election, would be eager for statehood as they are today. Statehood on the one hand and independence on the other seem to appeal to some of the leaders of the minority parties, not as desirable goals, but as convenient pegs on which to hang parties.

There can be no doubt, however, that a number of men advocate statehood as a hedge against independence, which would be even worse for the island and which is still *legally* possible, no matter how impossible it may be economically, morally, or politically. The political device of accusing Muñoz again and again of being secretly for eventual independence is used as a means for angling for statehood votes, as our Civil War was fought over the issue of "once a state, always a state."

Mr. Menshikov could understand that reasoning, but he was still not satisfied. "Parties need votes to survive," he said, "and I understand that in the 1956 election the Republican Statehood party won more than twenty per cent of the total vote. There can't be that many industrialists and large land-owners. Who votes for the party and why?"

There are those who vote for the minority parties because they honestly believe that either statehood or independence would be better for Puerto Rico than Commonwealth status. Others are employed by the Statehood party's leaders. Still others yearn for what they call "full citizenship," even at the cost of social hardship and physical hunger. Then, too, there are many who merely want to cast a protest vote at election time.

I explained to my fellow journalist from the Soviet Union that the Popular Democratic party has been in power since 1941, and that it is impossible for a party to rule that long without making enemies. People are thrown into technological unemployment, or have their rents raised in low-cost housing projects, and express their indignation by voting against the party in the next election. "It is an odd situation," I said, "in which a man cannot vote against the party in power without apparently voting for either statehood or independence, neither of which he may want."

That pleased Mr. Menshikov. "I see," he said. "You mean that Puerto Rico actually has a one-party political system."

As of today, he is right. In its internal affairs Puerto Rico does have a one-party system, though by accident, rather than design. The Popular Democratic party has been so dramatically successful with its programs, which were "revolutionary" a few decades ago, and Muñoz Marín is worshipped so intensely, that it would be political suicide to oppose them on major internal issues. Many believe that the one-party system will continue until Muñoz either dies or removes himself from politics. In that event, they say, the Popular Democratic party may fall to pieces and divide itself into two or more parties—perhaps as a result of the internal

dichotomy between more jobs and greater productive efficiency, perhaps in a demagogic struggle for power between
its various leaders.

In 1959 the Popular Democratic party, through its Resident Commissioner, presented Bill H. R. 9234 in Congress,
designed to strengthen Commonwealth status by amending
and clarifying it somewhat. Among other things the bill provides that Puerto Rico henceforth determine the limits of its
debt-incurring capacity, which have hitherto been set by the
federal government. It stipulates that several kinds of federal laws affecting Puerto Rico should be formally accepted
by the Commonwealth before being applicable on the island,
and it also provides for certain financial contributions by
Puerto Rico to the federal treasury. After its first submittal
as the "Fernós-Murray" bill, the measure—and indeed the
entire Commonwealth "compact"—were questioned by some
senators on the grounds of constitutionality; the legislators
seemed to wonder whether Congress has the constitutional
right and power to cede, limit, or abrogate any of its powers
opposite Puerto Rico. Others wondered whether the bill,
which stipulates that it "shall be known and cited as the 'Articles of Permanent Association of the Commonwealth of
Puerto Rico with the United States,'" did not preclude the
island's possible future admission to the Union as a federated
state.

In Puerto Rico the bill threw the leaders of the opposition
parties into an uproar, in part because it again disproves the
politically convenient claim that Muñoz is secretly working
for independence, and in part because its passage will go far
toward establishing Commonwealth status as a *permanent*
form of relationship. Whereupon the *Populares* announced
a new attitude on the statehood question, which was immediately incorporated in the Fernós bill's present form.

As present objections to statehood are based on Puerto
Rico's inability to afford such status, the present bill provides for a review of the entire matter "at such time as the

per-capita income of Puerto Rico, as determined by the United States Department of Commerce, shall equal that of any member State of the Union." When Puerto Rico has progressed to the point where its per-capita income is comparable to that of the poorest state, the stipulations under which the Puerto Ricans pay no federal income taxes and retain for their own use the federal customs duties and excise taxes collected on the island "shall be subject to termination by the Congress." At such time, too, the people of Puerto Rico shall review the entire status question and may hold a plebiscite to decide whether they want statehood or prefer to continue with their present Commonwealth arrangements—with or without possible further amendments.

Understandably, the new policy did not suit the opposition parties. If it *had* suited them, those parties would no longer have reason to exist—the one because independence is not mentioned as one of the political alternatives, the other because one cannot clamor for "statehood now" while at the same time admitting that it may be well to wait until Puerto Rico comes a little closer to being able to afford it. Both parties therefore accused Muñoz Marín of acting in bad faith when he merely combined some hard economic common sense with the kind of political astuteness that has made him world-famous.

Earlier in 1959, before the ruckus over the Fernós bill, the Republican Statehood party quite correctly raised the issue that general elections do not result in the true expression of the people's will in the matter of status. The party began to demand a plebiscite, specifically on that issue. The Independence party opposed this plebiscite on the ground that independence is a sacred right, not to be subjected to the votes of the people. Muñoz Marín, who was quite safe in his stand, said that he had no objection to such a plebiscite, provided it gave the people a choice between statehood, independence, and Commonwealth status, and provided also that the two losing parties would agree ahead of time thereafter

to stop their propaganda efforts. The statehood people didn't
want that kind of arrangement, which might well have resulted in the death of their party. They not only demanded
a plebiscite on the simple question: "Statehood, yes or no,"
but they also insisted that the U. S. Congress arrange for it,
giving advance assurance that it will grant statehood if the
vote goes that way. Since the leaders of the opposition parties insist that Commonwealth status is not, and cannot be,
permanent, and that only statehood or independence may be
regarded as the ultimate solutions for Puerto Rico's problem
of political relationship with the United States, such a plebiscite would, in effect, give the voters a choice only between
those two final arrangements. However, as it is inconceivable
that any congress will commit itself ahead of time to grant
statehood after such a lop-sided vote, the chances for the
plebiscite seem to be extremely faint.

The present status, the present government and its fine
programs, are obviously the creations of one man. There is
much apprehension because Muñoz Marín has not "trained"
anybody for the role of successor. To be sure, his government contains a number of the finest public servants to be
found anywhere on earth, but how many of them have the
popular appeal, the qualities of leadership, that are needed
for winning elections? Moreover, the Popular Democratic
party's greatest single weakness stems from the fact that it
seems all but impossible for young men, new leaders with
new ideas, to rise to the top in the party's affairs.

In the years immediately following 1940, when the *Populares* had only a minute plurality in the legislature and were
beset by bitter enemies, and when, moreover, they had both
to learn and to teach concepts of government that were utterly new to the stricken colony, they had to close ranks
against their embattled opponents, as well as to discipline
themselves against internal dissentions. The strong disciplinary hold Muñoz began in those days to exercise on his party

—as a safeguard against mere demagogy—has never been relaxed and leads to repeated though false charges that he is a "dictator." Today the party is still a tightly knit organization, strictly ruled by its Central Committee.

Young men, ardent *Populares*, complain that they have no chance to rise in the party or in the government by their own efforts, their own fresh ideas. A "Young *Populares*" movement does not exist and seems indeed to be unthinkable unless sponsored by Muñoz and the Central Committee in a paternalistic fashion, which would defeat the very aim and philosophy of such a movement. The result is apprehension over the fact that a successor to Muñoz is not only not being "trained," but is even prevented from getting ahead by means of his own concepts of leadership.

Commonwealth status, designed to fit Puerto Rico's specific needs, is obviously best for the island, and by far the majority of voters realize that fact. But it is now becoming apparent that the final decision on status may yet rest with Congress, and that a number of congressmen—who see the present status only as Tugwell described it, as a means of having one's cake and eating it, too—may not care particularly about what is good for Puerto Rico. The question that they may want answered is: what is best for the United States?

That modern Puerto Rico has experienced an unprecedented social and economic development; that its current trends redound immeasurably to the good name of the United States; that it plays a powerful role in the important matter of assuaging Latin-American mistrust toward *el coloso del norte* and cementing inter-American relations; that its people are today "loyal" to the United States as never before; that it has become a new American industrial frontier; that its purchases from the United States have multiplied sevenfold since 1940; that it attracts eminent and admiring visitors by the thousands from all the free world's countries, who in turn spread America's good reputation—these are powerful arguments for continuation of the Commonwealth status that makes such facts possible.

While the political debate is raging, Muñoz Marín is doing everything in his power to maintain and support the opposition groups. For instance, under the Commonwealth's constitution, minority parties are assured representation in the legislature, even though, as happened in 1952, they don't win a single seat at the polls. By law, one third of the legislators must today belong to opposition parties, dividing their seats in a system of proportional representation; in the event that none of their candidates is elected, the legislature is simply enlarged to make room for them. Also unique is a recent law under which the government makes financial contributions to all the existing parties on a basis of complete equality, regardless of their electoral strength. It will be remembered that in 1940 Muñoz Marín broke the political control powerful financial interests had previously exercised through the wholesale purchase of votes. He did it by persuading people not to sell their votes. Now the amount of money any one individual or corporation may donate to a party is rigidly limited by law, while the public treasury gives money to all the legitimate parties.

Cynics have accused Muñoz of using such means to assure the continuation of weak opposition parties, thereby preventing the rise of a strong one. However, he has also insisted on a constitutional provision that might facilitate the creation of a new party. Under present law a party must in an election win ten per cent of the total vote in order to remain a true party and be able to go to the next election. However, if a new party is formed, or if a former one wishes to reconstitute itself, it now needs petition signatures totaling only *five* per cent of the total vote cast in the preceding election.

Whatever one says about the rigid control Muñoz Marín exercises over his government and party, there can be no doubt that he is ardently and even fanatically devoted to the principles of human freedom. Roger Baldwin, former head of the American Civil Liberties Union, and himself world-famous as an embattled advocate of freedom, has been retained by the Commonwealth government to advise it in the matter, and to organize a nonpartisan committee on civil liberties, which advises the government and is free, through its reports, to publicize any infringements of freedom which it uncovers. No other government in the world has ever paid money to skilled and impartial outside experts—to advise it in the matter of broadening and strengthening its basic democracy.

Puerto Rico's elections of 1952 and 1956 hinted at significant political changes. Four parties participated in 1952, one of which—the Socialists—won only three per cent of the total vote and died as a result. At the same time, the Republican Statehood party polled thirteen per cent of the total vote, the Independence party nineteen per cent, and the Popular Democratic sixty-five per cent. Four years later, partly because it had inherited much of the Socialist party's former vote, the Republican Statehood party garnered twenty-four per cent of the total, the Independence party slipped from nineteen to fourteen per cent, while the *Populares*, though gaining numerically more votes than in the previous election, slipped from sixty-five per cent to sixty-two per cent of the total.

The broadest conclusion to be drawn from such changes is that the people of Puerto Rico, though preferring their present relationship to federated statehood, are overwhelmingly and increasingly for continued relations with the United States.

Many important problems in that relationship remain to be solved, but the method of solving them in a free and democratic manner has been established—at the very time when the United States is under vicious attack from the world's Communist side as a grasping imperialist. Moreover, with the world in turmoil over the dual problem of abolishing colonialism and raising standards of living for the hundreds of millions of people who are still on the verge of starvation, Puerto Rico—with Washington's full co-operation—has set an important example of the manners in which those problems can be solved.

Thousands of visitors from all parts of the free world go to the island today, see what Puerto Rico has done and is doing, and return to their homes, saying: "This is America's answer to communism." In this they express Puerto Rico's greatest importance to the United States and to the modern world.

Index

acerola cherry, 185
advertising, 208, 213
A.F. of L., 85, 155
AFL–CIO, 216, 229, 230
Agricultural Extension, 271
agriculture, 12, 167ff; diversification of, 177; industrialization of, 177, 184; master plan for, 185, 200; mechanization of, 168, 176, 179, 186; see also citrus fruits, coffee, credit, dairy farming, land, pineapples, tobacco, sugar
Agriculture and Commerce, Department of, 172
airplane transportation, 30, 32, 37, 41
airport, San Juan, 209
Alaska, 310
Albizu Campos, Pedro, 70ff, 82, 89, 110, 117, 119, 120, 121, 130
Alegría, Ricardo, 286
Algeria, 8, 12
Amalgamated Clothing Workers, 216
Amazon basin, 176, 234
American Civil Liberties Union, 113, 318
American Forests, 175, 187
American Geographical Society, 237
American Legion, 154
American Mercury, The, 86

Americanization of Puerto Ricans, 26, 34, 248, 300
ammonium plant, 200
ancylostomiasis, 233
Aqueduct and Sewer Authority, 239
aqueducts, rural, 239
arbitration, 222f
Arbona, Dr. Guillermo, 232
Arkansas, 37
Army of Liberation, 72
Art of Politics, The, 151
Ashford, Dr. Bailey, 59, 233, 234
assassinations, 74, 100, 252
Atlanta Penitentiary, 74, 111
atomic radiations, 75

balance of trade, 61, 191
Baldwin, Roger, 318
Baltimore Sun, 88
Barceló, Antonio R., 69, 92, 94, 115f
bargaining, collective, 218
Barranquitas, El, 212, 269
Batey, El, 126f
Batista, Fulgencio, 95
Bayamón Health and Welfare Regional Program, 245
beef cattle, 182
beet sugar, 168, 178
Benét, William Rose, 86
Betancourt, Romulo, 18, 163
Bilharzia, 240
Bill of Rights, 218

Bird, Estéban, 56, 209, 232
birth control, 80
birth rate, 4, 10, 11, 12, 30, 52, 62, 63, 237, 296
bishops, Catholic, 259
Black, Ruby, 93, 95
Bolivar, Simon, 69
Bootstrap, Operation, 125
Borinquen, 32, 290
Boston, 37
bottles, factory for, 141
Bourne, Dorothy and James, 78
brassière industry, 200
Brazil, 24, 208
Bridge, The (film), 267ff
Bridgeport, 25
Brookings Institution, 56, 60
Brumbaugh, M. G., 248
budget: control of, 65; Puerto Rico's, 139
Bureau of Employment Security, 226
Bureau of Environmental Sanitation, 239
Bureau of Malaria Eradication, 235
Bush, Monroe, 175, 187
Bushnaq, Dr. Hussein, 18
bulk-loading, 203
Byrnes, Governor, 37

Camden, 37
Canada, 190
cancer, 236; virus of, 72
capital: American, 28, 161; for development, 140, 152, 153, 182; *see also* United States
capitalism, 6, 7
Caracas, 74
Carbon and Carbide Co. Union, 202
Caribe Hilton Hotel, 198, 207
Caribbean area, 17, 20, 63

Caribbean Commission, 20ff
Carlisle Indian School, 249
Carmen, Doña, 274
Casablanca, 289
Casals, Pablo, 208, 210, 263, 282, 287
casinos, 208
Castro, Josué de, 237
Castro, Fidel, 211, 295
Catecismo del Pueblo, El, 123
Catholic: bishops, 259; Church, 80, 171, 296; culture, 69, 71, 80; faith, 259; schools, 259; University, 258, 297
cement plant, 4, 98, 104, 141, 195, 200
Chardón, Carlos, 97, 99, 110, 136
Chardón Plan, 98f, 102, 109
Chicago, 25, 37, 146, 239
child labor, 218
children, status of, 34
"Children of Famine," 76
Chile, 140, 143
Chillicothe, Ohio, 78
China, 167, 276
Chinese labor, 45
cigar industry, 228
cities, growth of, 77, 291, 296
citizenship: Puerto Rican, 31; U.S., 14, 67, 130, 131, 303
citrus fruits, 58, 182
civic employment, 12, 265ff
civil liberties, 113, 318
Civil Liberties Union, American, 113, 318
clay-products factory, 141, 195
Cleveland, 25, 37
climate, 4, 33
clothing industry, 200
Coalition, 91, 92, 99, 102, 127, 143, 144
Coastwise Shipping Law, 90
coffee, 58f, 79, 98, 182, 203

Colgate University, 22
collective bargaining, 218
colonialism: Puerto Rico's, 9, 11, 12, 13; world, 6, 7
colonos, 53, 64, 119, 151
Colom, José Luis, 17
Comandante, El, 209
Commonwealth Day, 306
commonwealth status, 20, 152, 301*ff*
communism, 7, 14, 16, 18, 71, 319, 320
Community Education, Division of, 172, 266*ff;* posters made by, 274; publications of, 273; use of films by, 267*ff*
community garden, 270; participation, 239*ff*
compact with U.S., 131
conciliation, 222*f*
Conference, Governors', 19
conferences, international, 19
Congress, U.S., 51, 83, 303, 316; shooting in, 75
Congressional committees, 146
Connecticut, 29, 40, 42
conservation, 142
constitution, Puerto Rican, 218, 224, 305; U.S., 65
consultants, American, 161
contraception, 296
contracts, labor, 42
Co-operative Development Administration, 173, 266; Bank, 173
co-operatives, 79, 98, 103*f*, 139, 168, 172*ff*, 181, 184, 251
Costa Rica, 18, 163
Craig, Howard Reid, 246
credit: agricultural, 53, 54, 120; unions, 172, 174
crime, 295, 297
Cuba, 21, 95, 211, 295, 308

culture, Puerto Rican, 27, 82, 87, 150, 256*f*, 281*ff*
culture societies, 48, 160
customs duties, 302; receipts, 50

dairy farming, 180, 186
death rate, 10, 11, 30, 57, 236*f*, 241, 296
Debs, Eugene, 228
de Golia, Jack, 61
Delaware: University of, 22; Valley, 40, 42
delinquency, juvenile, 36, 77, 297
Democracia, La, 84, 86, 93, 95, 149
democracy, Puerto Rico's, 14, 46
Democratic party, 94
Denmark, 10, 167, 168, 180, 264
Department, of Agriculture and Commerce, 172; of Education, 254, 261, 262, 272; of Health, 239, 240, 244*ff;* of Labor, 223*ff*, 230, 267; of Public Works, 278; of State, 16, 19; of Tourism, 211
depression, world, 6*ff*, 63, 76, 77, 89
Descartes, Sol Luis, 104
Detroit, 37
Development Bank, 140, 197, 310
Development Company, 140, 141*ff*
diabetes, 236
diarrhea and enteritis, 57, 235
dictators, Latin-American, 14
Diffie, Bailey and Justine, 60
diseases, tropical, 231
distribution, geographic, 30, 202, 212, 213
Division of Community Education, 172, 266*ff*
dollar diplomacy, 18

Dominican Republic, 21, 91, 130, 158, 211, 300, 309
dope, in New York, 34
Dorado Beach Hotel, 209
double enrollment, 261
Drake, Sir Francis, 45
Dubinsky, 216
Dudley, Ed, 209
dumping, 190

Economic Development Administration, 160, 185, 199, 200, 201, 208, 210, 222
Ecuador, 213
Educación, 262
education: 12, 31, 68, 114, 135, 202, 222, 248ff; adult, 255; community, 265ff; double enrollment in, 261; expansion of, 253; language problem in, 256; policy on, 248; public hearings on, 255; United Nations report on, 255; use of radio and television in, 262; *see also* English language, schools, teachers
Education: Commissioner of, 68, 248, 253; Department of, 208
Educational Exchange program, 17
Egypt, 246
Eisenhower, Dr. Milton, 165
Eisenhower, President, 301
election: of 1932, 71; of 1936, 115; of 1940, 3, 29, 53, 102, 124ff, 151, 316; of 1944, 125, 144; of 1948, 149, 253; of 1952, 319; of 1956, 319
election law, 127
elections, dishonest, 66

electric power, 192
electrification, rural, 98, 142, 181, 194
Ellsworth, Elmer, 131
Employment Security, Bureau of, 224
English language, 34, 39, 78, 83, 114, 208, 249ff, 253, 254, 257ff
erosion, soil, 4, 175, 181, 184
Escuela, 262
excise taxes, 50
exports, P.R., 191
expropriation, 205, 219

factories, 139, 140, 175, 189, 193, 195ff, 215; *see also* industries, industrialization
Fair Labor Standards Act, U.S., 220
Fajardo, 212
family, role in P.R., 282, 289
Fanguito, el, 293
Farley, James, 94
Faubus, Governor, 37
FBI, 144
FERA, 78, 103, 130, 137, 173, 185, 190
Fernández García, Benigno, 101f; Rafael, 97, 109
Fernós Isern, Antonio, 148, 149, 313; *see also* Resident Commissioner
Fernós-Murray bill, 314
Ferré, Luis, 153, 195, 310ff
F.H.A., 295
Figueres, José, 18, 163
Firestone Rubber Co., 53
fishing, 80, 201, 209
Five-Hundred-Acre Law, 52, 53, 54, 55, 90, 101f, 118, 120, 123, 139, 140, 167f

Florida, 43
flour and feed mill, 200
Font Saldaña: Carmen de, 129; Jorge, 128
Ford, Henry, Sr., 286
Foraker Act, 51, 52, 53, 68, 306
Foreign Relations Committee, U. S. Senate, 156, 163
Foreign trade zone, 204
forests, 176, 183, 186, 200
fortifications, 45
Fortune, 88
France, 20, 21
Franco, General Francisco, 284
Frankfurter, Felix, 106
Fries, Charles C., 258
frontier, geographic, 35, 115, 177
Future Farmers of America, 251

Galapagos Islands, 201
Gallegos, Rómulo, 91
gambling, 208
Gandhi, 71
garden, community, 270
Gary, Ind., 39
Gbedemah, Kohla Agbedi, 8, 9
General Electric Co., 201, 308
Geography of Hunger, The, 237
Geological Survey, U. S., 206
Germany, 10, 37
Ghana, 8, 13, 18, 24, 253
Gilbraltar, 46
glass factory, 141, 147, 195, 200
Gold Coast, 8
Gompers, Samuel, 228
González, Rafael, 104
Gore, Robert H., 94f, 100
governor, elected, 15, 75, 148, 253
graft, 66
Great Britain, 20
Gregory, Horace and Marya, 86
ground water, 205

Gruening, Dr. Ernest, 99, 107ff, 135, 299
Guadalupe, 21
Gulama, Ella Koblo, 18

Haiti, 21, 32, 167
Haitianization, 168
Hanson, Earl P., 104, 110, 189
Harding, President, 68
Harlem, 15, 35
Harrisburg, 37
Harvard University, 70, 106, 157
Hartford, 25, 37
Haverford College, 22, 250
Hawaii, 28, 179, 310
Hays, Arthur Garfield, 113
Health, Department of, 77, 234
health instruction, 242
health, public, 12, 14, 30, 77, 139, 231ff
heart ailments, 236, 237
Henry VIII, 167
Herald Tribune, N.Y., 76
Hernández, Rafael, 290
Hitler, 8
Hoffa, 217, 230
hookworm, 233f, 240
Hoover, President, 76, 250
hospitals, 103, 235, 241
hotel school, 208
hotels, 19, 198, 207ff
House of Representatives, 74
housing: 33, 36, 77, 103, 266; aided self-help, 173; municipal, 292; project, San José, 294; rural, 14, 171, 295
Housing Authority, 142
humid tropics, 232
Hungary, 32
hurricanes, 45, 58, 98, 172, 177, 182
hydroelectric power, 4, 10, 12, 104, 142, 181, 192ff

IBEC, 216
Iceland, 25
Ickes, Secretary, 73, 107f, 134
Idlewild airport, 33
Iglesias, Santiago, 92, 109, 227
illiteracy, 202, 255
immigration into P.R., 28
imports, P.R., 191
imperialism, U.S., 20, 58, 73
Independence party, 309, 315, 319
independence: Puerto Rican, 31, 66, 68, 71, 88, 92, 98, 101, 106, 108, 111, 114, 116, 131, 218, 220, 258, 293, 307, 309, 315; economics of, 307; Tydings bill for, 107f, 115, 309
income, per capita, 12, 60
income tax, 50
India, 13, 143, 234, 253
Indians of P.R., 281
Indochina, 8
Indonesia, 13, 18, 24, 253
industrialization: 12, 65, 90, 98, 104, 120, 139, 140ff, 152, 161, 175, 177, 184, 191, 260; mortality in, 199; policies for, 196
Institute of Puerto Rican Culture, 286ff
Interior, Department of, 98, 102
International Co-operation Administration, U.S., 276
International Ladies Garment Workers Union, 216
International Latex Corporation, 201, 229, 308
Iraq, 13
iron works, 200
irrigation, 194
Irrigation Service, P.R., 192
Isabela, 131
Israel, 13

Jackson, Congressman, 309
Jamaica, 24, 32
Japan, 200, 220
jibaros, 59, 116, 122, 129, 130, 131, 132, 145, 213, 285
Jiménez, Juan Ramón, 282
Jones Act, 68, 306
Jones, Catesby, 185
Jordan, 13, 18
Juarez, 167
juvenile delinquency, 36, 77, 297

Kenworthy, Leonard, 257
Kenya, 8
Keyes, Dr. Scott, 185ff
King, Senator, 253
Korsa, Sir Arkuh, 18

labor: 215ff; agents, 41; cheap, 161; force, 31, 203; leaders, 102, 196, 216, 229; legislation, 218ff; racketeers, 34, 39, 41; troubles, 196, 216; unions, 39, 229ff
Labor: American Federation of, 85; Department of, 37, 40; Statistics, Bureau of, 227
La Concha Hotel, 211
Lafayette, Central, 103
"Lamento Borincano," 290
Land Authority, 140, 169f, 179
land: distribution of, 14, 120, 167, 168, 170, 175; reforms, 134, 139, 140, 170, 175
land law, 169ff
La Parguera Hotel, 212
latifundia, 167
Latin America, relations with, 9, 13, 14, 16, 18, 191, 58, 82, 159, 163f, 281, 284, 299, 317
latrines, 240, 275
lawyers, in PRRA, 106

League of Nations, 71
Leahy, Admiral, 135
Lee, Muna, 85, 88, 93
legislation: labor, 218*ff*; social, 139
legislature, P.R., 196, 317
Liberal party, 91, 92, 94, 99, 115, 121
Liberia, 53, 97
life expectancy, 10, 11, 31
limestone, 190
literacy, 202, 252, 255; *see also* illiteracy
Little Rock, Ark., 15
Lodge, Henry Cabot, 301
Los Caños mill, 103
lottery, 208
lunches, school, 242, 278
lynching of Nationalists, 74, 107

Maine (battleship), 49
malaria, 57, 233*f*
Malaria Eradication, Bureau of, 235
malnutrition, 235
manufacturing, 189, 191, 195*ff*; *see also* factories, industrialization, industries
market in U.S., 54; for U.S. goods, 190; *see also* United States
Markham, Edwin, 85
Martinique, 21
massacre, Ponce, 112
maternal-health program, 80
Matthews, Dr. Thomas, 299
May, Dr. Jacques, 238
Mayagüez, 204
mayoress of San Juan, 211, 294
meat, 181; *see also* cattle, slaughterhouse
medical geography, 237
Medicine, School of, 255

Mendoza, Inés, 113*f*
Menshikov: Mikhail, 311; Stanislav, 311*ff*
Mexico, 32, 45, 167, 168, 179, 205
Migration Division, 37*ff*, 226
migration, Puerto Rican, 25*ff*, 191, 203; *see also* New York
Miles, General, 49, 306
milk, production of, 180; *see also* dairy farming
mineral resources, 4
minimum wages, 123
Mississippi, 37, 310
Missouri, 31
monopoly, trade, 47
Monserrat, Joseph, 38
Morales Carrión, Arturo, 17, 44, 116, 304
Morro, el Castillo de, 45, 288
Moscoso, Teodoro, 141, 199
Moscow subway, 276
motion pictures, 268*ff*
Moulder, Morgan H., 31, 309
municipal housing, 292; *see also* housing
Muñoz Marín, Luis: 11, 12, 33, 53, 73, 76, 82*ff*, 105, 106, 134, 143, 154, 188, 215, 229, 241, 259, 266, 280, 290, 300, 304, 313, 314, 317, 318; acquisition versus creation, on, 157; A.F. of L. speech, 155; American Legion, speech at, 154; assassination, attempted, 74; Barceló, quarrel with, 115*f*; campaign of 1940, 118*ff*; Chardón Commission, with, 98; culture changes, on, 284; demagogy, on, 158*f*; dictators, on, 163; dictatorship, accused of, 158, 159; eco-

nomic aid, on, 165; Eisenhower, Milton, with, 165; federal contributions, on, 162; Gore and, 94ff; governor, elected, 75, 149; Gruening, quarrel with, 107; Harvard University, at, 157; Ickes and, 134f; independence, on, 109, 114f, 144, 285, 314; industrialization, on, 161; land law, 136; Latin America, on relations with, 19, 156; Latin American, as, 14, 159, 163f; legislature, messages to, 158, 161, 265; lobbyist, as, 107; nationalism, on, 154; New York, life in, 55, 85, 137; Nixon, with, 19, 165; Operation Serenity, on, 158, 290; philosophy, 150ff; poet, as, 84; political status, on, 84ff, 156; private enterprise, on, 155; PRRA, and, 101, 110; realistic, 143; Roosevelt, and, 95f, 133; Senate Foreign Relations Committee, at, 156; successor to, 316; socialism, on, 155; socialist, as, 85; sources of income, on, 265; Trujillo, versus, 168; Truman, visits, 15; writer, as, 55, 60, 61, 84

Muñoz Marín, Inéz Mendoza de, 113

Muñoz Rivera, Luis, 49, 67, 83, 85, 91, 304

music in P.R., 210, 287; see also symphony orchestra

Naguib, Demonstration and Training Area of, 246

Nation, The, 55, 86

National Resources Committee, 104

nationalism, 69, 154f, 254, 258

Nationalists, 72ff, 89, 106, 112ff, 283, 301

needlework industry, 34, 54, 57, 191, 199, 220

Nehru, 13

Negroes, 15, 28, 34, 35, 39, 46, 70, 71, 281; see also race relations

Nelson, Donald M., 147

neo-Malthusians, 7

Netherlands, 20

New Deal, 64, 96, 101, 134, 135

New Jersey, 29, 42, 43

New Republic, The, 86

New York, Puerto Ricans in, 9, 24ff, 110, 203, 293, 297, 308

Nigeria, 14, 253

Nixon, Richard, 18, 165

Nkrumah, Kwame, 13

Norway, 10

nuclear power, 194

observers, foreign, 9ff

one-party system, 313

Operation Bootstrap, 10, 15, 125, 139, 311

Operation Commonwealth, 158

Operation Serenity, 158, 266, 290

Organic Act, 51, 68, 102, 304

overpopulation, 7, 237

overproduction, 6

Padín, José, 94, 250, 252, 261

Pagán, Bolívar, 143, 144

Pagán de Colon, Petroamérica, 38, 42

painters, Puerto Rican, 286

Pakistan, 143

Palm Sunday, 112

Pan American Sanitary Bureau, 233
Pan American Union, 17
Panama, 70; Canal, 48
paper and pulp factory, 141, 195, 200
Parent Teachers Association, 251
Paris, Treaty of, 49, 71
pastures, 176
patronage, political, 54, 116
pava, 120
People's Catechism, The, 123
pepper, 185
Perloff, Harvey, 176, 296
Peru, 27, 163
petroleum refining, 190, 200
Philadelphia, 25
Philippines, 115, 200, 220
Phosphorescent Bay, 212
physicians, 241
Picó, Rafael, 104, 197, 310
pineapple cannery, 179
pineapples, 179, 186, 198
Piñeiro, José Ramón, 17
Piñero, Jesús, 148, 151, 196
Pizarro, 27
planning, 10, 104*ff*, 202
Planning Board, 105, 139, 160, 197, 206, 271, 295
Planning Division of the PRRA, 104
planters, sugar, 53; *see also* sugar
plebiscite on status, 131, 305, 315
Point IV, 15*ff*, 173
police force, 111, 298
Poland, 32
Ponce, 112, 204
Ponce de Leon, 201, 289
Pons, Dr. Juan, 232, 235, 236, 243
Popular Democratic party, 102, 119*ff*, 128, 133, 143, 146, 151, 195, 205, 211, 217, 227,

291, 293, 306, 313, 316, 319
population: 28, 52, 62, 63; density of, 4, 5, 7; movement of, 37
Porto Rico, 60
ports, 203, 204
posters, 274
Postosky, 216
power, electric, 12, 192*ff*
Prado, President Manuel, 163
PRERA, 78*ff*, 103, 130, 137, 173, 234
proportional profit farms, 169
proportional representation, 317
prostitution, 34
Protestant Church, 80, 171
PRRA, 56, 80, 98, 99, 101, 102*f*, 115, 128, 130, 135, 137, 141, 173, 190, 207, 234, 235, 305
P.T.A., 261
Public Health Service, U.S., 232
Public Law 600, 305
Public Welfare, Office of, 242, 251

Queensland, 232

race relations, 7, 14, 15, 28, 33, 34, 35, 46, 70, 71; *see also* Negroes
racing, 209
radio in education, 262
Ramos, Menendez, 97
Reconstruction Administration, *see* PRRA
referendum, 305
refining, oil, 190, 200, 204
reforms, land, 134
regional distribution, 30, 202, 212, 213
Reily, J. Montgomery, 68
Relief Administrations, 78*ff*; *see also* FERA and PRERA

Remington Rand, 201
renaissance, 6
Republican party (includes Republican Statehood party), 67, 68, 91, 94, 121, 145, 153, 297, 307, 310, 312, 319
research, 79, 141, 160
Resident Commissioner, 51, 83, 92, 109, 143, 148, 228, 303, 313
resources, natural, 4, 14
restoration of Spanish San Juan, 287
revolution, Puerto Rican, 3, 11, 12, 127, 290
regionalization of medicine, 246
restaurants, 210
rice, 202
Riggs, Col. E. Francis, 74, 100, 105, 106, 252, 283
Rincon de Gautier, Felisa, 211, 294
roads, 50, 204, 205
Roberts, Dr. Lydia, 296
Robinson, Edward Arlington, 86
Rockefeller Foundation, 233
Rockefeller, Laurence, 209; Nelson, 216
Romany, Marcelino, 146
Roosevelt, Franklin D., 64, 73, 80, 92, 94, 95, 107f, 133; Mrs., 73, 97
Roosevelt, Theodore, Jr., 60, 76, 250, 304
Rose, Dr., 59; Mrs. Glenola, 242
Rosenwald Fund, 266
Rubert Hermanos, Inc., 102
rum industry, 138, 141
rural aqueducts, 239
Russia, 37

Sampson, Admiral, 46, 227
San Juan, restoration of, 287

San Cristóbal, Fort, 45, 288
San José Housing Project, 294
Sarah Lawrence College, 22, 277
Sánchez Hidalgo, Dr. Efraín, 261
Sanitary Bureau, Pan American, 233
sanitary environment, 232
Santo Domingo, 46
Scandinavia, 175
schools: 50, 271; Catholic, 259; public, 259; Second Unit Rural, 250f; vocational, 252, 260; *see also* education, teachers
seaports, 55
Second Unit Rural Schools, 250f
Secretary of Education, 261
Self-Help Corporation, 103, 173
Semana, 262
Senior, Clarence, 40
Senate Committee on Foreign Relations, 19
shipping, 178, 203
shoe factory, 141, 195
Sicily, 37
Sierra Berdecía, Fernando, 37, 38, 42, 219
Sierra Leone, 18
Skinner, Constance Lindsay, 86
slavery, 45, 46
slaughterhouse, 181
slum clearance, 103, 123, 293
slums, 171, 197, 207, 291
smallpox, 233
Smith-Hughes Law, 260
smuggling, 44, 47
soap, 190
social legislation, 139
Social Programs Administration, 172, 266
social workers: U.S., 40; Puerto Rican, 79
socialism, 142, 143, 144, 152,

155, 174, 182, 193, 195, 198, 295
Socialist party, 85, 91, 94, 121, 144, 228, 319
Soil Conservation Service, 176, 271
Soil Sanitation, Section of, 240
South, U.S., 37, 42
South Africa, Union of, 12
South Carolina, 37
sovereignty, national, 69
Soviet ambassador, 311
Soviet Union, 164, 237
Spain, relations with, 44ff
Spanel, A. N., 229
Spanish-American War, 51, 227
Spanish language, 36, 41, 249
Spanish merchants, 47, 284
Springfield, Ill., 283
standard of living, 202, 206
State, P.R., Department of, 16, 19
statehood for Puerto Rico, 54, 64, 67, 87, 195, 217, 257, 293, 307, 315
Statehood party, *see* Republican party
status, political, 48, 63, 67, 87, 120, 151, 302ff
Stefansson, Vilhjalmur, 86
sterilization, 296
stevedores, 216
Stimson, Henry, 304
Stricken Land, The, 138, 238
strikes, 170, 196, 204, 216, 219, 222ff
sugar economy: 42, 48, 52, 54, 58, 84, 102, 115, 141, 170, 173, 308; beet, 168, 178; bulk-loading, 219; culture, 28, 186; labor, 222; mechanization of, 179; politics in, 55, 99, 105; production, 52; public utility, as, 120; regu-

lation of, 135, 139, 140, 167
summer workshops, 40
supermarkets, 174
Supreme Court, U.S., 65, 152, 303
Swope, Governor, 135, 136
symphony orchestra, 210, 287

Taft, Robert A., 147f, 193
tariff, U.S., 5, 28, 49, 50, 61, 90, 115, 308
taxes: 205, 310; excise, 139, 290, 302, 310; exemption from, 152, 153, 196, 201, 310, 311; income, 314; Washington, to, 50, 51, 162
teachers: 256, 259, 261; New York, 40; *see also* education, schools
Teasdale, Sara, 86
Technical Co-operation Program, 17
telephone service, 203, 204, 216, 219
television in education, 262
tennis, 209
tenure, land, 168; *see also* land
terrorism, 70, 74
Thailand, 11, 13, 253
timber resources, 4; *see also* forests
tobacco, 58, 184, 186
topography, 4
Tourism, Department of, 211
tourists, 4, 141, 198, 207ff
Towner, Horace M., 304
Toynbee, 64
trade: balance of, 61, 191; free, 47, 48, 50; monopoly, 47, 48; statistics on, 191
transportation, 30, 54, 205
Transportation Authority, 142

Travel Association, P.R., 141
Treaty of Paris, 49, 71
Trinidad, 21
tropical, climate, 231; diseases, 234
Trujillo, Generalissimo, 21, 46, 158, 212, 276, 300, 309
Truman, President, 15, 74
tuberculosis, 57, 235
Tugwell, Rexford: 86, 97, 105, 133*ff*, 150, 160, 238; *Art of Politics, The*, by, 151; commonwealth status, on, 302, 317; governor, as, 136*ff*; inaugural address, 139; land law, investigates, 136; resignation of, 148; *Stricken Land, The*, by, 138, 238; tax exemption, against, 196
tuna fish, 201
T.V.A., 142, 192
Tydings, Senator Millard, 107, 114, 309

unemployment, 77, 170, 183, 185, 187, 203, 215*ff*, 221, 226
UNESCO, 275
Union party, 67, 68, 85, 91
United Fruit Co., 53
United Nations, 9, 225, 255, 276, 301
United States: capital, 48, 52, 58, 152; expenditures in P.R., 191; market, as, 54, 115, 302, 308; politics in, 60; relations with, 5, 9, 13, 14, 16, 20, 29, 32, 49*ff*, 65*ff*, 86, 131, 257, 283, 301*ff*; trade with, 61, 302
Universal Declaration of Human Rights, 225
University of Puerto Rico, 17, 60, 73, 95, 98, 99, 104, 136, 141, 160, 173, 255, 258, 263, 271, 299
urban renewal, 292

vanilla, 185
Velázquez, Luis, 111
Venezuela, 18, 74, 163, 233
veto power of governor, 54, 127, 135, 152, 303
Virgin Islands, 21, 211
visitors to Puerto Rico, official, 9*ff*, 253, 319
vocational training, 38, 222, 252, 255; schools, 252, 260
votes, purchase of, 55, 57, 65, 116, 119, 124, 125, 129

wages: 56, 161, 185, 196, 197, 200, 215, 216*ff*; differentials in, 216; minimum, 123, 217*ff*, 311
Wale, Fred G., 266; Mrs., 274
Waldorf Hotel, 38, 208
War Department, 98
Washington, George, 69, 83, 89
Water Resources Authority, 142, 181, 193*ff*
water, ground, 205; urban and rural supplies, 238, 279
West Africa, 11
West Florida, 46
West Indian Federation, British, 20, 32
West Indies, 35, 42
Wilkins, Sir Hubert, 86
Williams, Fatayi, 14
Wilson, Woodrow, 67
Winship, General Blanton, 96, 111, 113, 127, 207
Winthrop, Governor Beekman, 236

Withrow, Congressman, 309
"wolf gangs," 77
women, role of, 201
workshops, summer, 40
World Wars I and II, 6, 8, 15, 29,
    41, 50, 53, 58, 138, 182, 260,
    284

Yager, Arthur, 67
yellow fever, 233
Youngstown, 25
Yugoslavia, 13
Yunque, El, 212

zoning, urban, 197

A NOTE ABOUT THE AUTHOR

EARL PARKER HANSON was born in 1899, in Berlin, Germany, of American parents. He was graduated in engineering from the University of Wisconsin in 1922, and later did graduate work in geography at the University of Chicago and at Columbia University. At various times in his life he has been an engineer in Chile; an explorer in Iceland, sub-arctic Canada, the Amazon basin, and the Andes; head of the first U.S. economic mission to Liberia; and professor of geography at the University of Delaware. In 1935 and 1936 he was in Puerto Rico as a consultant to the federal Puerto Rico Reconstruction Administration and organized its Planning Division, of which he became executive secretary. His interest in Puerto Rico grew parallel to the fascinating development of that society. He is now Consultant to Puerto Rico's Department of State and a columnist for the weekly newspaper *The Island Times.*

In his career as a writer he has frequently contributed to geographical and scholarly magazines, as well as to *Harpers,* and is the author of many distinguished books, such as *Journey to Manaos* (1938), *Chile, Land of Progress* (1941), *New Worlds Emerging* (1950). He is also the originator and editor-in-chief of the three-volume *New World Guides to the Latin American Republics* (1944, 1946, 1950).

Mr. Hanson has been knighted by Liberia and Iceland.

A NOTE ON THE TYPE

THE TEXT of this book was set on the Linotype in a new face called PRIMER, designed by Rudolph Ruzicka, earlier responsible for the design of *Fairfield* and *Fairfield Medium,* Linotype faces whose virtues have for some time now been accorded wide recognition.

The complete range of sizes of *Primer* was first made available in 1954, although the pilot size of 12 point was ready as early as 1951. The design of the face makes general reference to Linotype *Century* (long a serviceable type, totally lacking in manner or frills of any kind) but brilliantly corrects the characterless quality of that face.

In the designs for *Primer,* Mr. Ruzicka has once again exemplified the truth of a statement made about him by the late W. A. Dwiggins: "His outstanding quality, as artist and person, is *sanity.* Complete esthetic equipment, all managed by good, sound judgment, about ways and means, aims and purposes, utilities and 'functions'—and all this level-headed balance-mechanism added to the lively mental state that makes an artist an artist. Fortunate equipment in a disordered world . . ."

Composed, printed, and bound by H. WOLFF, New York. Paper manufactured by P. H. GLATFELTER CO., Spring Grove, Pennsylvania. Typography and binding design by VINCENT TORRE.

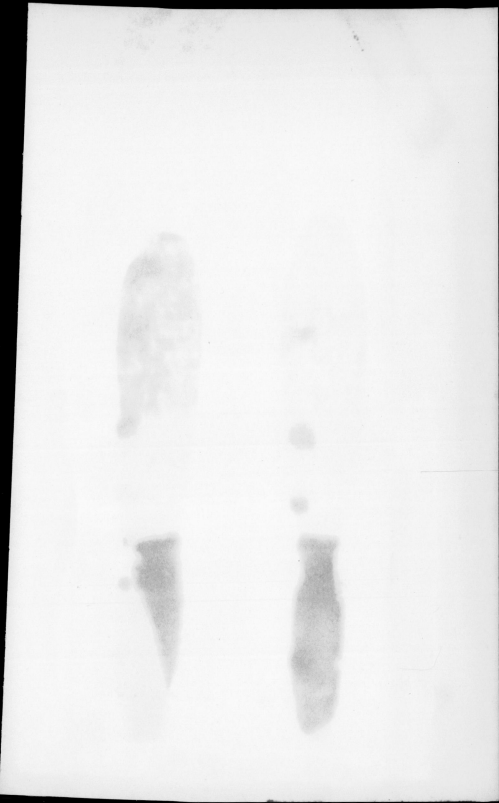